WITHDRAWN
UTSA LIBRARIES

THE TEXAS LAND AND DEVELOPMENT COMPANY

NUMBER 9 *The M. K. Brown Range Life Series*

THE TEXAS LAND AND DEVELOPMENT COMPANY

A Panhandle Promotion, 1912–1956

by B. R. BRUNSON

UNIVERSITY OF TEXAS PRESS, AUSTIN AND LONDON

International Standard Book Number 0-292-70038-5
Library of Congress Catalog Card Number 70-117722
© 1970 by B. R. Brunson
All Rights Reserved
Manufactured in the United States of America

TO MY MOTHER

Lura Hazel Early Brunson

PREFACE

In the summer of 1958 Mrs. Luther Bain of Plainview, Texas, whose late father had been a long-time general manager of the company, donated a group of Texas Land and Development Company records to the Southwest Collection at Texas Tech University. Earlier, the late Mr. Peyton Beaumont Randolph of Plainview, who was the attorney for the Texas Land and Development Company from 1912 to 1954 when the company was dissolved, had donated two groups of records to this collection. A third group, not to be legally disposed of until 1960, was then in the possession of the late Mr. Hugh R. Partridge of New York City, who had been a trustee for one of the parent trusts of the Texas Land and Development Company, the Staked Plains Trust, Limited, from 1920 until the trust was liquidated in 1956. Although the Bain and Randolph collections, numbering over ten thousand pages, seemed quite voluminous, a definitive history of the Texas Land and Development Company appeared impossible, since Partridge's collection represented an unknown quantity. Research was further limited because many employees and officers of the company were deceased or had moved from Plainview.

On the other hand, there were indications that a scholarly and worthwhile history of the company was possible from the available sources. Mrs. Bain graciously offered her father's personal papers, newspaper files, a miscellaneous collection bearing on the history of the company, and space in her home for conducting research. Mr. Randolph extended the courtesy of permitting the use of his extensive legal file, which partially bridged the correspondence gap in the history. Mr. Partridge kindly consented to make the records in his possession available on condition that they would be returned immediately on request. Finally there were many former employees of the Texas Land and Development Company still in the Plainview area, including Mr. Randolph, the company attorney; Mr. George T. Perdue, one of the early treasurers of the company; the late Mr. Fred Watson, the late Mr. David Dell Bowman, and Mr. Fred Lowe, all of whom had been farm superintendents for the company; and others who had served the company in such capacities as mechanics, carpenters, and painters.

An examination of available records encouraged me to locate former officials who were still living in 1960 or relatives of deceased officials. However, publicity about the project in numerous area newspapers, including the *Fort Worth Star-Telegram*, and an accompanying plea for information brought not one response. The silence was ominous, but a former colleague, Mrs. A. B. Cox, a long-time history teacher in the Plainview schools, was able to furnish names and addresses of former employees and others who might have knowledge of the early history of the area. One of these, Mrs. F. W. Clinkscales, possessed many valuable items, the most notable being the only copy found of a Texas Land and Development Company brochure compiled by the first general manager of the company, Milton Day Henderson. Interviews often provided not only a wealth of material and information but also the names and addresses of other former employees of the company. As a result the next two years brought 10 tape recordings, approximately 150 oral interviews, an estimated 100 telephone interviews, and approximately 100 letters. From the official records of the company obtained from Mrs. Bain, Mr. Randolph, and Mr. Partridge, from the information gleaned from the interviews and letters, from the files of Mr. Randolph and Mrs. Clinkscales, and from such other sources as contemporary newspapers and public records, the story of the Texas Land and Development Company slowly and painstakingly took form.

In preparing the history of the Texas Land and Development Company, I am especially indebted to many persons. It is not feasible to list all those who so generously aided, but the following exceeded the call of duty: Mrs. Luther R. Bain and the late Mr. Peyton B. Randolph for donating the records and for extending courtesies on numerous oc-

Preface

casions; the late Mr. Hugh R. Partridge for making the New York records available some two years ahead of schedule; the late Mr. David Dell Bowman, Mr. Fred Lowe, the late Mr. Fred Watson, Mr. Bob Martine, Mr. W. J. Williams, Mr. Hanley Wasson, Mr. Homer Rook, Mr. Clarence Rogers, Mr. Melvin Mise, and Mr. George T. Perdue, all of Plainview, for kindly assisting by submitting to long hours of tape-recording sessions; Mr. R. S. Charles of Richmond, Indiana; Mr. Clyde E. Craig of Raymondville, Texas, and Mr. A. B. DeLoach of Bentonville, Arkansas, for informative letters explaining the inner workings of the company in its early years and for their cooperation in answering many questions; Mrs. W. D. Pulling of Los Angeles, California, for her absorbing letters relating to her late stepfather, J. W. Grant, who was one of the first directors of the company; Mrs. Carolyn Pipkin of Los Angeles, California, for information relating to her late husband, J. W. Pipkin, who was a general manager for the company; the late Mrs. Charles F. Myers of Palo Alto, California, for much valuable information about her late husband, who was also a company general manager; Mrs. Sue D. Richardson of Houston, Texas, for information pertaining to her late father, George B. Doubleday, a company secretary; Mr. Ewen James MacEwen of Sarnia, Ontario, Canada, the Canadian lawyer who drew up the original charter and bylaws for the Texas Northern Land and Irrigation Company, Limited, for his several letters pertaining to the chartering process; Mr. and Mrs. A. B. Cox of Plainview, Texas, for suggesting persons to contact and for making available numerous clippings from the history department files at Estacado Junior High School; Mrs. F. W. Clinkscales for permitting the use of pictures, brochures, and newspapers; Mr. William F. Carter, irrigation engineer for Green Machinery Company for numerous interviews pertaining to irrigation wells, pumps, and engines; Dr. Seymour V. Connor, for his infinite patience, time, and guidance through this study; Dr. O. A. Kinchen, Dr. Ernest Wallace, Dr. William Pearce, Dr. L. L. Graves, and Dr. J. William Davis for the friendly suggestions they gave; my wife for her devoted patience, her suggestions for improving the manuscript, and her support; and a host of friends, relatives, and acquaintances for aid and encouragement.

CONTENTS

Preface ix
1. The Plainview Area before 1912 3
2. Organization of the Company 17
3. Sales and Advertising, 1912–1919 42
4. Development of Company Property 61
5. Reorganization of 1919 92
6. Consolidation under the Reorganization Agreement . . 109
7. The Depression Years 132
8. Retiring the Debt 153
9. Appraisal 169

Appendix I. Biographies 181
Appendix II. Officers of the Texas Land and Development Company 202
Appendix III. Investors before 1919 206
Appendix IV. The Land and Its People . . . 211
Bibliography 231
Index 239

PLATES

(Following page 112)

1. Lake Plainview Park Well, Plainview, Texas
2. Frederick Stark Pearson
3. Company Employees, c. 1930
4. Milton Day Henderson and Joe E. Lancaster
5. Lake Plainview, c. 1914–1915
6. Lake Plainview, c. 1914–1915
7. Winfield Holbrook, c. 1931
8. Slaton Well
9. Deep Tilling near Plainview

FIGURES

1.	Map of the Panhandle	4
2.	Henderson's Proposed Model Farm	63
3.	Company's Standard House Plan	76
4.	Floor Plan of Standard House	77
5.	Simplified Organizational Chart	95

TABLES

1. Estimated Value of Crops 48
2. Expenditures for Development (1912) 84
3. Comparison of Production: Dry-Land
    and Irrigated Farms 116
4. Profits and Losses (1920–1929) 119
5. Comparative Crop Acreage 120
6. Value of Company Property (December 31, 1919) . . 121
7. Company Sales (1920–1929) 124
8. Salary Schedule (1930) 133
9. Salary Schedule (1931) 134
10. Salary Schedule as of January 1933 136
11. Salary Schedule (1933–1934) 136
12. Funds in the Investment Reserve (1940–1953) . . 154
13. Comparison of Average Prices (1942 and 1943) . . 158

THE TEXAS LAND AND DEVELOPMENT COMPANY

1. The Plainview Area before 1912

ACCORDING TO THE traditional historical approach to the settlement of the American West, the various waves of frontier occupation ended with the establishment of permanent farmers who usually tilled small holdings that they owned themselves. According to one thesis, a frequently overlooked catalyst in the westward expansion of the nation was the land speculator, who bought large blocks of land cheaply and sold his purchases, in smaller tracts, more dearly. Especially during the closing years of the frontier era the presence of this catalytic agent is more easily detectable. In the region known as the South Plains of Texas, the frontier era came late and lingered until well after the turn of the twentieth century. Through the first decade, and even the second decade, of the twentieth century, numerous land companies flourished in the area, many carrying on large-scale operations that broke up the holdings of enormous ranches into tracts for sale to the "settled" farmer. Normally settlers bought these small farm-sized tracts with relatively low down payments and a term of years for the completion of

1. Map of the Panhandle showing the location of the Texas Land and Development Company.

The Plainview Area before 1912

payment. Many promoters were, therefore, also in the mortgage-finance business.

Typical of such operations were the Spur Ranch development under Clifford B. Jones, president emeritus of Texas Technological College, the Spade Ranch sales program, the Littlefield operations and the Yellow House Land Company, and the promotions of the once well-known W. B. Soash. These land companies advertised the South Plains lands broadly and, with the coming of the railroad to the area, introduced scores of special excursion trips, which brought prospective land buyers to the region from all over the country.

One such company, with its headquarters in Plainview, Texas, was the Texas Land and Development Company, an operating agent for a syndicate of eastern financiers. Only in its ultimate purpose, however, was this company similar to others; like all land companies, it hoped to profit by selling land. The company was unique because it started operations with relatively high-priced lands and attempted to sell fully developed, irrigated farms; it was substantially different from most because it realized very little profit from the venture in its early phase; it was more important to its zone of operations than were many other companies because it put capital into the region instead of taking money out; and it is of rather unusual historical significance because of the great financial ability of many of its backers and the complexity of its fiscal structure.

When the Texas Land and Development Company began operations in the Plainview area on the northern edge of the South Plains in 1912, the region had already passed through the principal phases of frontier development and was among the fastest growing population centers in West Texas. The initial waves of the farmers' frontier had already spread across the flat, treeless plains and had deposited in their wake a scattering of farms, stock farms, small ranches, and country towns. This development had occurred in the ten-to-fifteen year period immediately preceding the advent of the Texas Land and Development Company in 1912,[1] and even in the closing years of the nineteenth century, the region had been raw, unoccupied frontier.

[1] Jean Paul, "The Farmers Frontier on the South Plains" (master's thesis, Texas Technological College, Lubbock, 1958), p. 133.

To assess more completely the historical role of the company in the development of the Plainview area, as well as to fit the operation into proper historical perspective, it seems worthwhile to review in some detail the early settlement of the region and the beginnings of the town of Plainview, which the operations of the Texas Land and Development Company considerably affected.

The origins of Plainview were much like those of any other town in the surrounding region. When the Texas legislature in August of 1876[2] divided into additional counties the northwestern part of Texas, then attached to Bexar County, one of the new counties was Hale County in which the townsite of Plainview was to be located. The twenty northern counties of the divided area formed the region known as the Texas Panhandle; the seventeen adjoining southern counties, the South Plains. These two areas are part of the vast region known as the Llano Estacado or Staked Plains.[3] Hale County proper, which was named for John C. Hale, a hero of the battle of San Jacinto,[4] was located in the northern tip of the South Plains and in the center of the Staked Plains region. The area of the county at the time of its creation was 1,036 (today 979) square miles of gently sloping land, which ranged in altitude from 3,375 feet in the northwest down to 3,350 feet in the southeast.[5]

For some time prior to the arrival of the white man on the South Plains, Hale County was in the approximate center of an area dominated by the Comanche Indians,[6] who, no doubt, often camped under the hackberry trees in the groves that are now located in the townsite of Plainview. The Comanches made their last effort to hold the Panhandle–South Plains region in 1874. They lost the territory to troops led by Colonel Ranald Slidell Mackenzie on September 27 of

---

[2] Hans Peter Neilson Gammel, comp., *A Compilation of the Laws of Texas 1882–1897*, VIII, 1070–1073.

[3] *Plainview News*, December 20, 1912.

[4] Gammel, *Laws*, VIII, 1070–1073.

[5] *The Texas Almanac and State Industrial Guide*, p. 340.

[6] For a map of Comancheria see Ernest Wallace and E. Adamson Hoebel, *The Comanches: Lords of the South Plains*, p. 7.

The Plainview Area before 1912

that year.[7] Their defeat, which cleared the Plains of an Indian threat, was undoubtedly partially responsible for the division of northwest Texas into counties by the Texas legislature in 1876.[8]

Since the Indian menace no longer impeded settlement on the South Plains, a number of ranchers moved into the area. Only one ranch of consequence flourished, however; and only a portion of its lands were located within Hale County. The ranch was owned by the Runningwater Cattle and Land Company, which had been organized in Fort Scott, Kansas, by two brothers, J. W. and T. W. Morrison.[9] The absence of large landholdings in the county was to be an important factor in the subsequent real-estate boom at the beginning of the next century.

The first permanent white settler attracted to Hale County was Horatio Graves, a Methodist minister from Ausable Forks, New York. In 1882 Graves brought his family by train from New York to Eastland, Texas, and by covered wagon from there to the Quaker colony at Estacado, Texas, where they set up temporary housekeeping. Graves then freighted lumber for a home from Colorado City, Texas, to Hale County. He located approximately one and one-half miles southwest of the present town of Hale Center. Lured to Texas by cheap land and a milder climate, Graves planned his settlement as a Northern Methodist colony, and named it Epworth in honor of the birthplace of John Wesley. His plan miscarried, however, since most of the Methodists

---

[7] *Ibid.*, p. 28.

[8] Even though Mackenzie ended the Comanche barrier to South Plains settlement, fear remained that the Comanches would return. As late as 1891 there was an Indian scare in the Plainview area, and a messenger was sent throughout the region notifying settlers of the impending Indian attack. In the panic that ensued a large number of people fled into Plainview for protection. There they sought refuge in the county court house, where all available lumber in Plainview was used in an effort to build an additional defense. When the lumber supply proved to be insufficient, many people had no place to go except to their homes where they prepared to defend themselves with guns and clubs. The rumor that the Indians were coming proved to be false, but the event was not soon forgotten by those who had participated in the panic. Mrs. J. O. Oswald (one of the participants in the scare), oral interview, February 16, 1960.

[9] Hale County Deed Records, I.H.E., 132, County Clerk's Office, Plainview.

who moved into the area were members of the Methodist Episcopal Church South.[10]

The founders of Plainview, Z. T. Maxwell and Edwin Lowden Lowe, came separately to the Plainview area in 1886. Maxwell, who was born near Springfield, Missouri, in 1848, came to Bonham, Texas, with his family in or around 1862. After he married Laura Duncan in Sherman, Texas, in 1870, he lived in Fannin, Cooke, Montague, and Floyd counties.[11] He sold his homestead land in Floyd County in 1886, traded his cattle for two thousand sheep, and followed the Mackenzie trail out onto the Staked Plains. On the Runningwater Draw (the head stream of the White River) Maxwell found two groves of hackberry trees, which determined his location and the future location of the Plainview townsite. The hackberry trees, one grove of which still stands, were purported to be the only trees to be found anywhere on the Staked Plains at that time. In 1886 Maxwell dug a well between the two groves of trees and constructed a sod corral for his sheep. The following year he built a sod house.[12]

Edwin Lowden Lowe was born in Lowden County, Tennessee. After the death of his parents he lived with a brother in Hamburg, Arkansas, where he practiced law and became a member of the Arkansas legislature. There he met and married Virginia Archer, the daughter of a wealthy Louisiana plantation owner. Because of ill health, Lowe moved west in search of a higher, dryer climate. The trip, made in a covered wagon, proved fatal to his wife, who died at Buffalo Gap, Texas. When Lowe reached the area that was to become Plainview, he "seemed to feel that what he had been seeking was found" because of the "climate, location, and the purity of the water." Lowe "was much impressed with the beauty of the rolling plains, which stretched away in the distance as far as he could see."[13]

Maxwell and Lowe, on May 21, 1887,[14] each pre-empted adjacent

---

[10] Mary L. Cox, *History of Hale County Texas*, pp. 9–11 and 184.
[11] *Plainview Evening Herald*, March 6, 1935.
[12] *Ibid.*, May 18, 1938.
[13] *Ibid.*, May 16, 1934.
[14] Field Notes, Original Homestead Surveys, Book A-3, pp. 4–5, County Surveyor's Office, Plainview.

The Plainview Area before 1912

quarter sections, which included the hackberry trees, and on July 3, 1888, they appeared before the judge of Crosby County, under whose jurisdiction Hale County then operated, and deeded "streets, alleys, and a public square" to the judge and his successors. Their act on that date marked the founding of Plainview.[15] Lowe was credited with naming the town of Plainview, because he had a "plain view" of everything as far as the eyes could see in any direction.[16] Lowe did not live to see the town flourish but died in Plainview on July 13, 1889.[17] Nor did Maxwell long remain in the town he helped establish; he moved away in 1892 and died in Colgate, Oklahoma, in 1935.[18]

The officials of Crosby County organized Hale County as a separate legal entity in the summer of 1888.[19] In an election on August 4, the county chose its first officials and named Plainview the county seat.[20] Both Plainview and Hale Center grew steadily if not spectacularly. In 1890 the county had a population of 721;[21] in 1900, 1,680;[22] and in 1910, 7,566.[23] By 1906 the population of Plainview had grown to 600,[24] and by 1910 to 2,829.[25] The population almost doubled within the next two years, and on December 20, 1912, an estimate placed it at almost 6,000 people.[26] If this figure can be accepted as accurate,

---

[15] Hale County Deed Record, I. H. E., 372–375. The town was not incorporated until February 28, 1907 (Plainview Commissioner's Court minutes, Term 189, Vol. II, p. 117).

[16] *Plainview Evening Herald*, March 6, 1935.

[17] Hale County Probate Minutes, Book 1, pp. 1–2, Office of the Justice of the Peace, Plainview.

[18] *Plainview Evening Herald*, March 6, 1935.

[19] Hale County Deed Record, I. H. E., 1.

[20] Cox, *Hale County*, pp. 2–3.

[21] United States, Department of Commerce, Bureau of the Census, *Eleventh Census of the United States, 1890: Statistics of Population*, pt. 1, p. 784.

[22] United States, Department of Commerce, Bureau of the Census, *Twelfth Census of the United States, 1900: Population*, pt. 1, p. liv.

[23] United States, Department of Commerce, Bureau of the Census, *Thirteenth Census of the United States, 1910: Abstract of Census, Texas Supplement*, p. 620.

[24] *Plainview News*, December 20, 1912.

[25] Bureau of the Census, *Thirteenth Census*, p. 620.

[26] *Plainview News*, December 12, 1912; Texas Land and Development Com-

it was the highest for years to come. In 1914 there were only 5,500 people,[27] and in 1920, only 2,989.[28] The population did not again surpass 6,000 until some time in the nineteen-twenties, and the census bureau listed 8,834 residents in Plainview in 1930.[29]

During the first twenty years of Plainview's existence progress in all lines of endeavor was slow, in part because most of the first settlers were men of limited means. The first homes were tents, which the settlers occupied until they constructed half dugouts. For a short time the half dugout was the typical dwelling. Both the half dugout and its successor, the sod house, were comfortable, however.[30] By 1900 the inhabitants constructed houses of wood, but there were few if any brick homes in Plainview until the coming of the railroad in 1907. Before that time, two buildings, the Wayland Hotel and the Hale County abstract building, were constructed of concrete blocks that had been manufactured in Plainview.[31] There was only one exclusive residential street in the town, appropriately called Restriction Street, because there were no zoning restrictions in any other part of the city.[32] Prior to 1909, when Plainview installed public water, electric, and sewer systems, practically every family in town owned a windmill.[33]

The major problem facing the early settlers in the area was how to force a reluctant plains to yield a livelihood. Prior to the coming of the railroad in 1907, cattle raising was the chief industry, but it offered the settler a precarious living at best. Some attempted farming. The principal crops in the eighteen-nineties and early nineteen hundreds were

---

pany, brochure, "Texas Land and Development Company," Clinkscales Collection, Plainview.

[27] *The Daily Plainview Advertiser*, January (undated articles), 1914, Bain Files, Plainview.

[28] United States, Department of Commerce, Bureau of the Census, *Fourteenth Census of the United States, 1920: Population*, p. 999.

[29] United States, Department of Commerce, Bureau of the Census, *Fifteenth Census of the United States, 1930: Population*, pt. 1, p. 1072.

[30] *Plainview Evening Herald*, March 6, 1935.

[31] Bob Martine, oral interview, February 21, 1960.

[32] *Plainview News*, November 20, 1928.

[33] *Ibid.*

The Plainview Area before 1912

sorghum, millet, milo, and wheat. Those who could spare water from their windmills had gardens and orchards, which flourished since there were no bugs or worms.[34] Many original settlers obtained additional revenue through the sale of buffalo bones, which brought $20 per ton at the nearest railroad town. In some areas it was possible for a man to pick up two tons of bones in a single day.[35]

Obtaining supplies was another problem demanding solution. Prior to the opening of stores in Plainview, each person had to purchase his own supplies and then transport them from Amarillo[36] or Colorado City. Thornton Jones, a native of Virginia, established the first store in Plainview in the spring of 1887. Lowe and Maxwell offered a one-half section from lands they owned outside Plainview to the first person who would open a store within the limits of their town. To qualify as the first merchant, Jones opened his store in a tent but later freighted lumber and erected a wooden structure.[37]

The number of business establishments in town increased with the population. Among the early ventures were two hotels, two grocery stores, two drug stores, two hardware stores, two livery stables and wagon yards, blacksmith shop, one barber shop, and one millinery store.[38] A newspaper, the *Hale County Hesperian*, was founded as early as 1889. Another, the *Texan Press*, was established in 1890; it consolidated in 1892 with the *Lubbock Leader* as the *Texas Press-Leader* and was renamed the *Plainview News* in 1906.[39] Other papers

---

[34] Bob Martine, tape interview, August 19, 1959.

[35] R. P. Smyth (pioneer, surveyor, and congressman from Plainview), undated article in scrapbook, History Department Files, Estacado Junior High School, Plainview, Texas.

[36] *Plainview Evening Herald*, May 16, 1934.

[37] Ray B. Jones (son of Thornton Jones), oral interview, February 21, 1960. Jones, finding it impossible to tend his store, left a pencil and a piece of paper in a prominent place, and a person desiring merchandise waited on himself. If the customer paid cash, which was seldom, he deposited the money in the cash box; otherwise he recorded on the paper what he had taken (*Plainview News*, November 29, 1928).

[38] Martine, oral interview, February 21, 1960.

[39] The *Plainview News* operated independently until 1929 when it was con-

prior to 1912 were the *Epworth Chronicle*, founded in 1892; the *Hale City Globe*, founded in 1891; the *Hale Center Live Wire*; and the *Hale Center Messenger*, founded in 1903.⁴⁰ The first bank was chartered in 1900, and by 1912 Hale County possessed numerous banks, three of which were located in Plainview.⁴¹

Perhaps the greatest deterrent to economic progress in Hale County was the lack of an available market, which in turn was due to the absence of an adequate transportation system.⁴² By the late eighteen-nineties the forward-looking citizens of the area began trying to interest railroad companies in the town, and in 1903 a group raised $75,000 as a bonus to induce the Santa Fe Railway to build into Plainview from the north. The bonus agreement required the Santa Fe to reach town by twelve o'clock noon, January 1, 1907.⁴³ To meet the deadline, the company was forced to place down only half the proper number of railway ties for the last few miles.⁴⁴ Several ladies of Plainview entered a contest to determine which of them would drive in the last spike, which was to be made of gold. To the winner went the spike. The coming of the railroad opened Plainview and the surrounding area to outside settlers and industry.

About a year before the railroad arrived, Dr. James Walker Grant, a retired dentist who had entered the real-estate business, brought the first automobile into Plainview so that he could haul prospective customers over the countryside.⁴⁵ The following year there were five automobiles in Plainview, all of them owned by real-estate agents. Often the realtor induced a person to buy land farther out in the country than he real-

---

solidated with the *Plainview Evening Herald*. The *Plainview Evening Herald* still survives.

⁴⁰ Cox, *Hale County*, pp. 90–93.

⁴¹ Mrs. F. W. Clinkscales (whose husband was an officer in the Third National Bank of Plainview), oral interview, January 3, 1960.

⁴² Martine, tape interview, August 19, 1959.

⁴³ Cox, *Hale County*, pp. 67–68.

⁴⁴ *Plainview News*, November 20, 1928.

⁴⁵ Mrs. W. D. Pulling (Grant's stepdaughter and only child), letter, October 16, 1959, Brunson Letters, Southwest Collection, Texas Tech University, Lubbock.

The Plainview Area before 1912

ized, since he was not accustomed to the "high" speed of the automobile. This approach occasionally miscarried, however, especially when a car broke down, and the prospective buyer had to walk back to town.[46]

No reliable figures recorded the number of real-estate firms in Plainview in the early years. Probably many firms existed because the Panhandle–South Plains area of Texas saw the most activity in the real-estate "epidemic" that swept large portions of the United States in the early years of the twentieth century. The Panic of 1907 halted the boom in most sections, but not in the Plainview area.[47] Instead, the coming of the railroad to Plainview in 1907 increased the tempo of the land boom and staved off the depression that gripped most other sections of the country.[48] Immigrants came from every part of the United States and prices soared. Town lots jumped in value from $10 to $100 and in some cases to $500.[49] The acreage of land in cultivation more than doubled from 1910 through 1912.[50] By 1912, however, the boom was slowing down in Plainview, and the area was beginning to feel the effects of the Panic of 1907.

The years between 1907 and 1912 saw rapid cultural and economic expansion. Although the first hospital was not established until 1913, numerous physicians and dentists practiced in the county. The first public schools opened shortly after the organization of the county, and in September 1907 the Nazarene Church established the Central Plains Holiness College. Prior to its opening, its name was changed to Central Plains College and Conservatory of Music in concurrence with the recommendation of its first president, Dr. L. L. Gladney. Because of financial strains, the Nazarenes transferred ownership of the school to the Northwest Texas Methodist Conference in 1909. Renamed Seth Ward College in honor of Texas' first native-born Methodist bishop, it was operated by the Methodists until destroyed by fire in 1916.[51] In

---

[46] *Plainview News*, November 20, 1928. Several persons interviewed claimed to have brought the first car into Plainview.
[47] *Amarillo Record*, November 2, 1913.
[48] Fred Watson, tape interview, July 12, 1958.
[49] *Plainview News*, November 20, 1928.
[50] *Hale County Herald*, January 30, 1913.
[51] Cox, *Hale County*, pp. 82–83. Since the conference met in the fall there

the meantime, the Baptists opened Wayland Literary and Technological Institute (later Wayland Baptist College) in 1910, and by 1912 two business schools functioned in Plainview.[52]

The citizens of Plainview and Hale County, from the very beginning, participated actively in church work. It will be remembered that the first permanent white settler in Hale County, Horatio Graves, was a Methodist minister. By 1912 the following religious groups established churches in Plainview: Methodist, Episcopal, Church of Christ, Disciples of Christ, Catholic, Baptist, Presbyterian, and Nazarene.[53] That there had "never been a saloon or den of vice of any description in Hale County," and that Plainview was "recognized as one of the cleanest and most moral towns in the state" were two advantages listed in a brochure designed to sell Plainview to prospective settlers in 1912.

The brochure pointed with pride to Plainview and capsuled the city's progressive spirit. Located in the "wealthiest" agricultural district in West Texas, the city flourished as a population center of six thousand people, second in size only to Amarillo in the Panhandle—

---

was no time to name a Methodist president of the college and thus Gladney was retained until 1910 when Dr. Sam Barcus, former president of Stamford College, was chosen for the post. Dr. Barcus was succeeded by the Reverend William M. Pearce, who remained as president until the summer of 1914. Pearce was followed by the Reverend W. G. McDonald, a Methodist minister from Bovina, Texas. The last president of the college was the Reverend N. B. Johnson (Mrs. William M. Pearce, Sr., to Bill Brunson, telephone interview, March 1, 1960).

[52] Cox, *Hale County*, pp. 84–87.

[53] Dr. J. H. Crawford (minister of the First Methodist Church, Plainview), telephone interview, February 22, 1960; Betty Evans (secretary of Episcopal Church, Plainview), telephone interview, February 22, 1960; Fay English (secretary of First Church of Christ, Plainview), telephone interview, February 22, 1960; Mrs. Adella Drew (historian of First Christian Church, Plainview), telephone interview, February 22, 1960; Mrs. Jess Lockhart (early Catholic pioneer in Plainview), telephone interview, February 22, 1960; Leona Lloyd (educational secretary of First Baptist Church, Plainview), telephone interview, February 22, 1960; Mr. Frank D. Travis (minister First Presbyterian Church, Plainview), telephone interview, February 22, 1960; The Reverend Corbie Grimes (minister First Nazarene Church, Plainview), telephone interview, February 22, 1960.

The Plainview Area before 1912

South Plains area. The phenomenal growth, dating from 1907, as a result of the coming of the Santa Fe railroad, had changed the city from a cowtown to the "principal agricultural, educational and commercial center of the South Plains." The impressive facilities of Plainview that would make the settler's life more comfortable included three national banks, five lumber yards, three wholesale houses, an "excellent class of retail stores," a $30,000 opera house, cement sidewalks, a modern sewer system and water works, an electric and ice plant, three newspapers, and a business district primarily of brick and concrete construction. The public schools and the two private colleges were also assets to the community. The residential district, "artistic and up to date," housed the high caliber of people who lived in Plainview. These citizens, "sociable and refined" as well as "broadminded and enterprising," were "gleaned from every state and land." Plainview, according to the brochure, was "destined to become one of the important cities of the West" because of "her progressive citizenship" and her "unrivaled natural advantages."[54]

Although the boom that had brought this progress faded, in 1911 an event occurred that was to have even more far-reaching consequences for the region. That year marked the digging of the first irrigation well in Hale County. Some prominent citizens of Plainview, who had heard and read of the success of irrigation in California and other irrigation districts, decided to experiment. The chamber of commerce appointed a committee consisting of E. Dowden, J. O. Wychoff, Charles Malone, J. E. Garrison, W. A. Parker, and George Green to make tests to determine the availability of underground water.[55] Since digging a well and installing an engine and a pump were too expensive for an individual to risk, the committee circulated a subscription list among the Plainview businessmen.[56] Nearly every businessman in town contributed to the fund.[57] The well would be dug on the farm of John Henry Slaton, president of the First National Bank of Plainview.

[54] Texas Land and Development Company, brochure, "Texas Land and Development Company," Clinkscales Collection.
[55] *Plainview Evening Herald*, May 21, 1941.
[56] *Hale County Herald*, April 24, 1913.
[57] *Ibid.*, May 8, 1913.

If the project were successful, Slaton was to reimburse those who had contributed money to finance the scheme.[58] George Green, overseer for the test, supervised the setting of the casing and pump after J. N. McNaughten of Happy, Texas, had drilled a pit well[59] that was six by eight feet wide and twenty-six feet deep and reached into the first water-bearing stratum. Next, a twelve-inch hole was drilled for approximately one hundred feet through two other strata of water. Then Green placed the pump on the bottom of the pit. A shaft drive attached to a thirty-two–horsepower gas engine operated the well. Although limited by the capacity of the engine, the well produced a flow of 1,500 gallons per minute.[60]

Prior to the completion of the well, everyone apparently became disgusted except Wychoff, who refused to quit until the well was completed. Without a doubt the success of the well gave impetus to an idea that brought Eastern capital to the Plainview area for the purpose of land development. The *Hale County Herald* commenting later on the completion of the well and its effect on the area stated, ". . . the rest of the story is best told by the purchase of the Texas Land and Development Company of 60,000 acres of land around Plainview and their proposal to spend $2,000,000 developing this property into irrigated farms."[61]

[58] *Ibid.*, April 24, 1913.
[59] *Plainview Evening Herald*, May 21, 1941.
[60] *Hale County Herald*, April 24, 1913.
[61] *Ibid.*, May 8, 1913.

2. Organization of the Company

THE TEXAS LAND and Development Company, organized in Plainview, Texas, resulted from an idea that originated with Milton Day Henderson, a local real-estate agent. Prior to 1912, when the company was chartered, Henderson and his partner, Dr. James Walker Grant, had been actively engaged in the promotion of Plainview and Hale County lands. Henderson, foreseeing the great agricultural potential of the area, conceived a plan based on the premise that prospective settlers would buy land more readily if it were already developed when they saw it. The development process as he envisioned it would involve an organization's buying a large tract of land, dividing it into individual farms, and preparing each farm for occupancy. This preparation would include the erection of appropriate dwellings and, after adequate cultivation, the planting of at least one-quarter of each farm in alfalfa or sorghum. With great vision, perhaps stimulated by the success of the Slaton well, he planned to install an irrigation system. Only after each farm was fully prepared and productive, was it to be sold.¹

Henderson's plans were too extensive to be financed locally. It is not certain, however, whether he conceived his scheme and then by chance discovered his financial backer, Dr. Frederick Stark Pearson, or whether he evolved the scheme after he was aware that a man like Pearson, who was in a position to acquire funds for the enterprise, was in the area.² Whatever the case may have been, quite another project brought Pearson to the West Texas region where he renewed his acquaintance with the South Plains.

Pearson had first viewed the South Plains in 1886 when he and a companion traveled across them on horseback. Commenting on the trip many years later, he stated that the Plains at that time "gave little promise of becoming one of the world's great agricultural communities, supporting a population which only irrigated and intensified farming can maintain."³

Pearson was a stranger neither to promotional enterprises nor to the prospect of accepting a challenging task. A civil engineer, he had gained a noteworthy reputation as one who experimented with the impossible only to make it a reality. After graduating from Tufts College in 1883 and furthering his studies in mathematics and chemistry both at Tufts and at the Massachusetts Institute of Technology, where he was assistant professor of chemistry for one year, he and a fellow professor made prospecting trips across Texas and Mexico for a group of eastern financiers. It was then that he first saw the South Plains.

Pearson's reports to the financiers were so impressive that they sent

---

[1] Mary L. Cox, *History of Hale County, Texas*, p. 49; *Hale County Herald*, August 15, 1913, March 13, 1914; Peyton B. Randolph to Dr. Seymour V. Connor, tape interview, April 8, 1958; Robert S. Charles (engineer and officer for the Texas Land and Development Company 1912–1915), letter, November 1, 1958, Brunson Letters, Southwest Collection, Texas Tech University, Lubbock (hereafter cited as BL); and Mrs. W. D. Pulling, letter, October 16, 1959, BL.

[2] On April 17, 1962, Mrs. E. C. Perry wrote that she recalled "very vividly that their [Pearson's and Henderson's] meeting was by chance on a diner in the East." She did not remember either the date of their meeting or the name of the line on which they met (letter in author's possession).

[3] *Hale County Herald*, April 17, 1913.

Organization of the Company

him on similar trips to South America. During the next several years he diversified his engineering career and entered the areas of planning and developing city light plants, city water systems, and city transportation systems. After establishing his reputation in Boston and New York, he served as consulting engineer in several cities in the United States and abroad. By the turn of the century, he had attained a substantial name in his profession. His alma mater, Tufts College, conferred honorary doctorates on him both in 1900 and in 1905, and his associates fittingly labeled him "a steam-engine in trousers."[4]

Pearson's checkerboard acquaintance with many parts of the world probably gave him an opportunity to make valuable business connections, which at times led him to make personal investments. The extent to which he gave time, energy, and finances to personal enterprises can only be speculated upon, but an examination of one project, which converged with others under the label "Pearson Syndicate" and had some bearing on the present study, may serve as a good example. In the early nineteen-hundreds while he was consulting engineer for a Mexican power project, Pearson established a lumber-processing plant at El Paso, Texas, known as the El Paso Milling Company. He needed this plant because of an agreement with the Mexican government, which had awarded him a concession in the United States for the distribution of finished lumber milled from trees grown in the Mexican sugar-pine forests.[5] The El Paso Milling Company was a subsidiary of the "Pearson Syndicate," which was legally entitled the Pearson Engineering Corporation, Limited.[6] This seems to have been the parent organization through which Pearson funneled promotional funds for various ventures.

---

[4] M. O. Chenoweth (public relations director for the American Society of Civil Engineers) to Dr. Seymour V. Connor, letter, December 2, 1958, Texas Land and Development Company Papers, Southwest Collection, Texas Tech University, Lubbock (hereafter cited as TLDCP); and Robert S. Charles, letter, December 5, 1958, BL.

[5] Charles, letter, November 1, 1958, BL.

[6] There is no positive proof that the "Pearson Syndicate" was legally entitled the Pearson Engineering Corporation, Limited, but a close examination of the cash book of the Texas Securities Company would lead to this conclusion.

It was through the El Paso Milling Company that Pearson became involved in the Plainview venture. Twenty-five years after his prospecting trips in the South Plains area, Pearson investigated the possibility of building a railroad through West Texas to furnish transportation for the distribution of his lumber. Because the proposed railroad would connect with the Mexico Northwestern Railway, another enterprise of the Pearson Syndicate, Pearson was quite anxious that the plan prove practicable.[7] His interest in having a railroad built coincided with the plan of the Rock Island system, commonly referred to as the Frisco, to build a railroad.[8] In 1912 this company was about to embark on a reconnaissance survey of a proposed line from Quanah through Plainview to El Paso.[9] Engineers, who were working northward from El Paso, and another party, which was working southwestward from Quanah through Plainview, under the direction of Robert S. Charles, a young engineer from the Frisco, concluded that the proposed extension was not practicable, and the project was abandoned.[10]

Although the project was dropped, the surveys for it gave M. D. Henderson the chance he needed to acquire a financial backer for his land-promotion scheme, and Henderson was not one to let an opportunity escape. No doubt the Plainview realtor read about the proposed extension with interest and contrived a means to contact the man whose name had added prestige to the survey. But Pearson was at first uninterested, and he assured Henderson that the Pearson Syndicate would not invest in the Hale County promotion scheme. Henderson, however, was insistent and persuasive, and Pearson finally agreed to come to Hale County simply because Henderson "would not let him alone."[11]

[7] Randolph to Connor, tape interview, April 8, 1958.
[8] The Frisco system to Texas originated with the Paris and Great Northern Railway company in 1881. The St. Louis, San Francisco, and Texas Railway Company was chartered in 1900, and in 1903 all Frisco properties in Texas were brought into this organization by the parent company (see S. G. Reed, *A History of Texas Railroads*, pp. 423–433).
[9] Charles, letter, November 1, 1958, BL.
[10] *Ibid.*
[11] *Hale County Herald*, March 13, 1914.

Organization of the Company

Once he began to investigate the area, Pearson became as enthusiastic as Henderson. He saw many possibilities for development. The factor that had been lacking when he first visited the South Plains in 1886 was a workable irrigation system. Now he viewed a well and pumping system that was highly satisfactory but too expensive for farming operation. He carefully and systematically studied all aspects of farming in the area and talked not only with farmers but also with businessmen who provided services for the farmers. He held one such conversation with a young man named George Green, who was just getting started in the irrigation business. Green remembered Pearson as a small, rather unimpressive man whose looks were deceiving but whose penetrating questions were always pertinent to Pearson's investigation.[12] Another person observed that Pearson was "a tremendously inspiring person" who was "dynamic in his thinking" and "a power house in his mentality."[13] Plainview citizens were undoubtedly impressed with Pearson during his stay in their city. He had come to town in a private railroad car and was taxied about the countryside in his own chauffeured automobile.[14] These happenings, in themselves unusual for the citizens of the small community to observe, were undoubtedly the subject of much local talk.

Since funds for purchasing the land were the first requisite for organizing the enterprise, Pearson initiated an unbelievably complex series of financial maneuvers. The initial funds, which totaled over $1,500,000, were sent to Plainview through his main syndicate organization, the Pearson Engineering Corporation. This company obtained the first flow of money, approximately $250,000 between May and October, from another of Pearson's syndicate subsidiaries, the Pacific Securities Company, Limited, from Pearson personally, and from J. H. Dunn, one of Pearson's British associates. The bulk of capital needed for the land purchases came, however, during November 1912 from groups referred to in the company's ledger merely as "London"

---

[12] George Green, oral interview, October 25, 1958, BL.
[13] Charles, letter, November 1, 1958, BL.
[14] Green, oral interview, October 25, 1958, BL.

sources. The first deposit in the amount of $15,000 arrived at the First National Bank of Plainview on May 3, 1912.[15]

Immediately thereafter, Henderson began buying the land. Henderson and Pearson engaged a local attorney, Halbert Cyrus Randolph, and his son, Peyton Beaumont Randolph, to examine land titles. The Randolphs were to write a check for the land Henderson wished to purchase after confirming that the title was clear. Henderson delivered the first prospective title to the Randolphs on May 12, 1912, only nine days after the trustee account had been opened in the Plainview bank.[16]

From May 12, 1912, until the end of his land-buying spree, Henderson purchased 61,360 acres of land in Hale, Floyd, and Swisher counties. Of the amount, 18,175 acres were already under cultivation and 306.5 miles were fenced.[17] It is possible that Pearson's recent excursions in the area around Plainview complicated Henderson's job by driving land prices up.[18] He paid an average of $25 per acre for the land, a higher rate than the going price in 1912. In the final accounting, he spent over $1,500,000 for the land. From May 3, 1912, to December 3, 1912, Pearson interests sent a total of $1,557,000.00 to Plainview. Of this amount the Randolphs authorized payment of $1,518,617.60 for the purchase of the South Plains land. H. C. Randolph and John Henry Slaton, who had been appointed as trustees for the Canadian company that Pearson had formed to buy the lands, received $9,500.00. The remaining amount of $28,882.40 was transferred to the books of a new company Pearson and his associates had established in Canada to control the Plainview operations.[19]

The Canadian company, the Texas Northern Land and Irrigation

---

[15] Texas Securities Company, Limited, 1912–1914, ledger, Pearson Engineering Corporation, account, TLDCP.

[16] Peyton B. Randolph, oral interview, March 13, 1960, BL.

[17] Texas Land and Development Company, field book no. 360, Field Notes, Original Surveys, Office of County Surveyor, Plainview; a copy also in the Texas Land and Development Company Papers donated by Mr. W. J. Williams, Hale County Surveyor.

[18] W. J. Williams, tape interview, August 22, 1959.

[19] Texas Securities Company, Limited, 1912–1914, ledger, M. D. Henderson Trustee account, TLDCP.

Organization of the Company 23

Company, Limited, had been chartered in Toronto, Ontario, on April 25, 1912. The company was empowered to offer for sale 100,000 shares valued at $100 each to give it a capital stock of $10,000,000. For an unknown reason the Texas Northern Land and Irrigation Company, with the approval of the secretary of state of Ontario, changed its name to Texas Prairie Lands, Limited, on August 30, 1912.[20]

Texas Prairie Lands was set up by Pearson specifically to buy, develop, and sell the Texas lands that the Pearson Engineering Corporation was to buy and that were to be held by Slaton and Randolph as trustees for Pearson and his associates. If Texas Prairie Lands successfully carried out its mission of developing and selling the Texas lands, Pearson and his associates stood to make substantial profits. However, if the company failed, they would be liable for a maximum of $10,000,000, since in Canadian corporations designated as "limited" each shareholder or investor is liable for and/or "limited" to the par value of the stock owned (or to any amount that has been predetermined by a guarantee). Pearson, either as an afterthought or more probably on the basis of advice from his associates, therefore undertook another financial maneuver fairly common in the early part of the twentieth century; he limited to $1,000 the total liability to himself and his backers by establishing a holding company. There are two puzzling aspects about the establishment of this holding company: first, why did Pearson delay its establishment for over six months, and second, why did he not utilize the Pearson Engineering Corporation, already in existence, for the purpose? These questions can only be answered by conjecture, but it seems possible that he originally planned to make the Pearson Engineering Corporation the holding company for Texas Prairie Lands and was dissuaded by his associates, who lacked Pearson's enthusiasm for the land speculation. If such were the case, obviously Pearson's next move would have been to charter a new holding company.

For whatever reasons, the Texas Securities Company, Limited, was chartered on October 11, 1912, in Toronto.[21] The holding company

[20] *Documents 1917*, pp. 5–15, TLDCP.
[21] Books with retroactive entries for Texas Securities Company were made up. Many transactions involving the Plainview enterprise had already trans-

was authorized to issue four hundred shares valued at $100 each to create a potential capital stock of $40,000. But, since only ten shares were ever subscribed, the company had a capital stock (and liability) limited to $1,000.[22] If this company were to go bankrupt, the maximum for which Pearson and his associates would be held responsible would be $1,000.

Pearson then had this company sell the Texas lands, which J. H. Slaton and H. C. Randolph were still holding in trust, to Texas Prairie Lands. By a written agreement on October 16, 1912, probably a contract of sale which has not been located but the existence of which is implied in the Texas Securities Company account book, Texas Prairie Lands agreed to pay the Texas Securities Company $1,800,000.00 in cash to acquire title to the property on the South Plains.[23] The agreement, according to the Texas Securities Company ledger for the investment account, also provided that a block of thirty-five thousand shares of stock, each $100 par value, of Texas Prairie Lands would be transferred to the Texas Securities Company. Since no other shares were ever sold by Texas Prairie Lands, Pearson and his associates, through the Texas Securities Company, actually owned the Texas Prairie Lands company. By means of a Supplementary Letters Patent, on February 28, 1913, the capital stock of Texas Prairie Lands was reduced from $10,000,000.00, the original amount provided for in the charter, to $3,500,000.00,[24] the amount held by Pearson and the "London" group

---

pired prior to the formal chartering of this company. Thus, perhaps in order to show the Texas Securities Company as the owner and parent company of the enterprise in preparation for the land sale to Texas Prairie Lands, a set of books had to be made up for the Texas Securities Company as if it had existed since May 1912.

[22] Texas Securities Company, Limited, *Annual Report*, 1918, BL.

[23] Barrow, Wade, Guthrie, and Company, Staked Plains Trust, Ltd. *Memorandum* re Capital Stock Tax Returns, August 29, 1928, under that part entitled "Historical Résumé," 1, Wallet 27, TLDCP.

[24] Texas Prairie Lands, Limited, 1913–1915, ledger, p. 42, TLDCP. It seems likely that one of the schemes for financing the venture was to sell the additional stock but that this plan was abandoned in favor of the bond issue described later in this chapter.

Organization of the Company

through the Texas Securities Company. Thus, for their $1,000.00 "limited" liability in the Texas Securities Company, Pearson and his associates had sold the Texas land for $1,800,000.00 (for which they had paid $1,518,617.60 plus administrative expense) besides acquiring thirty-five thousand shares of stock in the Texas Prairie Lands. On paper this was a substantial profit, but it was paper profit only.

When the land was sold to Texas Prairie Lands on October 16, 1912, that company was virtually penniless. The sum of $1,800,000 was merely transferred on the books of the Texas Securities Company. It remained for the directors of Texas Prairie Lands (that is, the owners of the Texas Securities Company) to raise the money to convert the paper transfer into reality. If Texas Prairie Lands proved successful, the backers would not only realize their profit from the $1,800,000 sale, but would also secure additional returns from the profit of the operation. If it failed completely, the backers stood to lose more than $250,000 already invested, without realizing any of the $1,800,000. Enough money was raised on a bond issue to repay the initial investments, but it is doubtful whether there was ultimately even the smallest margin of profit for the backers of the Texas Securities Company, which finally wrote off a large proportion of the paper purchase price of $1,800,000.

While financial matters were being arranged, Pearson and his advisors had two other matters of importance to settle. First, he had been obliged to appoint trustees in Texas to hold title to the 61,360 acres Henderson had purchased, so that his corporations might legally operate in Texas. Such an arrangement was necessary because under Texas law a corporation was prohibited the ownership of land unless the land were necessary to enable the corporation to conduct its business, or unless the land had been received in the payment of a debt in the ordinary course of its business.[25] Hence the holding company appointed as trustees H. C. Randolph, the company's legal consultant in Plainview, and J. H. Slaton, the president of the First National Bank of Plainview, where the company maintained a sizable account. These two

---

[25] *Vernon's Texas Statutes*, 1893, Title 32, ch. 4, art. 1359, p. 512. This prohibition was repealed by the 57th Legislature in 1961.

trustees would assume absolute title to the land and were to convey it to the prospective purchaser. Deeds were duly drawn up by the company with the trustees as owners.[26] It was clearly understood by the trustees, however, that they were acting for the company and that in the event of their death no land held in trust by them would pass to their heirs. Instead, the company's directors would appoint new trustees.[27]

Pearson and his associates then made final arrangements for the formation of the Texas Land and Development Company, an operation company to handle the development and sale of the Texas lands. Such a company had been provided for in the charter of Texas Prairie Lands[28] and was to be established in Plainview. The preliminary meeting of the Texas Land and Development Company was held in Plainview, on October 19, 1912, in the office of M. D. Henderson. Robert S. Charles, M. D. Henderson, W. H. Mason, and James Walker Grant, the four men who organized the company and who became its first officers, were present.[29] Henderson was included in the group because of his position as originator of the development scheme and purchaser of the lands. His future duties entailed setting up the sales program and managing the development operations. His real-estate partner, J. W. Grant, had, no doubt, helped him locate and arrange purchase for the lands and was thus in the organizing group of the Texas Land and Development Company because of his connections with Henderson. R. S. Charles, who had first encountered the working of the Pearson Syndicate as a reconnaissance engineer for the Frisco, joined the group upon the recommendation of Harry Irving Miller, who had been Charles's immediate supervisor as a vice-president of the Rock Island–Frisco System and who had become a director of Texas Prairie Lands.[30]

---

[26] Even though Henderson, as an employee and trustee of the Texas Securities Company, bought the land, the titles to the land were never drawn up in the name of Henderson as trustee of the Texas Securities Company. Instead, the original titles bore the name of Slaton and Randolph, trustees.

[27] *Documents 1917*, pp. 159–167, TLDCP.

[28] *Ibid.*, p. 9.

[29] Texas Land and Development Company, minutes, October 19, 1912, TLDCP.

[30] Charles, letter, November 1, 1958, BL.

Organization of the Company

W. H. Mason, a New Yorker and a qualified comptroller, was no doubt hired by the directors of Texas Prairie Lands and transplanted to Plainview to keep the company's financial matters straight. It was the prime duty of the Texas Land and Development Company to act as a legal entity representing Pearson and the other owners of the Prairie Lands.[31]

The capital stock of the Texas Land and Development Company was $5,000, divided into fifty shares, each with a par value of $100.[32] Of the $5,000 Charles and Henderson each subscribed $1,300, and Mason and Grant each $1,200.[33] Actually, none of these men owned Texas Land and Development Company shares, since none of them spent his own money to cover the subscription cost. Instead, Texas Prairie Lands paid the fee for them. Texas Prairie Lands carried on its books an account for investments from which payment for the shares was drawn.[34] Each man simply held enough shares in trust for the shareholders of Texas Prairie Lands[35] so that he could act legally in organizing the company.[36] Since the Texas Land and Development Company charter provided that half the amount subscribed by each individual was to be paid into the company treasury immediately, $2,500 was taken from the investment account of Texas Prairie Lands and deposited in the First National Bank of Plainview on December 31, 1912.[37] The other half was to be paid within two years from the date the charter was issued.

H. C. Randolph, legal counsel for Texas Prairie Lands, became the attorney for the Texas Land and Development Company as well. To

[31] *Ibid.*

[32] Texas Land and Development Company, minutes, October 19, 1912, TLDCP.

[33] *Ibid.*

[34] Texas Prairie Lands, Limited, 1913–1915 ledger, p. 40, TLDCP.

[35] The Texas Securities Company paid one-half of the subscription price for the Texas Land and Development Company shares, which amounted to $2,500. However, this amount was repaid to Texas Securities on December 31, 1912, by Texas Prairie Lands, which owned the full amount until 1914 (Texas Securities Company, Limited, ledger, account of Texas Prairie Lands, Limited, TLDCP).

[36] Charles, letter, November 1, 1958, BL.

[37] Texas Prairie Lands, Limited, 1913–1915, ledger, p. 40, TLDCP.

obtain the company's charter, he prepared the necessary papers for submission to the secretary of state in Texas.[38]

Basic to the contents of the Texas Land and Development Company charter were a few routine provisions. The company was chartered for twenty years. It was to have its headquarters in Plainview. Its stated purposes were "construction, maintenance, and operation of dams, reservoirs, lakes, wells, canals, flumes, laterals, and other necessary appurtenances for the purpose of irrigational development." On the board of directors for the first year were Charles, Henderson, Mason, and Grant.

The organization of the Texas Land and Development Company was completed on October 21, 1912. Officers were elected and a committee appointed to draw up the bylaws of the company. Henderson was elected president; Charles, vice-president; and Mason, secretary and treasurer. Grant and Mason comprised the committee to prepare the bylaws.[39]

When the directors met on October 29, 1912, they unanimously accepted the bylaws, which reiterated the purpose of the company and the duties of the directors. A restatement of the stock-holding policy coincided with the charter's arrangement for shares in the amount of $5,000 to be held by the directors of the Texas Land and Development Company for Texas Prairie Lands. One clause provided for increasing the number of directors if the stockholders requested it and stated that should a vacancy occur on the board, the remaining members were immediately to elect a successor to serve until the next annual meeting of the stockholders. The stockholders were to meet on the first Tuesday in October of each year primarily to elect directors for the ensuing year. Special meetings might be called by the president or by any two directors after giving a twenty-day written notice to each stockholder. A president, vice-president, treasurer, and general manager were listed in the bylaws as officers of the company, and their respective duties were iterated.[40] In practice, the titles given to the various officers did

[38] Texas Land and Development Company, minutes, October 19, 1912, TLDCP.
[39] *Ibid.*, October 21, 1912.
[40] *Ibid.*, October 29, 1912.

Organization of the Company

not always signify what their real duties were. For example, the first president, M. D. Henderson, was in fact the sales manager.[41] The first vice-president, R. S. Charles, was in reality the engineer in charge of installing wells, of completing land surveys, of constructing buildings, roads, and fences, of preparing the land for irrigation, and of supervising the farms until they were sold.[42]

Business matters handled at the directors' meetings were purely routine. The directors determined no policy unless the directors of the controlling company, Texas Prairie Lands, predetermined it. The work of the directors, therefore, was strictly perfunctory in nature.[43] In fact, a later officer, who was also a director of the Texas Land and Development Company, reported as follows: "I never attended a directors' meeting, nor do I believe a directors' meeting was ever held in Plainview during my service [May 12, 1919 to August 2, 1920] with the Company. I have a dim recollection of having been introduced to one of the [other] directors, but do not remember his name."[44] When an officer or a director resigned, however, some kind of directors' meeting was necessary. The directors perfunctorily accepted and appointed a successor. Actually the directors of the parent organization had already appointed the successor, and the directors of the Texas Land and Development Company simply confirmed the choice. Since most of the business of Texas Prairie Lands was carried on in the New York office,

---

[41] When Henderson assumed his duties as president of the Texas Land and Development Company in October 1912, he was actually functioning in a dual capacity. He continued to buy land for the Texas Securities Company and to function as its trustee. At the same time he initiated a sales program as a part of his duties as an officer of the Texas Land and Development Company and thus an employee of Texas Prairie Lands. It was not until December 1912 that all the land was purchased and the business transaction transferring the land from the Texas Securities Company to Texas Prairie Lands was completed. At that time Henderson was serving as vice-president and general manager of the Texas Land and Development Company.

[42] Charles, letter, November 1, 1958, BL.

[43] *Ibid.*

[44] A. B. DeLoach (secretary-treasurer and director of the Texas Land and Development Company, May 12, 1919, to August 2, 1920), letter, November 25, 1958, BL.

it was only natural that the replacements for officers who resigned their positions with the Texas Land and Development Company were often easterners.

Early in the first year of the company's operation, the directors of the Texas Land and Development Company met in a called session on December 7, 1912. Harry Irving Miller,[45] a director of Texas Prairie Lands, was elected to succeed Henderson as president of the company.[46] Miller, as the Frisco official in charge of arranging the survey that was to determine whether or not the railroad would build an extension through West Texas, first became personally acquainted with Pearson and his syndicate operation in 1911 during preliminary planning for the survey.[47] The two men must have been mutually impressed with each other, because in 1911 Pearson invited Miller to join him in directing his enterprise. His main duty seems to have been that of manager of the Pearson enterprise. In that position he directed, from a New York office with occasional trips to the site, any enterprise to which he was assigned. Not only did he assume charge of the Plainview operation for Pearson,[48] but he also became president of the Madeira Company, Limited, and vice-president of the Mexico Northwestern Railway,[49] both of which were Pearson organizations. Possibly other enterprises were also under his supervision.

Miller brought with him many years of managerial experience connected with railroading. After holding several minor positions, he became general manager of the Rock Island system in 1903, and in 1906 he became president of several smaller midwestern lines.[50] It was from these positions that he joined Pearson. Surely the new job must have offered Miller an unusual challenge or Pearson could never have enticed him to make the change.[51]

[45] Although Miller maintained a house in Plainview, he did not live there much of the time. His other interests were too demanding.
[46] *Documents 1917*, p. 101, TLDCP.
[47] Charles, letter, November 1, 1958, BL.
[48] *Ibid.*
[49] *Who Was Who in America*, 1897–1942, I, 841.
[50] *Ibid.*
[51] Mrs. Miller usually accompanied her husband to Plainview whenever he came there on business. They always traveled in their special railway car. Mrs.

Organization of the Company

When the directors appointed Miller president of the Texas Land and Development Company, they shifted Henderson to the position of vice-president and general manager. Charles, Grant, and Mason resigned their respective positions.[52] A. M. Treub, representing the interests of Texas Prairie Lands, replaced Mason as secretary; and U. de B. Daly, representing the Empire Trust Company of New York and London, took over Mason's duties as treasurer.[53] At the same time, the directors adopted a proposal to increase the board of directors from four to six. The resignation of Grant and the increase of two members created three vacancies. Pearson, who now emerged from the comparative anonymity of his syndicate, and two of the new officers, Harry Irving Miller and A. M. Treub, became the three new directors.[54]

Thus, more experienced financiers, in name as well as in fact, gained control of the Texas Land and Development Company. A financial arrangement by the parent company, Texas Prairie Lands, necessitated the radical shift, probably not contemplated when the company was organized in October. On November 10, 1912, the necessary financial support, undoubtedly promoted by Pearson, came when the Texas Prairie Lands sold a complete bond issue to Messrs. Dunn, Fisher and Company, a London banking and investment firm. The London company acquired first mortgage 6 per cent bonds against the assets of the Texas Prairie Lands to mature in five years (on December 1, 1917) in the total of £500,000 or $2,433,333.33.[55] From 1912 through 1914, Dunn, Fisher and Company was to make installment payments of the

---

Miller, who was French, was always accompanied by her French maid. She showed the Plainview ladies how "the other half lived" since she did no work. In fact, she did not rise until around noon. Those who attempted to contact her by telephone were informed that Mrs. Miller had not yet gotten up and that they should call after lunch.

[52] Charles was retained as chief engineer, but upon Henderson's resignation on August 14, 1913, he became general manager. Mason was retained as assistant secretary, since U. de B. Daly did not move to Plainview. Grant was no longer with the company.

[53] *Documents 1917*, p. 101, TLDCP.

[54] Texas Land and Development Company, minutes, December 7, 1912, TLDCP.

[55] *Documents 1917*, pp. 29–30, TLDCP.

£500,000 to the account of Texas Prairie Lands in the Bank of Scotland.[56] The company made the first such payment, amounting to $1,097,820.00, on November 25, 1912.[57] Apparently Dunn and Fisher agreed to sell the bonds to various individuals and firms for a commission of 9 per cent of the £500,000 since Texas Prairie Lands paid them such a commission, which amounted to £45,000 or $219,000.00, on January 6, 1913.[58]

The Empire Trust Company of New York and London acted as trustee for the bondholders[59] and itself invested in bonds worth £20,000.[60] Dunn, Fisher and Company held bonds amounting to £10,000. The rest were issued to individuals and firms primarily in Great Britain, Canada, and the United States. F. S. Pearson himself invested £19,000 in the bonds.[61] The large amount of money these men invested in bonds of Texas Prairie Lands suggests that they had great faith in the success of the venture.

The Empire Trust Company, in order to oversee the bondholder's interests, required Texas Prairie Lands to include their representative, Leroy W. Baldwin, as a third trustee to work with J. H. Slaton and H. C. Randolph, who held title to the Texas lands that the Texas Land and Development Company was to develop for Texas Prairie Lands. After December 5, 1912, when he officially assumed his duties, no transfer of title to any of the company's property was valid unless Baldwin signed and acknowledged it as a cotrustee.[62]

Before the end of 1914, the company had almost depleted the money that Dunn and Fisher of London had acquired. Of the $2,433,333.33 deposited to the account of Texas Prairie Lands as a result of the

[56] Barrow, Wade, Guthrie, and Co., *Memorandum*, p. 1, TLDCP.
[57] Texas Prairie Lands, Limited, 1913–1915, ledger, p. 6, TLDCP.
[58] *Ibid.*
[59] *Documents 1917*, pp. 29–74, TLDCP.
[60] See Appendix III for a complete list of all owners of securities.
[61] Pearson's investment is listed under two different accounts: under the Canadian Bank of Commerce and under Pearson's own name. See Appendix III.
[62] *Documents 1917*, 159–161, TLDCP.

Organization of the Company 33

bond sales, $1,537,750.95[63] had been used to fulfill in part the monetary obligations of $1,800,000.00 which had been incurred when that company had purchased the Plainview property. During November and December 1912, Texas Securities had expended additional funds to complete purchase of the lands, bringing the total spent by the original backers through the Pearson Engineering Corporation and Texas Securities Company to $1,537,750.95. At this point there was no profit to the promoters, but the holding company, the Texas Securities Company, was still owed the amount of $262,249.05. Of the remaining amount acquired from the negotiated bonds ($895,582.38), $219,000.00 was paid in commission to Dunn and Fisher. The rest of the money, which totaled $676,583.38, was fast being spent to put the operations of the Texas Land and Development Company into motion. In the first five months, the Texas Land and Development Company, operating for Texas Prairie Lands spent $153,463.53,[64] a sum that represented only the initial expenditures for sales and development. An accelerated development program was still in full swing in late 1914 when the directors of Texas Prairie Lands realized that the company would soon have no more available funds. By the end of November 1914 the company had spent $618,561.06 for total operation of the Texas Land and Development Company,[65] which left operating capital of $58,021.32. This meant that the $262,249.05 still owed to the Texas Securities Company could not be paid. Also complicating matters was the fact that interest on the bonds was due.

The directors of Texas Prairie Lands realized that the local development must have additional operating capital and the parent company must pay interest on its indebtedness. Three factors prevented immediate bankruptcy: first, a new agreement was entered into with the Empire Trust Company whereby Texas Prairie Lands was able to defer

[63] Texas Prairie Lands, Limited, 1913–1915, ledger, p. 70, account of Texas Securities Company, Limited, TLDCP.

[64] Texas Prairie Lands, Limited, 1913–1915, ledger, TLDCP.

[65] Baldwin, Slaton, and Randolph and Staked Plains Trust, Limited, 1913–1918, general ledger, pp. 59–62, Texas Land and Development Company account, TLDCP.

payment of interest on all bonds for a period of four years dating from and including December 1, 1914, or until the proceeds from land sales enabled the company to resume the payment of interest on the bonds, whichever was the shorter period. The Empire Trust Company waived any default in the payment of interest in the meantime.[66] Second, the Texas Securities Company canceled its claim to the $262,249.05[67] still owed to it. Pearson and his financial backers, who operated Texas Prairie Lands probably canceled the debt so they might give Texas Prairie Lands a chance to continue operations. Certainly it would have been to the backers' advantage for the company to continue since they owned all its common stock. Third, the company successfully negotiated the sale of $500,000.00 worth of prior lien notes on December 12, 1914. The London County and Westminster Bank, Limited, and the Old Colony Trust of Boston were to act as agents for this procedure. As the notes were sold, the $500,000.00 was to be made available. Holders of prior lien notes were to receive profit-sharing certificates, "by way of a commission for subscription." There were to be three series of profit-sharing certificates—A, B, and C. Each subscriber to prior lien notes, upon complete payment of his subscription, was issued 25 per cent of the amount he subscribed in Profit-Sharing Certificates A. Holders of these certificates would receive the amount of the certificates plus accrued interest after the redemption of the prior lien notes but before the redemption of the first mortgage bonds. The subscriber would receive 75 per cent of the amount he subscribed in Profit-Sharing Certificates C. These were not redeemable until the first mortgage bonds as well as the prior lien notes and interest accrued thereon were paid in full.[68] If a subscriber paid only one-half of the amount he had obligated himself to pay, he received one-half of the amount he paid in Profit-Sharing Certificates B.[69] The Profit-Sharing

---

[66] *Documents 1917*, p. 79, TLDCP.

[67] Texas Prairie Lands, Limited, 1913–1915, ledger, account of Texas Securities Company, Limited, TLDCP. The last entry is dated October 31, 1914. Two cents were marked off the books for some unknown reason; thus, the ledger showed that only $262,249.03 had been marked off.

[68] *Documents 1917*, p. 111, TLDCP.

[69] A study of the list of investors, Appendix III, confirms this point.

Organization of the Company

Certificates B were not redeemable until the principal amounts of the prior lien notes and first mortgage bonds were paid but were redeemable before accrued interest thereon was paid.[70] The Old Colony Trust of Boston acted as trustee for the owners of these notes[71] and brought yet another firm into an already intolerably complex financial structure.

So that they might enter into an indenture of trust with the Old Colony Trust, the directors of Texas Prairie Lands had to provide security. In order to do so and still maintain security for the first mortgage bonds held in trust by the Empire Trust Company, the directors of Texas Prairie Lands transferred their holdings to the Staked Plains Trust, Limited, which they formed at this juncture. The plan involved the transfer of the Plainview lands, all improvements thereon, and all contracts of purchase therefor; in other words all assets except, of course, those assigned to the Old Colony Trust as security for the prior lien notes. When the new company, the Staked Plains Trust, Limited, was chartered on December 12, 1914, its directors issued thirty-five thousand shares valued at par at $100.00 each, coincidentally the same amount as had been issued by Texas Prairie Lands.[72] The shares of the new company were deposited with the Empire Trust Company in order to maintain security for the first mortgage bonds for which Texas Prairie Lands had obligated itself in 1912. Thus, Texas Prairie Lands without liquidation had transferred all liabilities and assets to the Staked Plains Trust. Next the indenture of trust held by the Old Colony Trust, which was acting as trustee for the holders of the new prior lien notes, had to be secured. The bondholders (through their trustee, the Empire Trust Company) agreed to an amendment to the bond indenture that would permit Texas Prairie Lands to mortgage (or sell) certain assets with permission of the bondholders' agent, who was authorized to make such arrangements as might be necessary to provide security and protection for the bondholders. Under this amendment to

---

[70] *Documents 1917*, p. 215, TLDCP.

[71] *Ibid.*, p. 109.

[72] The shares of Texas Prairie Lands, which were held by the Texas Securities Company, were at this point, one would suspect, valueless. It does not seem plausible that anyone would ever realize a profit from the shares of a company that was inactive.

the original indenture, the Staked Plains Trust was established, and the indenture to the Old Colony Trust was secured. A first mortgage on the Demonstration Farm and its improvements, valued at $165,000.00, was given to the Old Colony Trust, and the trustees reaffirmed the mortgage. In addition, Texas Prairie Lands gave as security contracts of purchase, valued at $376,082.61 on the 3,361.52 acres already sold, and a pledge of future contracts of purchase. Again the Staked Plains Trust reaffirmed the agreement.[73] Thus, Texas Prairie Lands saw that both the Empire Trust Company and the Old Colony Trust Company were provided with acceptable security to cover the monetary obligations assured by the Staked Plains Trust.

It seems worthwhile to note at this point that despite the unusual complexity of the operation (and the fact that the original backers had limited their liability) there is no evidence that there was any fraud involved. All operations had been open. The companies maintained complete, although confusing, financial records throughout this and subsequent reorganizations. The backers (Texas Securities Company) had denied themselves a profit for the sake of the operation in 1913, and now gave up their control of the venture in an attempt to provide sufficient security for refinancing.

In order to operate within the limits of Texas law, it was necessary for the Staked Plains Trust to set up a trusteeship that would hold the lands in its name for the owners of the company. The trustees appointed included Minor Cooper Keith, the founder of the United Fruit Company of Central America and president of the Empire Trust Company; Harry Irving Miller, then president of the Texas Land and Development Company; Ward Edgerly Pearson, a director of the Texas Land and Development Company and a son of Dr. Frederick Stark Pearson; Francis R. Hart of Milton, Massachusetts; and Bradley W. Palmer of Boston, Massachusetts.[74] With the exception of Hart, who probably represented the Old Colony Trust interests, the trustees were investors in the Plainview enterprise.[75] The land was officially trans-

---

[73] *Documents 1917*, pp. 77–85, 87–105, 139–149, TLDCP.
[74] *Ibid.*, pp. 89 ff.
[75] See Appendix III.

Organization of the Company

ferred from Slaton, Randolph, and Baldwin, trustees for Texas Prairie Lands, to the five trustees on December 12, 1914.[76] The men were to hold the land in trust and to sell and convert it to cash when feasible. In the meantime, they were to manage the property for the owners. The new trustees also assumed all liabilities and obligations of the Texas Land and Development Company and of Texas Prairie Lands.[77]

Texas Prairie Lands did not officially liquidate itself when its directors formed the Staked Plains Trust. It simply became inactive since, by a provision in the charter of the new trust, Staked Plains Trust was to carry on all operations previously handled by Texas Prairie Lands.[78] Many key investors in the Plainview enterprise had been consistent backers. Some, mainly British, had originally invested through the Texas Securities Company, which had bought the Plainview land. Because these investors held thirty-five thousand shares of Texas Prairie Lands stock as part of the agreement when the Plainview land was sold to Texas Prairie Lands in 1912, they wished to reinforce their original investment by further investing in the new company when it issued first mortgage bonds in 1912 and prior lien notes in 1914.

After the issue of the first mortgage bonds, which brought investments from New York and Boston in addition to those from Britain, the backers were consistently divided into the original three groups—the British group, the Empire group, and the Boston group. The personality of the groups varied from investment to investment, but the three nuclei were stationary. When the Staked Plains Trust assumed its duties as trustee for the holders of the Texas Prairie Lands securities, it obligated itself to operate for the benefit of these holders. Only by keeping the enterprise in an operating state could the investors hope to make a profit from their original investment. The New York group of backers, which included the Empire Trust Company, controlled the new company. Harry Irving Miller, as one of their group, was to continue to supervise the Plainview development. F. S. Pearson, as a result of the formation of the new company, lost direct control of the Plainview operation.

[76] *Documents 1917*, pp. 89 ff., TLDCP.
[77] *Ibid.*, pp. 119–123.   [78] *Ibid.*

Apparently, the control passed from Pearson's hands with his consent, for his son, Ward Edgerly Pearson, who had become a trustee, represented his interests in the new company. Perhaps Dr. Pearson was relieved that he no longer had the main responsibility for the enterprise. He had been struggling to acquire capital all along. His main source of capital for all his projects had been British investors. Even as the final plans for the Texas land development scheme were being consummated, his source was cut off.[79] When the Balkan wars broke out in the summer and fall of 1912, war preparedness tied up much of Britain's capital. By the time World War I began in Europe in the summer of 1914, it was no doubt even more difficult to obtain capital in England for investments in such endeavors as the one being attempted in Texas. Pearson's syndicate matters became so entangled that he traveled to England to look after his investment and was among those who were lost when the *Lusitania* was sunk.

Not entirely heedless of the world crisis but supported by new capital, the directors of the Texas Land and Development Company carried on operations. Development continued on the farms already sold. An accelerated sales program led to additional land sales of 6,325 acres.[80] Although the selling program had been designed to furnish additional operating capital, the company soon discovered that there would not be enough. The $500,000 operating capital that had been obtained in 1914, even with the installments paid by the land purchasers for their real estate, was not adequate to complete development of the newly sold farms. Selling the additional land had simply compounded the company's problems. In order to furnish a temporary supply of capital so that development could continue, some of the backers, who had tried to protect their original investment by further investing in both the first mortgage bonds held by the Empire Trust and the prior lien notes held by the Old Colony Trust, arranged a loan of $100,000 for a two-month period. The backers could only give their personal guarantee as security for the temporary loan.[81] During the in-

---

[79] Charles, letter, November 1, 1958, BL.
[80] *Documents 1917*, pp. 293, 301, 303, TLDCP.
[81] *Ibid.*, p. 321.

Organization of the Company 39

terim, representatives of some of the principal English and American investors conducted a survey to determine how much money the operating company needed to develop the lands already sold. The survey turned up an estimate of $400,000. The figure was only approximate since ever-increasing prices, precipitated by the activities of World War I, made estimates difficult. After long consultation among the representatives of the investors, a tentative solution was accepted. All sales operations were to end until conditions became more conducive to the sale of land.[82] In the meantime, of course, it was necessary for the Staked Plains Trust to raise additional money to pay for the obligations already contracted.

As a first measure for raising the money, all contracts of purchase, including those sold since 1914 and those sold before 1914 and held as security by the Old Colony Trust Company, and the mortgaged demonstration farms were sold on December 1, 1916, to a newly organized trust, the Prairie Lands Trust, Limited. This move was agreed to by the Old Colony Trust in a new indenture. Control at this juncture shifted from the New York backers to the Boston backers of the enterprise.[83] The unsold lands, whether they were rented to tenants or uncultivated, remained in the hands of the Staked Plains Trust; the new company bought only land that was being developed or needed to be developed. An agreement was made between the two trusts providing that the "Old Trustees shall . . . transfer . . . to the New Trustees such further contracts of purchase, vendor's lien notes, or lands as the New Trustees may deem necessary to insure the fulfillment of this guaranty."[84] As trustees for the Prairie Lands Trust, Minor Cooper Keith, Ward Edgerly Pearson, and Charles H. Zehnder agreed to undertake the obligations incurred by the trustees of the Staked Plains Trust who

---

[82] *Ibid.*, pp. 321–322.

[83] It should be recalled that there were three groups of original backers—a group from New York, one from Boston, and one from the British Isles. Since the New York and Boston groups were close at hand, they seemed to vie for control, that is for the privilege of investing more money in order to keep the enterprise operating.

[84] *Documents 1917*, p. 273, TLDCP.

had been obliged to sell a part of their assets because of insufficient capital with which to continue land development.[85] The Texas Land and Development Company was to act as agent in the future for both the Prairie Lands Trust and the Staked Plains Trust. Both companies were to share, in a proportion to be agreed upon, the expenses incurred by the Texas Land and Development Company.[86]

Keith, Pearson, Zehnder, and other backers who were actively spearheading this attempt to keep their investments sound, estimated that $375,000 would be required for the completion of their development program. It would, therefore, be necessary to raise that amount. To do so, an agreement was made on December 5, 1916, between the new trustees and subscribers, who agreed to purchase trust certificates of the Prairie Lands Trust. The issue of these certificates was oversubscribed by $50,000 because pledges amounted to $425,000 instead of the estimated $375,000. Subsequently, the subscribers received 4,250 certificates upon receipt of the full amount of their subscriptions. Actually, by advancing $425,000 in cash, the subscribers acquired title to mortgaged assets whose book value was approximately $700,000 to $800,000, although their market value at the time was questionable.

That a profit was anticipated for the risks involved is evident by the prospectus for these subscriptions, which explained that, "If all of the contracts of purchase are fulfilled, it will be seen that there is a possible profit of over $300,000 after repaying the prior lien notes, the profit sharing certificates of Class A and the subscriptions."[87] Of the $425,000, subscriptions by former investors amounted to $340,000 and $85,000 by new investors.[88] It is significant that the men connected with the enterprise were of such repute that, even at this point after the company had twice been on the verge of bankruptcy, they were

---

[85] Keith and young Pearson were also trustees for the Staked Plains Trust, Limited.

[86] *Documents 1917*, pp. 267–308, TLDCP. Apparently the Prairie Lands Trust, Limited, and the Staked Plains Trust, Limited, agreed upon the proportion of Texas Land and Development Company expenses each was to share, but no reference to such an agreement could be located.

[87] *Document 1917*, p. 325, TLDCP.

[88] *Ibid.*, p. 325.

Organization of the Company

able to raise any money from people who did not already have an interest in the enterprise. These subscriptions, with the property acquired by the Prairie Lands Trust, were pledged to the Old Colony Trust Company as collateral for a six-month loan of $375,000.[89] The money received enabled the new trustees to pay back the $100,000 that had been loaned temporarily by some of the American investors and to continue the development of farms. It was the intention of the trustees to renew the $375,000 loan until conditions improved or until their property in Texas yielded a sufficient return to repay it.[90] The loan was due on June 29, 1917, but since the trustees of the Prairie Lands Trust were unable to pay it at that time because the subscriptions had not been paid, the loan was renewed.[91] The renewal agreement did not state when the new extension was due, but the loan was paid as soon as the $425,000 subscribed for trust certificates was collected.[92]

The active operation of the enterprise remained in the hands of the Prairie Lands Trust until December 1, 1919, when a total reorganization plan was officially adopted. The Staked Plains Trust, which had been created in 1914 and had sold part of the holdings to the Prairie Lands Trust in 1916 as a result of a maneuver to gain more operating capital, was to initiate the movement to consolidate the operation. Certainly, such an act was in order since confusion had been heaped upon confusion by the previous reorganizations. Each company had issued securities, and so much interweaving of financial negotiations eventually led to a confusing, if not intolerable, situation. It was not surprising, then, that the investors in the three companies were anxious to bring order through a large-scale reorganization that would consolidate the operation financially as well as functionally; such a reorganization did not occur until December 1919.

[89] *Ibid.*, pp. 251 ff.
[90] *Ibid.*
[91] *Ibid.*, pp. 359–361.
[92] Staked Plains Trust, Limited, v. Commissioner of Internal Revenue, Transcript of Record (5th Cir., 1937), Randolph Files, Plainview.

3. Sales and Advertising, 1912–1919

WHILE FINANCIAL BACKERS of Texas Prairie Lands acquired capital for the Plainview enterprise, M. D. Henderson organized the Texas Land and Development Company to operate Texas Prairie Lands holdings locally. Even before the Texas Land and Development Company was chartered, Henderson had acted as a trustee and employee of Pearson's syndicate organization. In that capacity he was responsible for purchasing and holding in trust what finally amounted to 61,360 acres of Hale, Floyd, and Swisher county land. He was connected with the group that formed the Texas Securities Company until arrangements to sell the land to Texas Prairie Lands were completed. Three months elapsed between October 16, 1912, when the two companies made the agreement, and the last of December, when Henderson purchased all the land for them and saw it transferred to the trustees. During that time Henderson functioned both as president of the Texas Land and Development Company, a duty which he assumed on October 19, 1912, when the new company was chartered, and as trustee of the Texas Securities Company, a position he retained until some time in the following year.

As one of the terms of sale, the Texas Securities Company was to hold thirty-five thousand shares of Texas Prairie Lands stock. Since no other shares were issued, the Texas Securities Company owned the new company. It was, therefore, the backers of the Texas Securities Company who operated Texas Prairie Lands and who were responsible for acquiring capital to be used by the Texas Land and Development Company for development sales. When the backers completed financial arrangements for operating capital in December 1912, they deemed it necessary to have one of their number in a supervisory capacity as president of the Texas Land and Development Company. Harry Irving Miller filled this position, and Henderson became vice-president and general manager. Since Miller, who also had other personal interests, held a liaison position between the backers and the local operations, he did not spend much time in Plainview but operated mainly from New York, where the Pearson firm had one of its offices. Consequently, Henderson was to remain in direct charge of the local office although he was more closely supervised. The closer supervision was not surprising since the backers sent a large amount of capital into the area for the use of the local company. R. S. Charles, who at first was vice-president of the Texas Land and Development Company, lost his title as a result of the officer switch, but he continued as chief engineer in charge of development. With Charles taking the lead in development, Henderson assumed a more active role in the organization of the sales program, a position for which he was well suited because of his real-estate experience.

The terms of Henderson's contract when he became general manager were definitely geared toward those of a sales manager. He was employed as the company's "agent and representative" to sell the lands in the Plainview area. While the contract was in force, he was "to devote his entire time to the sale of said lands." The company was to pay Henderson a yearly salary of $10,000 plus 3 per cent commission of the gross amount of all land sales whether they were made by him or by his subagents. The commission was to be paid outright on cash sales but to be deferred on term sales until payment was made. Henderson could hire as many subagents as he considered necessary to assist him in selling the lands. Their commissions were not to exceed 10 per cent of any land sale and were to be paid in the same manner as were his. Henderson was to pay each subagent's commission, and the company in turn would reimburse him. The company allowed Henderson $30,000 each year for advertising and office expenses. He was to prepare all "advertising matter, subject to approval of the Company." He also received a traveling expense account of $3,000 a year to conduct company business. Either Henderson or the company could terminate the contract under which he worked subject to a sixty-day notice.[1]

Both aspects of the company's operation, sales and development, were set into motion simultaneously. The development program went forward under Charles's enthusiastic leadership, and the sales program took shape in the same vigorous vein under Henderson. Even though each complemented the other, their divergent paths of operation were so clear that they should be considered separately.[2]

Henderson acquired a staff to assist him with the sales and advertising department. Joe Hess became local sales manager, and Zenas E. Black took direct charge of publicity.[3] Although other sales agents were no doubt hired from time to time as the need arose, no record of their activities was kept.

Henderson evolved several schemes to promote the sale of company lands. He made available to local papers educational articles that company employees had prepared to explain farm development. These articles, which carried a Texas Land and Development Company by-line, were designed to inform the public about good farming methods and

[1] Texas Land and Development Company, contract, Wallet 2, Texas Land and Development Company Papers, Southwest Collection, Texas Tech University, Lubbock (hereafter cited as TLDCP).

[2] The development operations and connected subjects of the same period will be discussed in Chapter 4.

[3] Because the records of the sales department were scant, much of the early workings of the department had to be pieced together from newspaper accounts. It was impossible to ascertain when some members of the staff were hired and what their duties might have been. That they were on the scene at certain periods of the company's existence can be confirmed by newspaper accounts and reports.

to convince people to try some of the methods discussed. Such an article appeared in the *Hale County Herald* on May 8, 1913, and depicted the South Plains as a great stock-raising region, where there was no longer a conflict between the ranchman and the farmer. It expressed the need for a better type of stock. Further, it pointed out that there was a possibility for infinite profits from stock farming in the Plainview country and predicted that the area would become one of the great dairy centers of the nation. The article also drew attention to the advantages of diversified farming and poultry raising. In conclusion, the article portrayed the stock farmer as the happiest person in the world.

The stock-farmer of the Plainview country . . . is the most independent person on earth. His garden, his farm and his orchard, his dairy, his flock and his herds will return almost all of his household needs. He is getting the greatest amount of revenue from his investment because there is absolutely no waste or leakage in the little Empire of which he is sole Monarch. (Perhaps, though, we had better pay tribute to his wife who is the very important Queen of the Realm.) This royal pair is happy, and they are getting rich. Big red barns, sleek, high-grade stock, the latest farm machinery and irrigation equipment, and a rapidly swelling balance in the bank testify to the fiscal condition of their little empire. They should be happy . . . comfortable, luxurious farm homes, all modern conveniences: the telephone, good schools, nearness to colleges, rural mail deliverys [*sic*], automobiles, excellent roads, convenient churches, and congenial educated neighbors, make for conditions in the rural districts of the Plainview country superior to the advantages of modern city life.[4]

One of Henderson's major contributions to the sales program was an attractive brochure that he compiled and that a Kansas City firm published.[5] The brochure, simply entitled "Texas Land and Development Company," was published for the use of the sales agents when

[4] *Hale County Herald*, May 8, 1913.
[5] The brochure was published by the F. P. Burnap Stationery and Printing Company, Kansas City, Missouri, some time between December 7, 1912, and August 14, 1913, since those were the dates between which Henderson was general manager and vice-president of the Texas Land and Development Company.

they were attempting to convince prospective buyers of the advantages of purchasing Plainview lands. Before the potential buyer learned the terms of sale, which were listed in the back of the brochure, he was almost certain to examine the preceding pages, which excelled in convincing platitudes that presented Plainview as the garden spot of the world. The brochure assured him that he would be just as capable as anyone else of sharing in the profits to be gained by the yield of the land. In the introductory remarks the author emphasized that the brochure was written "in simple style" for the "benefit of the plain American farmer." It was quickly added, however, that the "local conditions appeal equally as strong to the man who is somewhat a scientist" since "under irrigation methods only can true scientific farming be practiced." The Plainview area was strongly recommended for those who wanted to "secure the future for their sons" as well as for those who were "tired of the pressure of city life" and wished to "join the multitudes" who were returning to the country. The brochure, it seemed, was supposed to convince people of all types that the lands offered an excellent opportunity for investment.

The brochure used the irrigation system as its biggest selling point. It represented the area's water supply as inexhaustible since a water shield, located thirty to sixty feet below ground, appeared to extend down several hundred feet more. The expense of irrigating did not seem great since it cost less than one dollar per acre-foot for pumps operated by gas- or oil-burning engines. The levelness of the land also helped to reduce irrigation prices. To convince further the prospective purchaser, the brochure pointed to irrigation farming as gaining in favor throughout the United States. The well owner could supply his crops with water at exactly the right time and in exactly the right amount. Irrigation experts who had visited Plainview claimed that the area had the cheapest and the best irrigation system in the world. One well could supply water for 160 to 320 acres of crops, depending on the variety of crops cultivated. The "most valuable crops, the highest-priced land, the best roads, the most compact and most prosperous communities," were found in irrigated areas. The same area could be expected to contain the "best schools and churches, social and business facilities," because it was inhabited by "only the most cultured, most ambitious and enterprising types of people." Because no other irrigated district in the world had a "shade" of advantage over Plainview, how long would it be before the prices of Plainview lands would "be enhanced to their true value"?

Sections of the brochure discussed truck farming, horticulture, and stock farming. To point out the advantages of truck farming, it emphasized the large number of first premiums captured by Hale County farmers at the Dallas State Fair in 1912. They took firsts in Jonathan, Roman Beauty, Limber Twig, Crab, and Storm Proof apples, several varieties of peaches, Irish potatoes, string beans, carrots, cabbage, cauliflower, radishes, celery, pumpkin, cantaloupes, onions, sugar beets, several varieties of wheat, broom corn, white kafir, and alfalfa. The growing season of the Plainview area was long enough and mild enough to grow all but the most tropical crops. Such crops as strawberries, asparagus, peas, cabbage, potatoes, beets, turnips, tomatoes, cauliflower, artichokes, eggplants, radishes, kale, lettuce, okra, spinach, rhubarb, and squashes had been grown successfully in Plainview. Included was a table (Table 1), "carefully and constructively compiled" to show the possible profits in the raising of the various crops.

The section devoted to horticulture emphasized that the Plainview area possessed the ideal combination of soil, water, climate, and marketing facilities for profitable fruit growing. It predicted that the area would shortly become one of the most versatile orchard districts in the country.

The Plainview area was also visualized as a stockman's paradise. It was profitable for every farmer to keep stock because all farm animals did well in the district. No extra expense would be incurred since favorable climate eliminated the necessity for shelters and since the residue from the crops would furnish food for the stock.

After the prospective buyer perused the first pages of the brochure and looked at the accompanying pictures, which had been aptly chosen to enhance the selling points, he then was told the terms under which land in the Plainview area could be his. It was hoped, of course, that he would be in a buying mood. It was first stated that the company offered its lands for sale in units of 40 acres. Prices ranged from $100 per acre for an improved stock farm of 160 acres or more, to $250

Table 1. Estimated Value of Crops

Crop	Value per Acre
Beans	$ 75 to $ 100
Cabbage	400 to 600
Strawberries	700 to 1,000
Cantaloupes	250 to 500
Grapes	300 to 500
Tomatoes	200 to 400
Onions	250 to 500
Sweet potatoes	200 to 350
Irish potatoes	200 to 400
Lettuce	250 to 500
Watermelons	250 to 500
Asparagus	750 to 1,000
Sugar beets	75 to 150
Celery	750 to 1,000
Turnips	75 to 150
Cucumbers	250 to 500
Parsley	600 to 800

Source: Texas Land and Development Company, brochure, "Texas Land and Development Company," Clinkscales Collection, Plainview.

per acre for a 40-acre unit. The developments and improvements on a given unit determined the price. If a buyer could not purchase the land with cash, a condition much to be preferred, the agent arranged terms. The company required one-fourth of the cost as down payment, the balance to be due within one to five years, depending on the terms. Interest was 6 percent, payable annually. Default of any interest payment for more than thirty days after it was due matured all the remaining unpaid notes.[6]

There was no way to determine the extent to which the company used the brochure in its advertising program. Because it was compiled before development was well under way, the sales policy it presented was possibly altered more than once to fit the rising cost of develop-

[6] Texas Land and Development Company, brochure entitled "Texas Land and Development Company," Clinkscales Collection, Plainview.

Sales and Advertising, 1912-1919

ment.⁷ The educational material it presented would remain valuable, nonetheless, when a sales agent was trying to convince a prospective buyer of the area's assets. A great portion of $5,941.45 spent by the sales and advertising departments in the first five months of the company's operation was no doubt spent on the brochure. A breakdown of the expenditures of the two departments was listed.⁸ In the Advertising Department $800.00 was spent on salaries, $42.95 for traveling expense, $1,141.80 for publications, $2,963.68 for printed matter, $99.00 for postage, $64.12 for miscellaneous expenses, and $242.98 for camera and photo supplies, making a total of $5,354.53 spent on advertising. The Sales Department added $586.90 to this account, bringing total expenses to $5,941.45. Salaries of salesmen were listed at $332.14, office expenses at $55.68, and traveling expenses at $199.08. The $2,963.68 for printed matter under the advertising department expenses probably represented the cost for printing the brochure. At least a portion of the camera and photo supplies division would have to be credited to the publication of the brochure since it contained so many pictures. Portions of other entries could also be allotted to the expense of the brochure.⁹ The bookkeeping system used by the Texas Land and Development Company allowed very general entries to be placed in the main ledger. As a result, amounts spent for specific items were seldom accurately determined. Much of the money spent was labeled with one of the following general entries in the ledger: expenditures for the month of January, cash, sundries. No doubt more detailed records were kept in another place, but only the main ledgers and cash books survive.

Advertising in publications formed an important facet of the company's land-selling campaign. In the first five months of operation, the

---

⁷ Robert S. Charles, letter, November 1, 1958, Brunson letters, Southwest Collection, Texas Tech University, Lubbock (hereafter cited as BL).

⁸ Texas Land and Development Company, Baldwin, Slaton, and Randolph, and Staked Plains Trust, Limited, general ledger, balance sheet, TLDCP.

⁹ Even though no record was found of the number of brochures printed, surely several hundred were. The sales agents would be expected to use many of them in their attempts to sell land, and many others could be mailed to persons who sought information about the land.

company spent $1,141.80 on this type of advertising.[10] Perhaps typical of the advertisements inserted in local newspapers was a half-page notice that appeared in the *Hale County Herald*. A picture of the irrigation system operating on the company's experiment farm was followed by information designed to inform the people about company activity.[11]

SOME THINGS THE TEXAS LAND AND DEVELOPMENT CO. is doing—planting 65,000 fruit trees and grape vines. Planting 90,000 tamaracs for shade. Developing a pleasure park for Plainview. Maintaining a 630 acre experiment farm with experts in charge for the benefit of Hale County farmers. Fully improved, planted and irrigated tracts of 40, 80, and 160 acres will be sold on easy terms. Write for illustrated literature. Office in Denver, Kansas City, and Columbus, Ohio.

TEXAS LAND AND DEVELOPMENT CO.
M. D. Henderson, Manager
PLAINVIEW, TEXAS

Possibly similar advertisements appeared in newspapers in Denver, Colorado, Kansas City, Missouri, and Columbus, Ohio, where the company established sales contacts during the early months of operation.

To make effective use of the large advertisements placed in local and out-of-town publications, the agents made trips to key cities to attract prospective buyers. The agent, who was sent from the Plainview office to a designated city, probably used the methods of contemporary traveling dentists and salesmen of various types. The company would announce the agent's presence in the city in the classified section of the newspaper and would designate the place, probably a hotel suite, where interested parties could contact the agent. In May 1913 Joe Hess, the local sales manager, made a trip to Denver, Colorado, no doubt typical of all sales trips. Hess reported, "They wouldn't let me rest a minute." The morning after he registered in a Denver hotel, he found two callers waiting. All that day and until he left the following day, visitors came to inquire about the Plainview area. Hess's trip was not confined

---

[10] Texas Land and Development Company, Baldwin, Slaton, and Randolph, and Staked Plains Trust, Limited, general ledger, balance sheet, TLDCP.
[11] *Hale County Herald*, May 8, 1913.

Sales and Advertising, 1912–1919 51

to Denver. He also went to Fort Collins, Boulder, and Walsenburg. Everywhere he went he found inquirers who were "anxious to know about the Plainview country."[12]

As a result of these and similar trips made by Hess and other agents during the first years of the company's operation, the company organized excursions that transported groups of "prospectors"[13] by train to Plainview to look over the land. Most often the prospectors came free; however, there were occasions when the company charged a nominal fee of $25.[14] This method of selling land was not unique with the Texas Land and Development Company. Of the forty real-estate agencies[15] operating in Plainview during the period, several organized excursions to bring in prospectors. Even the Santa Fe Railroad sponsored an "Educational Special" in November 1913. The Texas Land and Development Company chauffeured a party about the Plainview area that was headed by the agricultural demonstrator of the Santa Fe system, Amarillo, Texas.[16] The local newspaper devoted ample space to reporting "Excursion days" held by the various land promoters. Names of promoters other than the Texas Land and Development Company were often prominent in the reports. Some others whose firms often appeared in the newspaper accounts were J. J. Lash, DeLay and Burch, Alley Brothers, W. R. Hall, J. B. Nance, Price and Boswell, Hess-Wilkes-Otto Company, and J. L. Vaughn.[17] The Texas Land and Development Company, however, held a prominent place in most of the newspaper accounts. If sheer numbers be proof, the Texas Land and Development seemed to attract far more people to its excursions, and its prospectors came from a much greater area of the United States. The important role of the Texas Land and Development Company is not surprising because its operation was of far greater consequence than

---

[12] *Ibid.*, May 29, 1913.

[13] The term "prospector" was used by the Texas Land and Development Company and by the Plainview newspapers.

[14] *Plainview Evening Herald*, February 19, 1915.

[15] *Daily Plainview Advertiser*, January 1, 1914.

[16] *Hale County Herald*, November 21, 1913.

[17] *Plainview Evening Herald*, sporadic articles throughout 1913, 1914, 1915, and 1916.

was that of any other promoter. Typical of newspaper accounts of the early excursions was the following:

Today is excursion day, and there are many prospective land buyers in the county. The Texas Land and Development Co. are entertaining more than twenty men, while J. L. Vaughn and W. R. Hall took nearly as many men from here into the Littlefield section. The dining room of the Hotel Missouri looked very metropolitan when all these visitors assembled for their meals.[18]

The company decided to extend its sales territory and accelerate its use of the excursion system. Late in the summer of 1913, it chose to open a permanent office in Chicago, a farm-belt city accessible to people who might be interested in buying land. A man who had previously worked in the Chicago area, Walter S. Ayres, was available within the framework of the Pearson Syndicate to open the office. The syndicate hired Ayres to operate the office for two of the Pearson organizations, the Texas Land and Development Company and the Medina Valley Irrigation Company, an offshoot of the Medina Dam project, that had sixty thousand acres of land to sell in the San Antonio area.[19] Ayres's previous connection with Chicago had been as the member of the passenger department of the Rock Island Railroad who dealt principally with the Oklahoma and Texas areas. The department was also active in promoting the "Gulf Coast Country," especially the Lower Rio Grande Valley area. While bringing people to that area, Ayres became acquainted with the organizers of the Gulf Coast Irrigation Company and was invited by them to become its vice-president in charge of land sales. He successfully sold some sixty thousand acres of land in a four- or five-year period. It was then that he joined the staff of Pearson's Medina Valley Irrigation Company,[20] on which Pearson was consulting engineer. When Ayres accepted the Chicago position, he was put under a contract that was, no doubt, similar in many ways to Henderson's.[21]

[18] *Hale County Herald*, April 17, 1913.
[19] *Hale County Record*, November 14, 1913.
[20] Clyde E. Craig, letter, October 5, 1959, BL.
[21] Although a copy of Ayres's contract was not located, pencil marks on a

The sales policy under which Ayres operated seemed more flexible than the Henderson policy, however, and he exercised more freedom than had Henderson in arranging terms. The company still sought, but did not always demand, a down payment of one-fourth the cost of the land, and the buyer had ten years instead of five or less to pay off notes. The buyer benefited from a lower interest rate of only 5 per cent instead of the former 6 per cent.

The two groups no doubt shared the expenses of the Chicago office and of Ayres's salary since the Texas Land and Development cash book showed only sporadic entries concerning Ayres's office. The first record of money being advanced to Ayres was made in July 1913, when the company disbursed $1,000 to him for salary and office expenses.[22]

Shortly after Ayres opened the Chicago office, Henderson terminated his association with the company, his resignation becoming official in August 1913. Although it was not known whether Ayres's employment was related to Henderson's action, Mr. Peyton B. Randolph alluded to the fact that Henderson could not "get along" with some of the eastern backers of the company and had a "row" with them.[23] What the "row" was about could not be ascertained. With Henderson's departure, the company shifted the bulk of the sales operation to Chicago, and Ayres officially became a vice-president of the Texas Land and Development Company. Henderson's duties and title, general manager, were attached to those of the chief engineer in charge of development, R. S. Charles.[24] Zenas E. Black, who continued to

---

copy of Henderson's old contract show strong evidence of proposed revisions for Ayres's contract. Such terms as "Chicago," for the base of operation, and "July 1913" (the approximate date of Ayres's employment), as the date the contract was signed, were superscribed over the original terms of Henderson's contract.

[22] Texas Land and Development Company, cash book, July 1913, TLDCP. This record book was kept in the New York Office.

[23] Peyton B. Randolph to Dr. Seymour V. Connor, tape interview, April 8, 1958.

[24] Texas Land and Development Company, minutes, August 14, 1913, TLDCP.

function as publicity agent, moved to Chicago, and Joe Hess remained in charge of the Plainview sales department as local sales manager.[25]

Typical of listings that began to appear in the local newspaper while Hess supervised sales was a full-page advertisement in which the company drew a comparison between the prices of irrigated lands in other parts of the country and those in Plainview. Following the list of lands for sale elsewhere was a listing of Texas Land and Development Company properties for sale. The reader, of course, was to come to the conclusion that he would be getting a "bargain" if he purchased land from the Texas Land and Development Company. Further, the implication was that he should "buy while the buying was good." Some samples quoted suggested the differences between the two groups.

Imperial Valley, California—raw lands from $80 to $100. Improved lands from $350 to $600.

Salem, Oregon—Raw lands $60 to $300. Improved lands from $150 to $500.

Boise, Idaho—Raw lands including water right $80 to $150. Improved lands $250 to $1000.

Fort Collins, Colorado—Raw lands with water right $75 to $125. Improved lands $125 to $500.

Texas Land and Development Company listings emphasized the low cost of initial investment.

No. 125. 60 acres, about 20 acres in orchard, balance in cultivation; a mile and a half from Plainview, near Seth Ward College. This would make an ideal small irrigation farm. Price $80 per acre.

No. 104. An improved quarter section five miles out of Hale Center, near school, has four room house, well windmill, nice shade trees, all fenced. One hundred acres in cultivation. Price $35 per acre.

No. 108. An unimproved section of land seven miles east of Happy, on the Ceta draw, no finer soil anywhere in Texas. Near school. Price $18 per acre, terms given on part.[26]

---

[25] *Hale County Herald*, August 26, 1913.
[26] *Ibid.*, April 17, 1914.

Sales and Advertising, 1912–1919

Ayres's main approach to the land-selling venture was a continuation and acceleration of the system carried on by Henderson. Large advertisements were placed in newspapers, and magazines with a national reading public such as *Sunset* and *Country Gentleman* also carried advertisements.[27] While Ayres and his agents contacted potential customers in the midwestern states and arranged and conducted excursions from that area, Hess made similar contacts in Oklahoma[28] and Colorado,[29] as well as in other parts of Texas and the Southwest.[30] As a result of the sales agents' trips, excursion trains brought in several hundred potential buyers. By December 1913 fifteen of the Texas Land and Development Company's farms had been sold.[31] By December 1914 contracts of purchase had been issued for 5,712.69 acres.[32]

During 1914, 1915, and 1916, the years in which the greatest attempts were made to sell Plainview lands, the Texas Land and Development Company conducted monthly excursion tours. From June 1915 until June 1916, the company conducted semimonthly tours. In 1915 and 1916 approximately one thousand potential buyers came to the Plainview area on company-sponsored excursion trains.[33] As a result of the land-selling efforts in 1915 and 1916, the company issued contracts of purchase for an additional sixty-one farms representing approximately 6,235 acres of land.[34] From the beginning of 1913 to

[27] *Ibid.*, August 26, 1913.
[28] *Ibid.*, March 13, 1914.
[29] *Ibid.*, December 30, 1913.
[30] *Ibid.*, November 21, 1913.
[31] *Ibid.*, January 20, 1914.
[32] *Documents 1917*, p. 181, TLDCP.
[33] Information concerning the tours, dates, and number of people who came to Plainview was reported in the *Plainview Evening Herald* during the years mentioned. Unfortunately, the number of prospectors brought into the area was not always reported. Thus, only an estimate can be given. Although many of the newspaper accounts stated that only the best caliber of person was brought to look over the land, one of the company's lawyers, Peyton B. Randolph, stated that some of those who came were simply "railroad station loafers" who were picked up to add to the number. How extensive this practice was is not known (Randolph to Connor, tape interview, April 8, 1958).
[34] *Documents 1917*, pp. 279–281, 293, 301, 303, TLDCP. Only an approxi-

July 1916 the total number of contracts of purchase was ninety-two. The total number of acres represented in the contracts was approximately 12,038. The total amount that the company would receive if all contracts were paid in full was approximately $1,090,000.[35]

During the time the company was bringing in excursion trains, there was one recorded occasion on which another land promoter tried to take advantage of the Texas Land and Development Company's system. The Texas Land and Development Company never commented on the situation,[36] but the promoter, because of his advertising methods, incurred the wrath of some of the townspeople. The townspeople carried on a battle with the promoter in the local newspaper. Dr. R. R. White of Temple, Texas, the realtor in question, had placed 2,000 acres of land in the Plainview area for sale. On the principal routes leading into Plainview, White had placed large signboards that read: "See Dr. White's irrigated farms before you buy, nearer town for less money; no cash payment required, twenty years time." Obviously prospectors brought into the area by the Texas Land and Development Company saw the signs. Apparently the company made no formal protests, but seven citizens of the town did. A telegram sent to White by Knight, Slaton, Anderson, Hughes, Lancaster, Garrison, and Gidney, claimed that the signs were "demoralizing the handling of prospectors by the Syndicate" and they felt that "in justice to them and the Plainview District" it would be "wise" for White to "change the wording of them" so the signs would not "interfere with the handling of prospectors in this territory." The gentlemen who sent the telegram claimed that, in making "this suggestion," they had "only the best

---

mate number of acres can be recorded here since the twelve contracts of purchase (p. 303) did not carry a listing of acres contained in them.

[35] This figure was arrived at by checking the lists of contracts of purchase in *ibid.*, pp. 105, 279–281, 293, 301, 303. Again, one of the lists (pp. 279–281) was incomplete. Since it represented 2,365.51 acres, a figure of $354,826.50 was arrived at by assuming that the average cost of each acre was $150.00. The other amounts listed were $376,082.61 (p. 105) and $359,217.89 (pp. 293, 301, 303), making a total of $1,090,127.00, which was rounded off here to $1,090,000.00.

[36] At least no record was found to this effect.

Sales and Advertising, 1912–1919

interests of the Plainview district at heart." White, in his reply[37] to the seven men, stated that he had no fight with the syndicate, that he appreciated their development contributions but that he also realized that business interests and not "philanthropic motives" influenced syndicate activities. He further clarified the situation by contending that his purchases of land antedated those of the syndicate and that he had paid his own money for his property and for his improvements. White claimed he would not use the signboards with which to advertise if no prospectors came to Plainview except through the efforts of the Texas Land and Development Company. "Fortunately," he continued, "there were other prospectors, and it was to those that his advertisements were directed." Further, White's "interests" suggested that he "aggressively endeavor" to make such sales as he might "legitimately be able to make." However, White promised that he would sell to no one who was under obligation to the Texas Land and Development Company unless the person so obligated first discharged his debt in full to the syndicate.[38]

A few days after White had clarified his position in advertisements, he inserted another advertisement in the *Plainview Evening Herald*. The advertisement opened in this manner:

> DR. WHITE'S IRRIGATED FARMS
> Since Our First Advertisement Appeared, Someone Has Torn Down Our Signs On Which We Offered Lands Nearer Town for Less Money. Can You Guess Who Did This—And Why?

Apparently there was some fear among the Plainview citizens that the Texas Land and Development Company would abandon the Plainview project if White continued his advertising campaign. White admonished the citizenry to be calm.

Do not be afraid that someone will abandon the Plainview country because some other fellow offers land for sale "nearer town for less money." They

---

[37] *Plainview Evening Herald*, June 15, 1915.
[38] The same advertisement appeared in the *Herald* again on June 18, 22, and 25.

could not afford to leave if they wanted to. Don't be an easy mark. Speculators and development companies buy land to sell—they can't eat it, and they do not want to keep much of it, so do not be annoyed by any hot air talk that any of us are going to withdraw from the Plainview country. If the future and permanent value of the Plainview country is dependent on any one interest or concern, then we advise you to let the lands alone, for as soon as such interests have cleaned up and gone, you will have dead property on your hands.[39]

Apparently little more came of the incident. No doubt, White and other promoters continued to carry on their individual advertising campaign in healthy competition with the Texas Land and Development Company.

During the great push to sell developed farms, Ayres, operating from Chicago, spent the major portion of the money allotted to the sales program. The total amount paid by the company toward maintaining its part of the Chicago office was $65,981.75.[40] The company, it will be remembered, paid only a part of the expenses since Ayres also represented the Medina Valley Irrigation Company.

Some time during 1915, Joe Hess resigned, and E. Dowden, who had been in charge of cultivation on the unsold farms, succeeded him.[41]

In 1916, the Boston group of investors, who wanted to save their investment in the enterprise, gained control of the Texas Land and Development Company because of financial difficulties among the New York backers brought on by the tight money market of World War I.[42] They planned to cut out any unnecessary expense, and they endorsed a recently adopted policy (date unknown) that forbade improving

---

[39] *Plainview Evening Herald*, June 29, 1915. The same advertisement also appeared on July 2, 1915.

[40] Texas Land and Development Company, cash book, TLDCP.

[41] *Plainview Evening Herald*, May 21, 1915. E. Dowden was referred to as the local sales manager in the *Hale County Herald*, June 19, 1914.

[42] *Plainview Evening Herald*, September 12, 1916. This statement taken from a newspaper account indicates, and accurately so, that the Boston backers of the company now asserted control over the Plainview operation. For a review of the association of the company with the parent organizations, see Chapter 2.

property until it had definitely been sold. Their major change in the operation of the company was to discontinue the Chicago sales department and to terminate Ayres's employment with the Texas Land and Development Company. All future sales were to be local in nature. Charles F. Myers, as the general manager and vice-president of the company, was to be in direct charge of the local sales as well as of all other phases of the operation.[43] He was to be closely supervised, no doubt by Charles J. Hubbard, president of the Old Colony Trust of Boston and choice of the Boston group for president of the Texas Land and Development Company. On October 7, 1916,[44] shortly after his election to the Texas Land and Development Company post, Hubbard came to Plainview on business and issued a statement to the *Plainview Evening Herald* regarding the company's selling policy: "At this time we cannot take on more obligations, there being enough contracts now to keep all of our men busy for a year. Consequently the sales department has been temporarily discontinued."[45]

It became the company's aim for several years to fulfill the obligations for which it had already contracted and to attempt to make a profit from the enterprise. Between October 1916 and the end of 1919, when a plan for reorganization was put into effect, the company was run by the Prairie Lands Trust, which was controlled by the Boston backers. After October 1916 the company discontinued the sales program for some time. Even so, between 1916 and 1919 it negotiated eleven sales of dry-land farms, which were not to be developed and which represented 2,621.70 acres valued at $82,498.[46]

The company's overall success during the early years was nebulous. It sold only a small portion of the 61,360 acres owned by the trust. Contracts of purchase for the pieces of land sold usually contained term payment clauses. Whether the buyers would pay out their contracts or whether there would be a series of repossessions was yet to be deter-

[43] *Plainview Evening Herald*, September 12, 1916.
[44] Texas Land and Development Company, minutes, October 7, 1916, TLDCP.
[45] *Plainview Evening Herald*, October 24, 1916.
[46] Staked Plains Trust, Limited, Plainview office ledger, December 1, 1916–September 30, 1918, p. 265, TLDCP.

mined. Already some of the purchasers were asking for and receiving extensions of time to make payment.[47] A large amount of money was expended, yet the company realized no profit from the operation. Surely an assessment of the sales program would lead to the conclusion that the sales department spent far too much money, some perhaps wastefully, since the company had thus far gained no real profit.

[47] Randolph to Connor, tape interview, April 8, 1958.

4. Development of Company Property

ONCE TEXAS PRAIRIE LANDS decided to embark upon the Plainview enterprise and purchased most of the land, the Texas Land and Development Company started developing the land. The original plan was to have the company's entire land holdings developed within a five-year period.[1] R. S. Charles was on hand to supervise development from the day the Texas Land and Development was chartered in October 1912. He was already familiar with the Plainview terrain since he had been in charge of one of the engineering reconnaissance crews that had been sent out earlier in the year to survey the possible route for an extension of the Frisco line. Although the railroad had turned down the area, Charles had been "fascinated" by the land because he felt it had a "great future if it could actually be irrigated." If he had not been convinced that the land could be irrigated and that he was the man to do it for Pearson and his associates, Charles received the confidence he needed from Pearson himself when Pearson asked him

[1] *Plainview Evening Herald*, June 25, 1914.

to accept the job as chief engineer in charge of development. As Charles said, "If Dr. Pearson believed it [the Plainview development] practicable and in my ability to do it, why doubt him?"[2] Charles acquired three supervisory assistants. John Walter Longstreth, an experienced irrigation farmer from Kansas, took charge of breaking the ground and cultivating crops. R. C. (Chess) Dublin, an expert well driller from East Texas, supervised the well-drilling rigs both for household use and for irrigation. W. H. Mason, the company auditor and purchasing agent, as part of his duties ordered and disbursed equipment. In the beginning Pearson's New York engineering office, headed by Jules Hirt, served as consultant and helped to select mechanical equipment for the local company.[3]

The 61,360 acres of land that Henderson purchased, represented approximately 153 separate titles. It is not known what standards Henderson used as a guide for purchasing the land, except that each tract should contain a lake.[4] The value of a lake for drainage during rainy seasons was obvious. Perhaps Henderson felt, too, that the water stored in the lake would serve as a "recharge" for the underground supply used for irrigation.

The company designated two of its choice acreages to be developed as demonstration farms. They were to be made ready as quickly as possible to serve as models for prospective purchasers to view. These two farms, which were called the Pioneer Park Farm and the Demonstration Farm, were actually experimental farms, but the company avoided the term "experimental" for fear of the adverse effect it might have on prospective buyers. On them "everything adaptable to the climate was tried and/or demonstrated."[5] Regardless of what they were called, the farms served their purpose well since it was convincing for a farmer, upon his arrival in the area, to see his favorite crop in a flourishing state. Using the demonstration farms for its experiments provided the company with much valuable information. It found that

[2] Robert S. Charles, letter, November 1, 1958, Brunson Letters, Southwest Collection, Texas Tech University, Lubbock (hereafter cited as BL).
[3] *Ibid.*
[4] Peyton B. Randolph to Seymour V. Connor, tape interview, April 8, 1958.
[5] Charles, letter, September 14, 1959, BL.

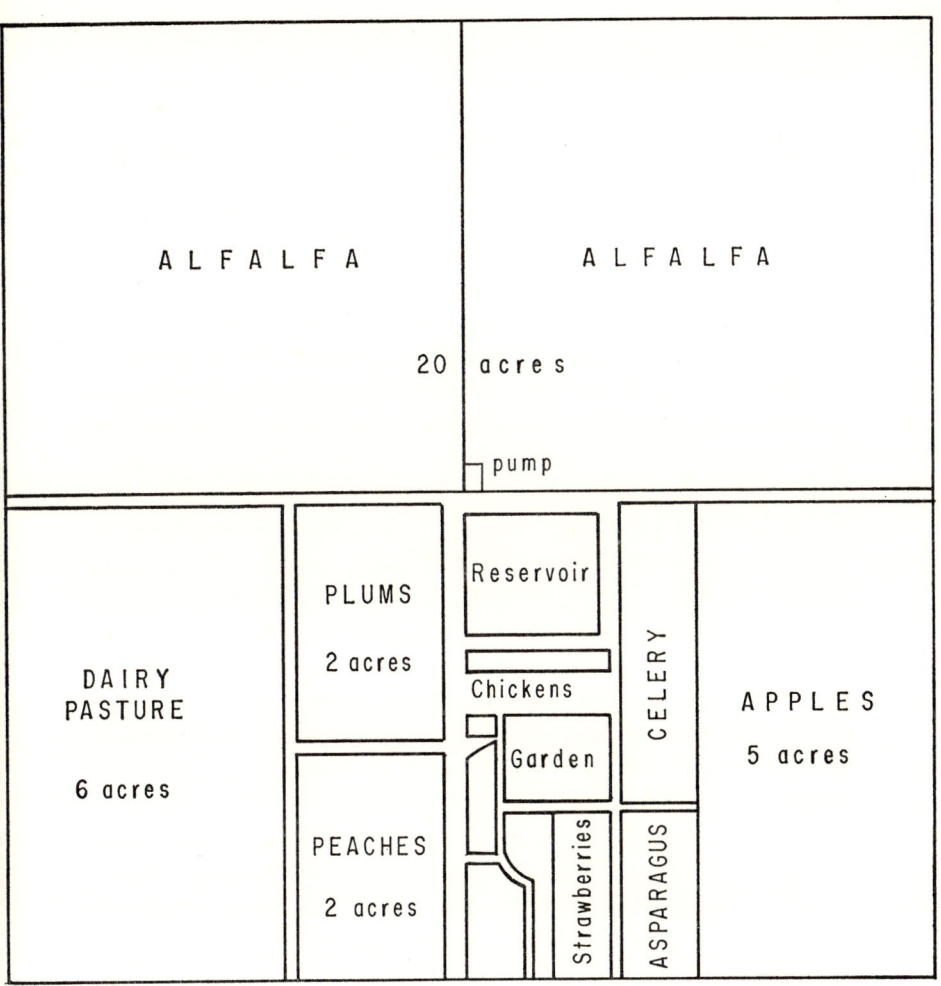

2. Henderson's proposed model farm.

several crops could be grown profitably under irrigation and that others proved "either uneconomical . . . or non-competitive with those crops raised elsewhere."[6]

The Pioneer Park Farm, three miles southeast of Plainview in the White River bottom, was located in an extremely fertile area with an

[6] *Ibid.*

abundance of good irrigation water. The farm was one section in size although the company operated a section adjacent to it as part of the farm. The main experiments on the farm were with fruits.[7] Even before John Walter Longstreth and A. M. Krueger, who worked under Henderson as supervisor of the demonstration farms, arrived, M. D. Henderson had started an orchard on the farm. In carrying out his pet project, Henderson tried to grow many varieties of fruit trees.[8] In the spring of 1913, the company planned to set out sixty-five thousand of them. Labor scarcity, however, prevented the completion of the job.[9] The fruit trees, which demanded much special attention, flourished as long as they were well attended.[10] Perhaps the outstanding failures among the fruit demonstrations were Tokay and Malaga grapes.[11]

The Demonstration Farm, also used for company experiments, was located one mile east of Plainview and was approximately one section in size.[12] Longstreth, Krueger, and their crews used the farm primarily for experiments in truck crops, grains, fibers, and forage.[13] Since Krueger was interested in extensive use of trees for shade, windbreaks, and other functional purposes, he planted tamaracks around the farm in the spring of 1913.[14] Krueger felt that in addition to their utilitarian value, trees would make the area more attractive to prospective settlers.[15]

For the most part, truck crops grown on irrigated tracts proved successful. The biggest failure proved to be the growing of Irish potatoes. Luxuriant plants flourished on ten acres and produced a

---

[7] Fred Lowe, tape interview, July 12, 1958.
[8] Charles, letter, September 14, 1959, BL.
[9] *Hale County Herald*, May 8, 1913.
[10] Lowe, tape interview, July 12, 1958.
[11] Charles, letter, September 14, 1959, BL.
[12] *Documents 1917*, p. 104, Texas Land and Development Company Papers, Southwest Collection, Texas Tech University, Lubbock (hereafter cited as TLDCP).
[13] Charles, letter, September 14, 1959, BL.
[14] *Hale County Herald*, January 2, 1913.
[15] *Ibid.*, January 30, 1913.

Development of Company Property

beautiful sight above the ground, but when the potatoes were dug, they yielded a crop of "hardly a bushel of hickory nut size potatoes."[16] Early in 1913 Krueger had urged Hale County farmers to take up the cultivation of celery and sweet potatoes. He was convinced that both crops would yield large returns.[17] In fact he was so sure of large profits that he guaranteed a market to any farmer who would join him in a celery experiment. He offered to give advice on seeds, cultivation, planting, and harvesting of celery. Krueger also urged the cultivation of beans and peanuts, because he considered them better-paying crops than kafir, maize, cotton, oats, or wheat. Beyond this, they enriched, rather than impoverished, the soil.[18] Harvest time in August 1913 proved that watermelons, cucumbers, cantaloupes, squashes, Mexican green chiles, cabbages, lettuce, tomatoes, and radishes did well on the Demonstration Farm. Whatever happened to Krueger's celery, sweet potatoes, beans, and peanuts was not recorded, but several loads of vegetables were sold locally as well as in Fort Worth and Waco as a result of the August harvest. Gratifyingly, the demand actually exceeded the supply, probably because South Plains vegetables "come in" after those farther south have "burned up," and the produce buyers in Central Texas were always anxious to purchase them.[19]

Company experiments stimulated the growth of alfalfa. Although alfalfa had been grown prior to the formation of the company, few individuals could afford to install the expensive irrigation system under which the crop was more likely to flourish. Since alfalfa was to be the principal crop on company farms, it was one of Longstreth's duties to demonstrate that it could be successfully grown.

Longstreth found that area farmers who grew alfalfa were convinced that newly broken "sod land" would not produce a successful crop. They believed that row crops should be planted two or three years to prepare the soil for the planting of alfalfa. Longstreth set out to prove this widely held belief a fallacy. Using a Spalding plow, Longstreth's crew tore up the soil to a depth of fourteen inches and planted

[16] Charles, letter, September 14, 1959, BL.
[17] *Hale County Herald*, January 2, 1913.
[18] *Ibid.*, January 30, 1913.
[19] *Ibid.*, August 1, 1913.

alfalfa with a regular drill. The first cutting yielded almost two tons of hay per acre.

Since deep plowing was slow and expensive, Longstreth tried the conventional method of plowing, which was to turn the sod two inches deep and then disc the surface. Again he used an ordinary drill to plant the seeds. The seeds came up promptly, and at the end of the year the alfalfa on the shallow plowed sod looked as good as that on the deeply plowed land or on any of the tracts that had been cultivated for two years in the conventional method.

Longstreth also demonstrated that a farmer might obtain a yield of wheat and a field of alfalfa on the same tract of land within the same year. The scheme proved feasible. If it were not sown so thickly that the wheat plants choked out the alfalfa plants, the wheat protected the young alfalfa plants from the strong spring winds.[20]

Alfalfa grew best under irrigated conditions, and once the initial cost of installing irrigation equipment was met, operational expenses were not excessive. The lift of the pump ranged from thirty to sixty feet, and the cost of pumping one acre-foot of water was approximately $1.80. A well that flowed from 1,000 to 1,500 gallons a minute was adequate to care for 160 acres of South Plains alfalfa.[21] When there was an inadequate rainfall, alfalfa needed to be irrigated twice a month. The annual cost of growing one acre of alfalfa, including watering, mowing, marketing, and other operations, was approximately $25.00.[22] Up to six cuttings of alfalfa a year were possible depending on the length of the growing season. An acre usually produced a minimum of one ton per cutting,[23] and from four to six tons per year.[24]

After the alfalfa matured, Longstreth planned to demonstrate to Hale County farmers that it could be used profitably as feed for livestock. He estimated that one acre of irrigated alfalfa grazed by hogs would produce approximately one thousand pounds of pork, valued

[20] *Plainview Evening Herald*, October 26, 1915.
[21] *Hale County Herald*, April 10, 1913.
[22] *Plainview Evening Herald*, October 26, 1915.
[23] Charles, letter, September 14, 1959, BL.
[24] *Plainview Evening Herald*, October 26, 1915.

Development of Company Property

at between $60 and $70.²⁵ Longstreth planned to raise hogs by grazing them on an alfalfa pasture to near maturity and then finishing them for market by feeding them grain.²⁶ His scheme seemed to work, for the hog-raising business flourished in the Plainview area²⁷ until hog cholera struck in 1916.²⁸

The demonstration farms fulfilled quite well the two-fold purpose of their original design. They served as excellent showplaces that were impressive to the prospective buyer, and they also yielded experimental crops that helped Longstreth and his staff to decide which crops were best suited for the area and which methods of cultivation were desirable. During the first five months of the company's operation, while these two farms were in the early stages of development, they were an expensive drain on the company. The company spent a total of $33,560.27 on the Demonstration Farm, which had undergone most of its initial development. The Pioneer Park Farm operation, which was in the very earliest stages, cost $2,058.14.²⁹

The demonstration farms, as important to the company's program as they were, did not compare as showplaces to Lake Plainview, a Texas Land and Development Company attraction beheld by anyone passing through Plainview on a train. The lake, in part artificial, was perhaps the most impressive construction in Northwest Texas. Harry I. Miller, company president from 1912–1916, who was "strong in showmanship," conceived of the lake. His idea called for the installation of a typical irrigation well in front of the Santa Fe railway station in order to demonstrate to prospective buyers of company land the tremendous amount of underground water available for irrigation in the Plainview area. It was the duty of R. S. Charles, as the company's engineer, to make the project practicable.

Before the plan could be taken seriously, the Texas Land and Development Company, ironically, had to purchase a small wet weather

---

[25] *Ibid.*
[26] Charles, letter, September 14, 1959, BL.
[27] *Plainview Evening Herald*, April 9, 1915.
[28] *Ibid.*, April 18, 1916.
[29] Baldwin, Slaton, and Randolph, and Staked Plains Trust, Limited, general ledger, balance sheet, TLDCP.

lake, about thirty acres in size, in order to dispose of the water brought to the surface by its demonstration pump.[30] The tract obtained was located just north of the Santa Fe railway station in Plainview.[31] There the company drilled and installed a pump.

The lake, which held over fourteen million gallons of water, was full by July 1, 1913, after the engine had pumped over 158 hours, a period believed to be a record for continuous operation of an irrigation pump and engine up to that time.[32] When completed, it was the largest body of water in Texas supplied by a well.[33] It covered thirty acres[34] and had a depth of five to six feet.[35]

By constructing a concrete levee two feet wide entirely around the water, the company protected the artificially constructed banks from the waves, whipped up by the prairie winds.[36] It also built a well-kept graveled roadway around the lake[37] and enclosed the grounds with a fence that had two entrance gates, one operated by a mechanical triggering device touched off when a vehicle drove over it.[38] Between the lake and the Santa Fe station, there was a lush display of grass, shrubs, flowers, and trees. Concrete walks and a protective banister[39] provided the visitors a walkway through the exotic oasis of the Plains. Twenty-five sixty-watt electric lamps on high poles lighted the area for night sightseers.[40]

The company went "all out" to make the lake a playground as well as a showplace. It imported two motor boats and four row boats,[41] which, incidentally, brought a revenue of $1,374.49 from July 31,

[30] Charles, letter, September 14, 1959, BL.
[31] *Hale County Herald*, May 1, 1913.
[32] *Ibid.*, July 1, 1913.
[33] *Ibid.*, June 19, 1914.
[34] *Ibid.*, June 12, 1913.
[35] Homer Rook, tape interview, August 28, 1959.
[36] *Hale County Herald*, July 15, 1913.
[37] Rook, tape interview, August 28, 1959.
[38] Hanley Wasson, tape interview, August 19, 1959.
[39] Rook, tape interview, August 28, 1959.
[40] *Hale County Herald*, August 29, 1913.
[41] *Ibid.*, July 11, 1913.

Development of Company Property

1913, to September 25, 1916.[42] During the winter months the frozen lake became an ice-skating arena on which a person might skate as long as he wished for twenty-five cents.[43]

Partially for utilitarian purposes, the company imported giant bullfrogs from New Rhodes, Louisiana, to rid the lake of mosquitoes and other insects.[44] Simply for beautification of the lake, it brought in types of exotic birds including Indian cranes, black and white swans, peacocks, and sheldrakes.[45] It also installed artistic duck houses and a feeding place for wild ducks.[46]

The company then stocked fish of various types. For utilitarian purposes it brought in carp, which are vegetarians, to keep the water free of vegetable growth, and goldfish to eat any larvae that might appear, thus helping the frog population prevent mosquitoes.[47] For the sportsmen, it stocked catfish[48] and bass.[49] In the fall of 1913 Melvin Mise, a driver for the company, rescued a truckload of catfish from a creek bed that was fast drying up on the ranch of Judge L. S. Kinder and carried the fish to Lake Plainview.[50] By August 1914 the lake was overstocked with carp, bass, and catfish, whereupon the company sold fishing permits at the rate of twenty-five cents per person. It permitted only poles and lines and limited a person's catch to fifteen. The *Plainview Evening Herald* proudly announced: "You don't have to go to the canyons now to fish."[51]

From the beginning, Lake Plainview posed problems for the company. Before the lake was filled, people drove over the property in cars and buggies and damaged the grass and shrubs. After small boys con-

---

[42] Staked Plains Trust, Limited, ledger, p. 81, account 21, TLDCP.
[43] Rook, tape interview, August 28, 1959.
[44] *Hale County Herald*, June 19, 1914.
[45] *Plainview Evening Herald*, June 25, 1914.
[46] Rook, tape interview, August 28, 1959.
[47] *Hale County Herald*, August, 22, 1913.
[48] *Plainview Evening Herald*, July 16, 1914.
[49] *Ibid.*, August 11, 1914.
[50] Melvin Mise, tape interview, August 20, 1959.
[51] *Plainview Evening Herald*, August 11, 1914.

verted the lake into a swimming hole and destroyed a part of the concrete dam the company was constructing, the company temporarily closed the area to visitors.[52] The company solved another problem, loss of water from seepage, by a "puddling" process. First, the water level was permitted to go down. Then two hundred hogs were turned loose in the lake bottom and remained there until the bottom was thoroughly cemented.[53] The resulting smell touched off something of a furor in the city. Some of the citizens complained that the process was a menace to the health of the community. An editorial in the *Hale County Herald* defended the company and claimed that the people doing the complaining possessed "habits, traits, and characteristics akin to those of the hogs which are now puddling the big lake."[54] The county health officer, Dr. A. H. Lindsey, assured local citizens that there was no health danger and that the stirring up of the pond to rid it of moss, rather than the hogs, was causing the obnoxious odor.[55] Within a short time, the hogs cemented the lake bottom, chemicals were used to clear the water, and the lake was refilled.[56]

With the seepage problem solved, the company had to tackle the problem of flooding. The first big rain caused the lake to overflow and seriously flood adjoining lands. When the pump was stopped, however, the lake became an unsightly stagnant pool. Charles solved the problem by digging a second well in the middle of the lake down to the water-bearing sand. This well served as a disposal well. Despite skepticism, the disposal well worked perfectly and maintained the water level at the desired height.[57]

The company left no complete set of figures to represent the amount of money spent on Lake Plainview, but the total sum must have been impressive. In addition to the initial construction expenses, upkeep proved to be a drain. Employees had to be hired especially to look after the lake. During the winter months there was only one employee and

[52] *Hale County Herald*, June 3, 1913.
[53] *Ibid.*, April 21, 1914.
[54] *Ibid.*, April 24, 1914.
[55] *Ibid.*, April 28, 1914.
[56] *Ibid.*, May 1, 1914.
[57] Charles, letter, September 14, 1959, BL.

Development of Company Property

caretaker, Homer Rook, but during the summer months there were five or six employees under the supervision of Percy Hauck. The cost of operating the well added expense. The pump used fuel, which cost six cents a gallon, at the rate of approximately sixty gallons a day. The company bore the expense of frequently grading the road around the lake, a feat accomplished with teams of horses dragging split logs over the road.[58] During the fall of 1913, the company constructed a concrete abutment across the south end of the lake to protect the driveway from erosion. Before the concrete could dry, a rain washed out part of it, the replacement for which cost the company $500.[59] Prior to the time Charles engineered the disposal well for the middle of the lake, the company sustained additional losses to its grass, shrubs, flowers, and trees every time the lake overflowed.

Although it could not be determined with any degree of certainty when the company closed Lake Plainview, the final blow apparently came June 19, 1917, when a fire destroyed the pump station at the lake. The loss, estimated at $2,050, included the building, at $550; contents of the building, at $500; and the pump, at $1,000.[60] Insurance covered the loss, but as far as could be determined the company never contemplated replacement.

That the expense of upkeep on the lake was no small drain on the Texas Land and Development Company's resources was clear in the fact that the company manager R. S. Charles offered it to the city of Plainview, but the city declined,[61] although there was some sentiment for the city to help maintain the lake. A front-page editorial appearing in the *Plainview Evening Herald* in part declared:

> Plainview is proud of Lake Plainview; at least she is when Lake Plainview is well kept. If it were not for the improvements there, the traveler would be greeted on his arrival in Plainview by a typical Plains lake. The people of the town have spent many pleasant minutes at Lake Plainview. It is worth while.
>
> Lake Plainview has been and can be made again a beauty spot.

[58] Rook, tape interview, August 28, 1959.
[59] *Plainview Evening Herald*, September 28, 1915.
[60] *Ibid.*, June 19, 1917.
[61] Rook, tape interview, August 28, 1959.

It is privately owned, but its use is public, and it is nothing more than justice that the town of Plainview should contribute, even if in a small way, to its support. The expenditure necessary to make Lake Plainview beautiful and enjoyable is a mere mite compared with what it would cost to maintain a city park.

Though privately owned, Lake Plainview is a benefit to the entire citizenship of Plainview. We ought to help maintain it.[62]

Their first view of Lake Plainview, along with the pump gushing water, variously impressed prospective buyers. Many refused to believe that so much water was coming out of the ground. Those who held the most common belief that the water was being pumped out of the lake and right back in again often remarked: "Looks like you'd wear that water out pumping it out of the lake and pumping it right back in again."[63] A visiting newspaper editor commented, ". . . the water gushing from the Texas Land and Development Company's pumping plant adjacent to the station, and which fills an immense artificial lake, would cause any traveler, who has summered or wintered on the 'Lake Front' in Chicago, to catch his breath, and look for skyscrapers."[64]

Even though Lake Plainview closed in 1917, it had provided area citizens with many happy memories. In addition to the pleasures it gave, the lake served its purpose well as an impressive showplace for prospectors to see during the height of the sales operation.

Since it was very important to the success of the sales operation that the demonstration farms and Lake Plainview be completed quickly, the company concentrated much of the early development on these properties. Concurrently, it worked quickly to develop other farms for sale. Once the land survey was completed, construction and drilling crews began their operation. As soon as irrigation water was available, breaking the land, planting, and cultivation followed. Although the company brought in from other parts of the country some of the crew

[62] *Plainview Evening Herald*, June 2, 1916.
[63] Clarence Rogers, tape interview, August 21, 1959.
[64] The Plainview Chamber of Commerce, "The Great Plainview District Where There Is Nothing Shallow but the Water," Smyth Collection, Panhandle-Plains Museum, Canyon, Texas.

Development of Company Property 73

supervisors and farm superintendents, all of whom it considered experts in their fields, the crews consisted primarily of local men. There was an ample labor supply since the area had suffered from a severe drought for several seasons and many were in debt.[65]

The surveying crew worked under the supervision of the company's chief engineer. Originally R. S. Charles filled this position, but as his duties as general manager expanded, he put another engineer in charge as supervising surveyor. The engineers in charge of surveying were first W. S. Fife, until March 1916; then W. J. Williams, for approximately one year; and finally D. L. Alexander, until development stopped in 1917.[66] The surveying crew usually consisted of a supervisor and three assistants. Apparently the three assistants, who were chain carriers and rod men, were only temporary employees. Some were college students who wanted to work in the summer months. In 1913 Fife, as supervising surveyor, had as his assistants, Jennings Anderson, who was later to die in the flu epidemic during World War I, Joe Kunesh, who was a young English engineering student at the University of Wisconsin, and Keith Catto, who had just returned from a European tour and had come to Plainview to supervise his mother's land interests in the Hooper community. During good weather, the crew surveyed; during inclement weather, it remained in the office and did its drafting and mapping. The surveying crew drove back and forth to work every day. Purchasing the food for each day's trip was a duty assumed by Catto, whom Fife admonished "to go easy on the groceries." Fife, a Scot, was convinced that his crew ate too much.[67]

Hanley Wasson, as construction superintendent, was in charge of all construction of the company whether it was building a house or erecting some of the paraphernalia around Lake Plainview. Henderson hired Wasson, the only construction superintendent ever employed by the company, in September 1912. He kept that position until the company terminated construction in 1917.

When one or more pieces of land had been surveyed and were ready

---

[65] Fred Watson, tape interview, July 12, 1958.

[66] W. J. Williams, tape interview, August 22, 1959.

[67] Keith Catto to Mrs. L. R. Bain, tape interview, May 31, 1958, Bain Files, Plainview (hereafter cited as BF).

for development, the company's chief engineer instructed Wasson regarding the improvements to be placed on the property. It was then Wasson's duty to determine exactly what materials would be required for the job and to order them from the company's warehouse, which was located in the northeast part of Plainview.[68] The warehouses, under the supervision of Oscar Leroy Allen, were completely equipped for the construction of any type of building that the company might specify. Included in the warehouses were a lumber yard, oil tanks, and a machine shop. W. H. Mason, as purchasing agent for the company, kept a close check on warehouse supplies that the company purchased wholesale in various parts of the world.[69] Some of the supplies, especially lumber, came from Mexico,[70] very likely from Pearson's Mexican sugar-pine forest concession.

Once Wasson determined the materials needed for a particular job, he then saw to it that they were delivered to the proper place on a large Alco truck.[71] This truck was an unusual pre-World War I monster made by the American Locomotive Works. It had solid rubber tires and an iron steering wheel, but lacked headlights, windshield, and starter. The driver was required to sit over the motor since there was no cab. Melvin Mise, who drove for the company for fifteen months, later observed that in winter, the driver froze, and in the summer, he baked. Once the driver was on the road, the supplies were far from delivered. During wet weather, it was a common occurrence for the truck to get stuck in the soft mud, in which case it was the driver's duty to get the truck out the best way he could. It was not uncommon for the truck to be unloaded for this to be accomplished. Often a nearby farmer would help with one or more teams of horses or mules. When well casings started to slip off the rear of the truck, an altogether too common occurrence, the driver backed up against a telephone pole, and pushed the load back on. One driver, apparently because there was no convenient

---

[68] Wasson, tape interview, August 19, 1959.
[69] Williams, tape interview, August 22, 1959.
[70] Mrs. Oscar Leroy Allen, letter, September 16, 1959, BL.
[71] Wasson, tape interview, August 19, 1959.

Development of Company Property

telephone pole, backed up to a school house to push his load back onto the truck and instead pushed the school house off its foundation.[72]

After the drivers delivered the supplies to the site, Wasson moved in with his construction crews. He had two carpenter crews, two paint crews, and a concrete crew—a total of approximately forty men most of the time. A foreman supervised each crew, which also had its own cook. Two of the construction foremen were J. C. Jones and George Runyon, and the paint foreman was Karl Brask.[73]

The construction crews, provided with tents and bedding, camped at the site during the week. The company had two teams and two small wagons for hauling the men back and forth on weekends. Since the company developed more than one farm at a time, Wasson did not camp out with the crews, but drove every day from place to place. The company either paid the expenses on an individually owned car or furnished a car. Every Saturday Wasson made a report to the general manager in the Plainview office.

When the company tagged a farm for development, it carried on all construction simultaneously. Unless the purchaser specified otherwise, his land was to contain a standard set of improvements, which included a house, barn, outhouses, a domestic well and windmill, fencing, an irrigation system, twenty acres of land plowed for alfalfa, an orchard, and small tracts plowed for truck crops. If the purchaser did not want the buildings, domestic well, and windmill, the company allowed a $1,600 deduction from the price of the developed tract. If he did not want an orchard, he received a deduction of $50.[74] The company also had a standard house plan, which it used unless the buyer specified otherwise. The houses were well constructed as evidenced by the fact that many still stand and still make comfortable homes, almost half a century later.[75] The paint crew used the best available paint on all houses; it used cheaper paints on the windmill, greenhouse, and barn.

[72] Mise, tape interview, August 20, 1959.
[73] Wasson, tape interview, August 19, 1959.
[74] Elmer G. Johnson (land salesman) to Clyde E. Craig, letter, March 28, 1917, Wallet 13, TLDCP.
[75] Wasson, tape interview, August 19, 1959.

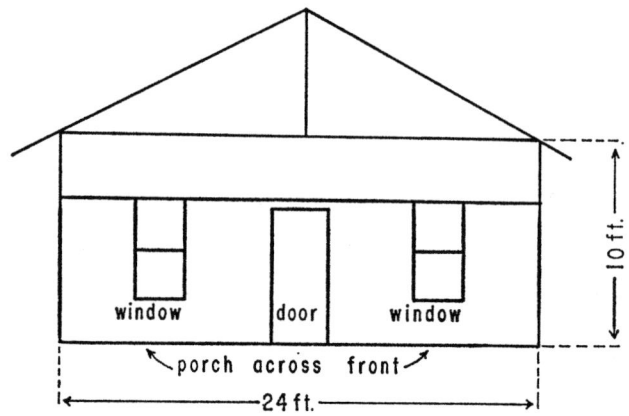

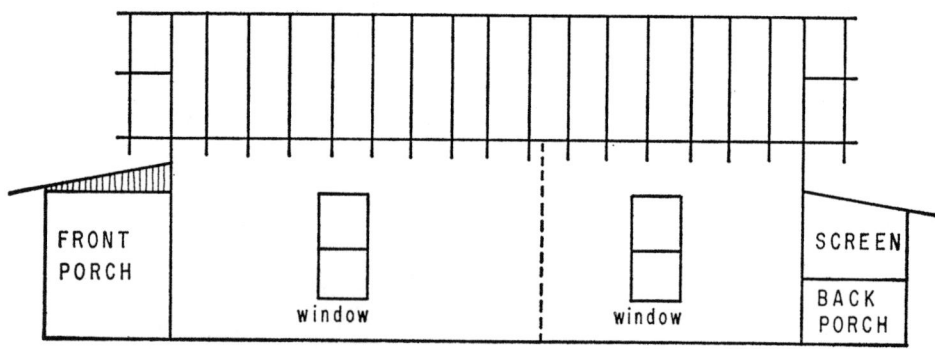

3. The standard house plan for company farms: front elevation; side elevation. Based on drawings by Hanley Wasson.

The first houses were painted a light cream color with white trim. Inside the house were varnished woodwork and solid wooden walls covered with cheesecloth and then wallpaper.[76]

While the construction of the houses, barns, greenhouses, windmills, derricks, and other outhouses was in progress, the fencing and drilling crews were busy with their respective jobs. There was reference to only one fencing crew, and that crew, consisting of four men, was under the supervision of an "old cowpuncher" named Love. His crew had

[76] S. O. Craig, oral interview, June 15, 1958.

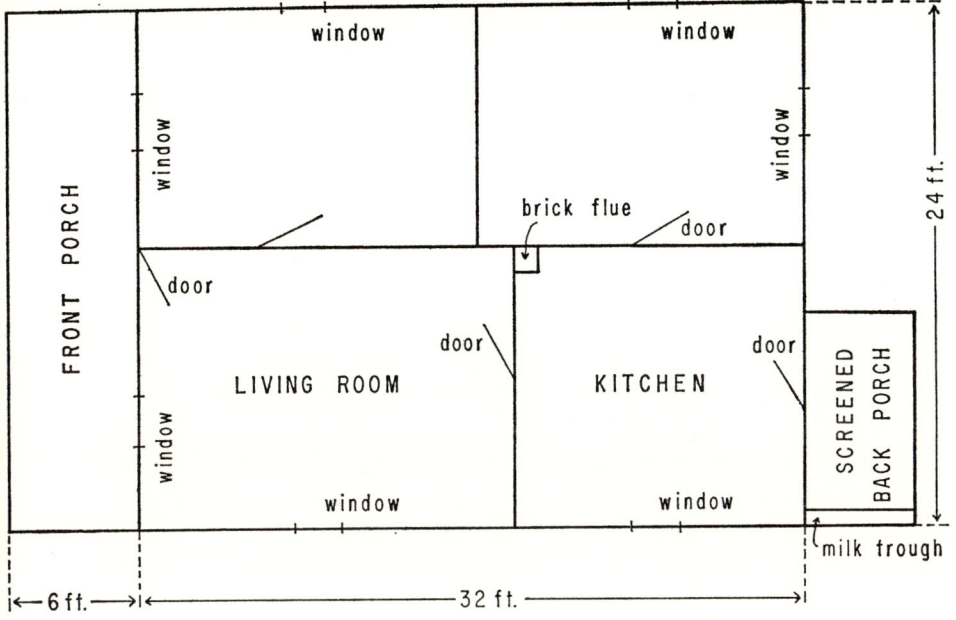

4. Floor plan for the standard company house.
Based on drawings by Hanley Wasson.

had a great deal of experience working on ranches prior to their working for the Texas Land and Development Company, and each man could punch about one hundred holes per day. Each hole was twenty inches deep and six inches in diameter. A man often spent half a day setting a corner post with its bracing since the average corner post supported a half mile of fence. Three strands of wire formed the fence. In each mile there were two hundred posts spaced at an average distance of twenty-six and one-half feet. The fencing crew, like the construction crews, camped out during the week, usually around a windmill. The fencing crew was never hard to find in the early morning since the coffee they brewed was so strong that it could be detected half a mile away.[77]

While construction crews did their work, R. C. (Chess) Dublin directed well-drilling operations.[78] His crew drilled water wells for

[77] Keith Catto to Mrs. L. R. Bain, tape interview, May 31, 1958, BF.
[78] Wasson, tape interview, August 19, 1959.

household use near the house site. Then it drilled irrigation wells. Perhaps the most important part of the operation was drilling the strategically placed wells and supervising pumps and engine installation.

Even before the Texas Land and Development Company started operations in Plainview, irrigation was beginning to take hold. The first well in Hale County had been placed on the farm of John Henry Slaton in 1911. Although the well proved to be an excellent one, many said that they knew the "draw" had plenty of water but they also knew "it could not be had on the up-land." Wells were subsequently completed for E. H. Perry, six miles southwest of Plainview; for Robert Alley, near Hale Center; and for P. E. Snyder, south of Plainview. The comment then was, "There is plenty of water in the draw and to the south, but how do you know there is water to the north?" Wells were placed on the farms of R. P. Smyth, R. Graham, a Mr. Holland, and E. H. Perry—all north of the draw. Holdouts then conceded, "We knew there was plenty of water, but it will kill the land; this country would not be practical to irrigate."[79] This statement, of course, proved to be false. By the time these first wells were drilled and pumps and engines installed, Plainview was on its way to being one of the great irrigation centers and one of the wealthiest agricultural areas of the world.

More than any other single factor, a workable irrigation system was responsible for the entry of the Texas Land and Development Company into the Plainview area. In fact, the heart of the company's program lay in the irrigation system. A workable well was one of the basic specifications on any set of improvements. Each contract of sale issued by the trustees of the company guaranteed that a well, which would produce sufficient water for irrigation purposes, must be placed on the land or the contract would automatically be void and any money received by the trustees in payment for the land would be immediately returned to the purchaser.[80]

The original plans of the company included digging 400 wells and installing irrigation pumps and engines on each of them.[81] If all 61,360

---

[79] George Green, "First Irrigation Well Near Plainview Was Started in 1911," *Plainview Evening Herald*, May 21, 1941.
[80] *Documents 1917*, inserted contract between pages 348 and 349, TLDCP.
[81] *Hale County Herald*, April 24, 1913.

Development of Company Property 79

acres of land that the trust owned had been brought under irrigation, there would have been one well for every 153.4 acres of land sold. Although the plan proved to be too ambitious, the company's accomplishments were quite admirable. The company installed at least 17 wells by November 21, 1913;[82] 39 wells by March 13, 1914;[83] 53 wells by July 28, 1914;[84] 66 wells by February 23, 1915;[85] and 127 wells by May 7, 1915,[86] at which time the company terminated all drilling. The company listed the original cost of all irrigation at $257,410.[87]

The company placed the first irrigation pumps and engines, which were installed on the Pioneer Park Farm and the Demonstration Farm, on hand-dug open pit wells,[88] no doubt similar to the Slaton well.[89] After some time the crew punched the wells into the ground with an instrument called a "spudder." Once the crew dug the well, it installed the pump and attached it to an engine by means of a flywheel and belt process. In the twenties and thirties various types of gearheads took the place of the flywheel and belt. Today several types of gearheads have been perfected and are used efficiently in most irrigation districts.[90] Both the company's crews[91] and private contractors handled digging wells and installing equipment. The Green Machinery Company of Plainview,[92] and the Layne-Bowler Pump Company of Houston,[93] two

---

[82] *Ibid.*, November 21, 1913.
[83] *Ibid.*, March 13, 1914.
[84] *Plainview Evening Herald*, July 28, 1914.
[85] *Ibid.*, February 23, 1915.
[86] Mary L. Cox, *History of Hale County, Texas*, p. 49.
[87] Staked Plains Trust Limited, *Annual Report*, 1936, TLDCP. These figures were given in an inventory made by the Staked Plains Trust, Limited, in 1935 in order to ascertain what the original developments had cost.
[88] Randolph to Connor, tape interview, April 8, 1958.
[89] See Chapter 1.
[90] William F. Carter (irrigation expert for Green Machinery), oral interview, July 9, 1960.
[91] *Hale County Herald*, March 13, 1914.
[92] *Ibid.*, November 21, 1913; George Green, oral interview, October 25, 1958. As of the date of this interview Green still had one of his original contracts with the Texas Land and Development Company, which he kept in his desk. After almost half a century he was still very proud of the fact that he had landed several of the company's early contracts.
[93] *Plainview Evening Herald*, July 28, 1914.

pioneer irrigation firms that were to become famous, did much of their early business with the Texas Land and Development Company. The first contract given to Layne-Bowler, which was let immediately after organization of the company, was for a group of ten or twelve wells. The contract was large enough to bring M. E. Layne, his most expert well-installation men, and his own drilling crew to Plainview to live for a time.[94] Before the Texas Land and Development Company terminated its irrigation operation, it owned four rigs of its own.[95]

After a crew dug a well and installed and satisfactorily tested the pump and engine, the owner's troubles had just started. The two types of engines, widely used in the early years, the Charter and the Ven-Severin, which cost on the average of $1,000 per engine,[96] were so large and so complex that two people were needed to start one of them. When an engine broke down, repairing the damage required an irrigation mechanic. Breakdowns were frequent, especially on the Charter, because it ran on a fuel containing a large amount of sulfur, which dissolved the iron in the engine and caused it to cease operation every two or three weeks.[97] The company maintained one and often more crews to act as "trouble shooters." The duty of these crews was to make irrigation as easy as possible for purchasers of company land.[98]

As soon as the water for irrigation was available, Longstreth instructed his land-breaking crews to begin operation. Teams and power tractors ditched, plowed, and planted in rapid succession.[99] The crews used a unique system for breaking some of the land. They placed two of a set of four steam engines, which had been imported from England, on each side of a tract to be broken or plowed. A cable then pulled the plow back and forth across a quarter of a mile of land. Mainly as an experiment, the company broke some of the land to a depth of twenty-

---

[94] Charles, letter, November 1, 1958, BL.
[95] *Plainview Evening Herald*, January 29, 1915.
[96] *Ibid.*, June 19, 1917.
[97] Williams, tape interview, August 22, 1959.
[98] Rook, tape interview, August 28, 1959.
[99] Charles, letter, November 1, 1958, BL.

Development of Company Property

four inches, though even today fourteen inches is considered deep plowing; as a result of the experiment the broken sod was so rough that the steam engine plow had difficulty getting over it a second time. No tractor could have plowed as deeply as twenty-four inches; the job was impossible for a team. The engines required four people for operation, one man for each engine. In addition, two teams hauled water to the site.[100]

Although the company did not have to contend with much interference from outsiders during the time it developed its land, it did encounter some instances when a few of the local citizens took advantage of it. During the early phases of development, a period of fence cutting and gate smashing took place. Apparently these acts were committed, not out of malice toward the company, but in an effort to graze cattle, free of charge, on company property. The trespasses became so flagrant that the trustees, J. H. Slaton and H. C. Randolph, inserted a warning notice in one of the local Plainview papers. In part, the notice read:

> In view of the depredations, of weekly occurrence, on the places belonging to the Syndicate, which we hold as trustees, we are compelled to notify all parties concerned that we will prosecute any further trespasses on the Syndicate property.
>
> The people owning this land have come into this country in good faith and are seeking to assist us in keeping down depredations upon the places owned by the Syndicate.
>
> We do not wish to prosecute any one, and use this notice as a final warning to the people to keep their stock off the premises owned by the Syndicate.

The notice further pleaded for persons living adjacent to the company to furnish the trustees with the names of parties "committing these outrages." The trustees expected neighborhood assistance, "for the development of the Syndicate property" meant "the enhancement of the value of their [neighbors'] property."[101]

[100] Rook, tape interview, August 28, 1959.
[101] *Hale County Herald,* April 3, 1913.

The local newspaper gave editorial support to the company shortly after the warning notice appeared. The editor chided the citizenry by asking, "Is it not possible for the fathers to teach their sons that law is not to restrict their freedom, but to insure to them personal rights? Indeed, is such instruction any less a sacred duty of citizenship?" The editor deplored the spirit of vandalism that had been loosed in the area. Private property, as well as that of the Texas Land and Development Company, had been destroyed; so had public school property. The editor thought that "the pride of manhood" would "ordinarily keep a grown-up" from acts of vandalism. He concluded, "Ordinarily the people who live in the West, are men and women. Plainview has no place for lawlessness in any form. Vandalism must cease."[102] Apparently the vandalism did cease since no more warning notices or editorials against such depredation appeared in the local papers.

Generally the city of Plainview was most friendly and cooperative toward the Texas Land and Development Company. During 1913, however, the Plainview city council passed an ordinance that inconvenienced the company. The law was not specifically directed toward the company, but was an attempt to save Plainview streets. It prohibited bringing into the city any heavy machinery since such actions had already torn up several new concrete crossings.[103] The ordinance, which forced the company to keep its heavy equipment in the country, posed problems in moving the machines from one piece of company property to another and in servicing and repairing the machines.

The company also faced the problem of outsiders' stealing its materials. For example, when a house was to be built, lumber and other necessary materials for the house were stacked near the place of construction. People in the area simply helped themselves to whatever they needed. These activities seemed to be justified on the basis that the company was a "big outfit" and "it wouldn't hurt" the company if only a board or two were taken. The company solved the matter in 1916 when it, perhaps for that reason and also for other pressing

---

[102] *Plainview Evening Herald*, March 2, 1915.
[103] *Ibid.*

Development of Company Property

financial reasons, placed construction on its property in the hands of local contractors. If a contractor did not have enough material because of stealing, he, not the company, was forced to buy more. "When people found out that they were stealing from their neighbors, they quit."[104]

The exact amount the Texas Land and Development Company spent for the development of its raw lands prior to 1920 is unknown. The only existing figure, $791,849.03,[105] was supposed to cover the original cost of all development. Since there was no specific breakdown available in the journals it was not possible to confirm what this sum actually covered.[106] That the company launched an extensive development program from the beginning is evident from a balance sheet for the first five months of operation.[107] During that time, it spent $49,335.26 on development alone. A division of the expenditures was recorded on the balance sheet (Table 2).

The figures revealed that the development of the Demonstration Farm took precedence in the first months of the operation. Fencing also was well under way during the initial period. The fact that some of the items listed as expenditures did not carry cost figures indicated what some of the company's future development costs were expected to be.

Of course, the money spent on the development of the lands would not represent a complete picture of the money spent on development during the first five months. Since purchasing construction materials was necessarily kept ahead of development, there was an inventory of

[104] Williams, tape interview, August 22, 1959.

[105] Staked Plains Trust, Limited, minutes, February 28, 1936 (I, 149), TLDCP.

[106] An inventory, made in 1935, recorded the original cost of construction as $451,851.87. The same inventory reported the original cost of irrigation equipment as $257,410.00. (Staked Plains Trust, Limited, *Annual Report*, 1935, TLDCP). The total expense represented by these two operations was $709,261.87, which left $82,587.16 of the quoted figure unaccounted for. It was possible that the remainder covered salaries and other administrative expenses.

[107] Baldwin, Slaton, and Randolph, and Staked Plains Trust, Limited, 1913–1918, ledger, balance sheet, TLDCP.

Table 2. Expenditures for Development (1912)

Development	Expenditure
General	
Wells, irrigation	$1,828.67
Wells, domestic	1,574.73
Buildings and Repairs	3,040.49
Fencing	6,380.81
Cultivating and farming	160.46
Cultivating and farming implements	572.75
Buildings and repairs	3,040.49
Ditches	....
Road improvements	....
Seeds, trees, etc.	....
Pumping and irrigation expense	1.00
Total	$13,558.91
Parks	
Pioneer Park	$2,058.14
Lake Plainview	157.94
Total	$2,216.08
Demonstration Farm (except land)	$33,560.27
Total Development (except land)	$49,335.26

Source: Staked Plains Trust, Limited, 1913–1918, ledger, balance sheet, TLDCP.

undistributed materials in the warehouse to be taken into account. These materials represented a total sum of $72,076.[108]

During the development period, the company was not entirely without income from the lands that remained unsold. The income did not in any way compare with the expenditures; however, it was not the intention at this point that it should. The dominant philosophy seemed to be that any scheme that might make money should be used to the advantage of the company. For instance, in the first five months the company

[108] *Ibid.*, 1913–1918, ledger, balance sheet.

Development of Company Property 85

realized $310.00 as profit from grazing-rights leases.[109] As the Demonstration Farm and Pioneer Park Farm began to produce their experimental crops, it gained a small income from them. Income from these farms and from other operations carried on by the company prior to the outbreak of World War I in June 1914 was listed in the account books.[110] Income for the period totaled $14,002.15. Of this amount grass leases brought in $1,320.96; the truck garden, $2,607.42; tenant-farming, $3,877.13; boat rental at Lake Plainview, $495.20; the Demonstration Farm, $3,440.02; the Merrill tract, $871.57; the Pioneer Farm, $586.63; and the broom corn crop, $803.22. Truck garden crops, one of the largest income items, went to markets in Fort Worth during the 1914 harvest season. The company employed an agent, Edward O'Brien, to handle their sale.[111] Tenant farming also proved to be a lucrative source of income. From 1913 the company financed each dry-land tenant by furnishing him seeds and machinery.[112] In return, the tenant was to pay a monthly rent and was to give the company a set percentage, usually one-third of the profits from the crops. The company employed a dry-land superintendent to direct this phase of the operation.[113]

On the day World War I began in Europe the Plainview office received a telegram advising that no more money for development was forthcoming. This pronouncement altered when the Staked Plains Trust and later the Prairie Lands Trust raised additional funds. The money raised, however, was for the development of lands already sold; the farming operation was to pay its own way. When war was declared, the company was in debt almost $200,000 for its farming operation. Since the operation was to pay for itself from that day on, it became the duty of the general manager, R. S. Charles, to pay off the debt. Charles declared that it had "always been a satisfaction that it [the debt incurred by the farming operations] was paid by the time all of the crops were

[109] *Ibid.*
[110] Staked Plains Trust, Limited, Plainview office ledger, accounts 18–25, December 1, 1916, to September 30, 1918, TLDCP.
[111] *Plainview Evening Herald,* August 27, 1914.
[112] Charles, letter, November 1, 1958, BL.
[113] Watson, tape interview, July 12, 1958.

gathered and sold in March of 1915." "That accomplishment," Charles added, "was due to the productiveness of the land and water, first, and second to the type of men on the job led by J. W. Longstreth."[114]

One method used to help raise the money needed was an incentive plan to promote an increase in crop efficiency and production among the company's tenants. The company offered prizes, divided into four categories and amounting to $310 in gold to the tenants. Class one embraced tracts of 250 acres or more; class two, tracts of 150 to 250 acres; class three, tracts of 100 to 150 acres; and class four, tracts of not less than 40 nor more than 100 acres. The best crop returns to the trustees after the tenant's share had been taken out decided the winners of the contest. The company, therefore, kept on file a record that was open to the inspection of any tenant at any time.[115]

When the company made the awards for the 1914 contest in April 1915, it announced plans to conduct a similar contest in 1915. It also added a separate contest for the children of the company's tenants. Thus all members of the family would be able to enter the contest and "put forth all their energy and brains to produce the greatest returns from the smallest acreage." The announcement, which appeared in the local paper, closed by saying, "So to our farmers, who are our friends, we say: Fly to it and do your best, and if you did not succeed in getting one of the gold coins in 1914, be sure and make good in 1915."[116]

Company policy on development as well as on sales underwent a change as a result of the outbreak of war in Europe. Because of the increasing costs of installing irrigation equipment and purchasing construction materials as well as rising selling expenses, the original plan of irrigating all the land within five years could not be fulfilled. Charles terminated his service when the company decided that it would place no irrigation system on a tract of land until it was sold and then only at the owner's request. Such a decision naturally slowed down irrigation development, and for the time being the company geared its operation to a farm program, which Charles felt could be adequately handled by

---

[114] Charles, letter, November 1, 1958, BL.
[115] *Plainview Evening Herald*, July 2, 1914.
[116] *Ibid.*, April 20, 1915.

Development of Company Property

J. W. Longstreth. Charles's resignation became effective on August 1, 1915.[117]

From the time of Charles's resignation in August 1915 until the spring of the following year, Longstreth functioned as general manager.[118] During his tenure as general manager company policy underwent another change. Longstreth's experiments with fruit trees, vines, and garden produce, which had been successfully, but expensively, grown under irrigated conditions, had to give way to a more realistic wartime market, which demanded such staples as alfalfa, hogs, and grain. Since Longstreth's specialty crops were being deemphasized, he was lured to Arizona where he again experimented with fruits and vegetables grown under irrigated conditions.[119]

The company hired Charles Frederick Myers, who had been associated with the Mexico Northwestern Railway in Juarez, Mexico,[120] to fill Longstreth's position as general manager. Myers was to assume his duties in March 1916.[121] He decided to terminate his position with the company in July, only four months after he had come to Plainview, when he went to Cuba to investigate a position as general superintendent of a Cuban railway. James Walkup Pipkin, who had been superintendent of the company's dry-land farms, was next to act as general manager,[122] and John F. Watson succeeded Pipkin as dry-land farm superintendent.[123]

[117] Charles, letter, November 1, 1958, BL.
[118] *Plainview Evening Herald*, March 14, 1916.
[119] Charles, letter, November 1, 1958, BL.
[120] Mrs. Charles F. Myers, letter, November 19, 1959, BL.
[121] *Plainview Evening Herald*, March 14, 1916.
[122] *Ibid.*, July 3, 1916. The official records do not show that Pipkin (who died in 1924) was hired as general manager. The account cited above refers to him specifically as such and several of the people interviewed (who were in a position to know), W. J. Williams, Homer Rock, and Fred Watson, attest to the fact that he functioned in that capacity. Correspondence in Wallet 12 of the Texas Land and Development Company Papers further bears out this fact. His wife, Mrs. Carolyn Pipkin, in a letter to the author dated September 16, 1959, also confirmed that he was general manager. She added that he resigned because he "became dissatisfied with the dirty politics being carried on among the higher personnel of the local office."
[123] *Plainview Evening Herald*, July 3, 1916.

In September 1916 Myers decided to return to Plainview, this time as general manager and vice-president in charge of sales.[124] The company also shifted the sales operations back to Plainview as a result of closing the Chicago office. Development on those farms already sold was to continue, but no development was to take place on the other tracts until they were sold. After Myers had been situated in Plainview for a month, the company again changed the operating procedure. It cut off sales altogether[125] and planned to do all future development on a contract basis, a situation that relieved the company of a large payroll and material inventory. The company needed crews for the development of farms already sold. It also needed some supervision for the farming operations, which took the form of repair work that a small crew could handle.[126] The Plainview job, with its policy changes, did not offer Myers the financial security he desired. He remained the second time for another period of four months, until February 7, 1917, when the company again accepted his resignation.[127] Myers then accepted the position that he had investigated previously with the Guantanamo and Western Railroad in Havana, Cuba, because he felt railroad work, which he preferred and in which he was most experienced, offered him a better future.[128]

For some time prior to February 1917, when Clyde Emerson Craig assumed the duty of the general manager and vice-president, the position had been in an unsettled state. Myers' ephemeral relationship with the company, the rising costs because of World War I, and the financial maneuverings of the backers of the company had caused a breakdown of the local operations.[129] Charles J. Hubbard, as president of the Texas Land and Development Company and immediate supervisor of the investments of the company backers, was anxious to find a competent man to oversee the local operations. It was the feeling of one of the

---

[124] *Ibid.*, September 12, 1916.

[125] *Ibid.*, October 24, 1916.

[126] Williams, tape interview, August 22, 1959.

[127] Texas Land and Development Company, minutes, February 7, 1917, TLDCP.

[128] Mrs. Charles F. Myers, letter, November 19, 1959, BL.

[129] Watson, tape interview, July 12, 1958.

Development of Company Property

local employees that a person well acquainted with the Plainview area and experienced and educated in the farming methods of the area should be hired to direct the operations.[130] Hubbard placed his trust, however, in Clyde Emerson Craig, a Michigan-born man who had had some experience with Texas lands as secretary-manager for the Gulf Coast Irrigation Company, with headquarters at Lyford, Texas. Walter S. Ayres, who had at one time been connected with the Gulf Coast Irrigation Company, recommended Craig to Hubbard.[131] Hubbard traveled to Plainview with Craig to look over the operation in the fall of 1916. At that time Craig accepted the position as general manager, but he did not report to work until February 1917. Craig remained in Plainview as long as Hubbard and the Boston group maintained control of the company under the Prairie Lands Trust. When in early 1919 the Staked Plains Trust initiated its move for reorganization and the control of the company shifted to New York, Craig resigned his position.[132]

During the two-year period that Craig remained in Plainview, he was faced with insurmountable problems. The cost of materials constantly increased during the war, and although Craig made every effort to find a profitable crop to increase the income for tenants, he had little success. The company hired P. B. Barber, an agricultural expert, who had made a success of a waning farm operation in Las Cruces, New Mexico, to work under Craig.[133] Craig and Barber experimented with a dairy herd to determine whether a large-scale dairying industry would prove profitable. The company purchased a herd, which consisted of twenty-three purebred Holstein cows and one registered bull, for $3,300 in May 1917. The herd, bred in Iowa, came directly from New Mexico. On the Pioneer Park Farm, crews constructed barns and sheds, installed a cream separator and other necessary equipment, and put the experiment into operation on fifty acres. The company planned to sell the butter fats and to feed the skimmed milk to the company's pigs.[134]

[130] *Ibid.*
[131] Clyde Emerson Craig, letter, September 15, 1959, BL.
[132] *Ibid.*
[133] *Ibid.*; *Plainview Evening Herald,* March 18, 1917.
[134] *Plainview Evening Herald,* May 22, 1917.

The dairy operation consistently lost money, and in 1918 the company instructed Craig to dispose of the herd at once even if he had to take a loss. The company felt that the loss it suffered every month by keeping the herd was greater than the loss it would incur by disposing of the herd.[135]

The company contrived several other schemes in an attempt to make money for the local farming operation. For instance, it experimented with raising hogs and sheep. Hogs had been successfully raised before in the area, but the industry had waned after a siege of hog cholera in 1916. The initial expense of these operations proved to be too great a drain on the company.

In another attempt to make money, the company began to operate several of its developed farms, namely the Valley View Farm, the Shady Glenn Farm, and the Merrill Farm. Grain was the principal crop grown on these farms as well as on the Demonstration Farm and the Pioneer Park Farm. The company also attempted to raise cattle, sheep, and hogs on the various farms.

During this time, there was no extensive use of irrigation. The company maintained some of the wells that were already installed but left most of them dormant. The high cost of irrigation equipment to replace worn-out parts caused the company to discontinue using most of its irrigation system as it depreciated. Although crops noticeably flourished for several seasons when planted near a formerly used irrigation ditch, farmers, not convinced that irrigation would be profitable, did not revive their wells for several years.[136]

The tenant proved to be the most lucrative source of income during the period.[137] Fred Watson, dry-land farm superintendent, faced many problems, however. He was responsible for finding a reputable tenant and then for seeing that the tenant lived up to his lease. Watson had to collect rents—not always an easy task. He found that some of the tenants, who appeared to be reputable, had misrepresented themselves and could not successfully farm. Watson was also expected to handle

[135] William F. Feeney to Henry S. Fleming, letter, November 25, 1918, BF.
[136] Williams, tape interview, August 22, 1959.
[137] Staked Plains Trust, Limited, ledger, TLDCP. The books for the years 1917 and 1918 recorded the operations of the Prairie Lands Trust.

Development of Company Property

the tenant's problems, whether they were concerned with repair work or crop management. The main crops grown by the tenant farms were sorghum grains and wheat.[138] The dry-land farm operations during the seventeen months that the Prairie Lands Trust handled the operation made a profit of $10,073.78.[139] The other phases of the farm operations made little or no clear profit.

It soon became obvious to the backers of the company that the Plainview operation was making no progress. Attempts to succeed with the local farming operations could in no way approach the profit that might have been realized had the original prospectus of developing the land and successfully selling it been carried out. Unforeseen deterrents— World War I, inflated prices on construction materials, a tight money market, inexperience with farming in the West Texas area, and other problems—had caused the company to become too deeply involved financially to hope for a profit for all its investors. Before the Prairie Lands Trust, which had handled the local operations since 1916, could even attempt to correct the situation, foreclosure by the Empire Trust Company, acting as trustee for the bondholders who had invested in Texas Prairie Lands in 1912, forced an active reorganization of the whole operation. The reorganization was to be carried out by the Staked Plains Trust since it had assumed direct responsibility from the time it was organized in 1914 for the liabilities and obligations of Texas Prairie Lands. Actually the reorganization sought to benefit equitably the backers of the enterprise.

[138] Watson, tape interview, July 12, 1958.
[139] Baldwin, Slaton, and Randolph, and Staked Plains Trust, Limited, 1913–1918, ledger, general profits and losses, p. 178, TLDCP.

5. Reorganization of 1919

A REORGANIZATION of the Plainview enterprise was necessitated when the Empire Trust, in 1919, foreclosed on behalf of the holders of first mortgage bonds issued in 1912 by the Texas Prairie Lands. Since security held for the bonds was thirty-five thousand shares of Staked Plains Trust common stock, the trust was obliged to take steps to meet the demands of foreclosure. Although the foreclosure was the immediate reason for the reorganization, it was apparent that some change in the operation should have been initiated even if the foreclosure had not taken place. The backers of the enterprise, in order to keep the local operation functioning, had entered into a series of financial maneuvers that had created a complex multiplicity of subsidiary companies and trusts. The maze of companies and trusts undoubtedly needed to be simplified and unified. The local operation also needed to be streamlined. Although money was being poured into the area to meet the cost of developing the land and administering the overall program, the Texas Land and Development Company, because of unforeseeable circumstances, from the outset of the operation had never successfully carried out its program of developing and selling all the Plainview land held by the enterprise. Only if the land could be sold, would the backers have any hope of realizing a profit from their investment. Thus it would seem that the foreclosure simply speeded up an inevitable reorganization.

Minor C. Keith, Francis R. Hart, and Charles H. Zehnder managed the reorganization.[1] Keith, as trustee for both the Staked Plains Trust and the Prairie Lands Trust and as a director of the Empire Trust Company,[2] was spokesman in the reorganization for all three trusts. Hart, a Staked Plains Trust trustee, represented that group; Zehnder, a trustee of the Prairie Lands Trust, acted as its representative. Keith, who held the most powerful position among the managers, became the chairman of the reorganization. The Empire Trust group, who held the balance of power since it was foreclosing, and other "interested parties" were responsible for appointing the reorganization managers.[3] Probably the other "interested parties" were the most influential backers of the Boston group and the English group who were at the moment out of control. It should be pointed out, however, that Keith, the most influential member of the reorganization group, had allegiance to the Boston group as well as to the New York group. Although the Empire group was in direct control, because of its move to foreclose on Texas Prairie Lands, the atmosphere created by the appointment of the reorganization managers was one of compromise. Henry S. Fleming, a consulting engineer, assumed the duties of secretary of the reorganization, and it was to his office in New York City that all preliminary reports pertinent to the reorganization were to be sent.

Preliminary reorganization proceedings actually began in November 1918 when the reorganization managers authorized an extensive investigation of the operation of the Plainview office. The managers sent

[1] *Documents 1917*, Reorganization Agreement, Texas Land and Development Company Papers, Southwest Collection, Texas Tech University, Lubbock (hereafter cited as TLDCP).

[2] *Who Was Who in America*, 1897–1942, I, 60.

[3] Peyton B. Randolph to Paul A. McDermott (attorney), letter, n.d., Randolph Files, Plainview (hereafter cited as RF).

William F. Feeney, an associate of Fleming's, to Plainview to conduct the investigation.[4]

It is questionable that a charge of mismanagement during the early years of operation could be leveled at the local company, but certainly the chaos, partially created by a rapid turnover in the general managership of the Texas Land and Development Company, hampered the company's efficiency. There had been six general managers from the time the company was chartered in 1912 to the time of reorganization. The first three general managers—Henderson, Charles, and Longstreth—had carried out specialized facets of the operation. Henderson had concentrated on the sales program; Charles, the development program, especially irrigation; and Longstreth, the agricultural operations. No doubt, these men had performed their specified duties with acumen. When the Prairie Lands Trust assumed control of the operation in 1916, that company's trustees tried to hire a general manager who was versatile enough to supervise the complete operation. Unfortunately the first man they hired, Charles F. Myers, discovered that the job did not live up to his expectations. While he was getting settled in a railroading position in Cuba, however, he made two attempts to carry on the work connected with the general managership of the Texas Land and Development Company. In the interim between Myers' two brief periods of employment, J. W. Pipkin had acted as general manager. Such a rapid turnover of managers could lead only to confusion among the subordinate officers and workers connected with the operation, since no permanent supervisory policy could be established. When Clyde E. Craig assumed the position of general manager in February 1917, he inherited a tedious job that demanded the stern hand of a good organizer. To add to his problems, he lost one of his key officers because of World War I. George Tolbert Perdue, who had been the assistant secretary and the treasurer of the Texas Land and Development Company from December 1916, went into the service in August 1918.[5] Others in key positions were called to the service also, and, in addition, the war caused labor shortages and a period of inflation.

[4] This fact is confirmed in William F. Feeney to Peyton B. Randolph, letter, November 25, 1919, RF.

[5] George Tolbert Perdue, tape interview, July 14, 1958.

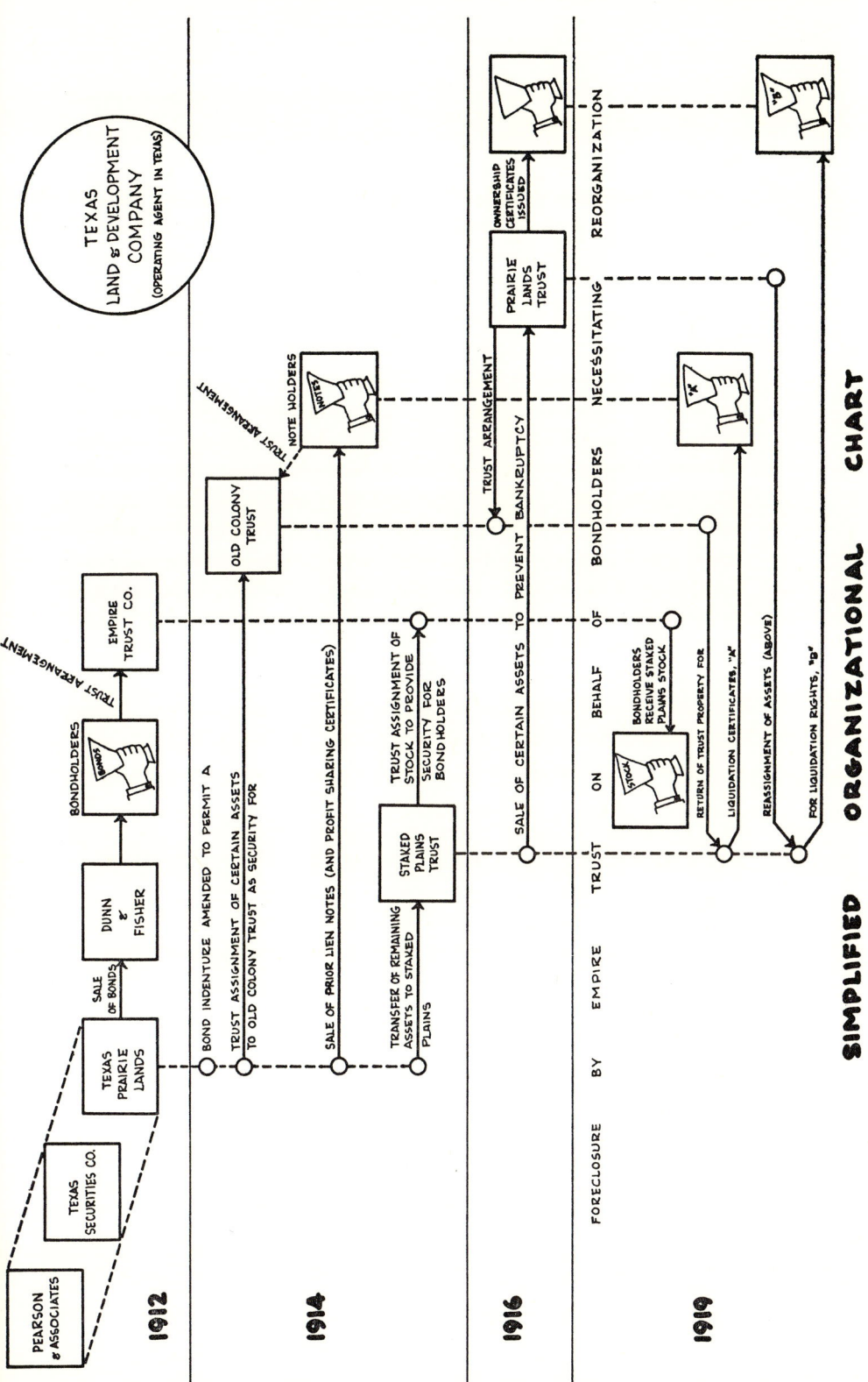

When the reorganization managers received the main report from Feeney, who had been sent to investigate the Plainview operation, it became clear that changes should take place. After an auditor named Monteith, who had accompanied Feeney to Plainview to assist in straightening out the records in the local office, had "put the books and records in good condition," Feeney suggested that "Mr. Craig be instructed to see that they remain that way."[6] He felt that if they were not closely checked, it would "only be a question of a short time before another overhauling" would be necessary.

After a thorough investigation of the company's operational procedures, Feeney critically analyzed the situation. He was of the opinion that Craig's subordinates possessed the necessary qualifications for their positions, but that they did not cooperate. Their lack of cooperation, he pointed out, was especially noticeable among the heads of the different farms. Inefficiency in all departments attended the bickering and could only result in unnecessary expenses to the company. As an example, Feeney reported that Fred Watson, the superintendent of the dry-land farms, seldom consulted with Craig concerning tenants, terms, collections, and extensions of contracts. Feeney did not question Watson's honesty or integrity. However, he was of the opinion that it was not "good business methods for one man to completely run his department, as follows":

1. Personally select the tenant.
2. Personally arrange the rental and terms of payment.
3. Personally draft the contract.
4. Personally grant extension on notes given for rental.
5. Personally collect notes, etc.
6. Personally make allowances against notes in exchange for labor performed.
7. Personally attend to harvesting Company's share of crops (when based on a one-third of crop basis).[7]

Feeney thought the general manager should be consulted about the

[6] William F. Feeney to Henry S. Fleming, letter, November 25, 1918, Bain Files, Plainview.
[7] *Ibid.*

selection of the tenants and the terms under which they were chosen. In the case of extensions of a note, he felt that Craig, not Watson, should be responsible for the decision. "These little things," together with other obvious ills he had seen, convinced Feeney that Craig allowed "altogether too much leeway with his assistants," resulting in "lack of cooperation and an inefficient organization."

Feeney discussed his feeling that P. B. Barber, who was in charge of the developed farms, was not fulfilling his role as an agricultural expert for the company. One of Barber's duties was "to consult with all the tenants and purchasers in an effort to secure more scientific [farming] methods." Feeney wrote that he had it from "good authority" that Barber was not adequately performing his job. One of the company's purchasers had requested instructions from Barber in reference to alfalfa planting. Barber's reason for not complying with the purchaser's request for help was "Oh, he would not listen to me." Feeney added, however, that Barber was advising a Mr. Wilson, a man who had no connections with the company. This arrangement led to Barber's employment as general manager for the Wilson farms while at the same time he retained his position with the Texas Land and Development Company. The arrangement should have been of short duration since Craig informed Barber that he would have to give up one job or the other, but "after this notice, two months elapsed before Barber finally gave up the position with Mr. Wilson."[8]

Feeney suggested that the Plainview office might take other steps to secure company efficiency. He would have stopped the practice whereby the foreman of the Demonstration, Pioneer, and Dairy farms went to the office or the warehouse several times a day for orders and materials. He was convinced that this practice led to work stoppage in the absence of the foreman since he knew "from experience, what to expect from men without supervision." He further suggested that the practice of lending company implements to farmers who had no connection with the company be stopped immediately.

In conclusion, Feeney stated that Mr. Craig either lacked "executive ability, or the firmness required to correct the faults." In order to help

---

[8] *Ibid.*

him Feeney suggested that Craig "arrange his time in the office to enable him to get around to the farms daily, if possible, in order that he might keep posted on what is going on." So that Craig might carry on more efficiently, Feeney outlined the following program.

- A: That he insist on regular hours being kept by the employees in the office, so that when it becomes necessary to dictate in the morning, he does not have to await the arrival of a stenographer.
- B: Arrange conferences with tenants, purchasers, agents, etc. where possible, for say, 11 a.m. to 12 m. [sic]
- C: Plan regular inspection trips with his Superintendents and occasionally have, say, the Dry Farm Superintendent accompany him when making an inspection of the Developed Farms with their Superintendent and vice versa.
- D: Every afternoon possible should be spent by him on the farms, as this is where close supervision will be reflected in reduced operating costs.[9]

The reorganization managers, after receiving Feeney's reports about the Plainview operation, were evidently convinced that they needed to change the personnel in charge of the Plainview operation. By February 25, 1919, the managers accepted resignations from all Texas Land and Development Company officers and appointed a new group of officers. Henry M. Keith[10] replaced Charles J. Hubbard as president of the company. Winfield Holbrook replaced Clyde E. Craig as general manager and vice-president. William F. Feeney assumed the duties of both secretary and treasurer from J. Lothrop Motley and George T. Perdue respectively.[11] Perdue had actually terminated his employment in August 1918 when he entered the armed forces, and his position had been vacant for several months. Neither Keith nor Feeney was to live in Plainview during his term of office; instead each would be more closely associated with the reorganization managers' office located in

[9] *Ibid.*

[10] It could not be determined whether Henry M. Keith was a relative of Minor C. Keith. One would suspect that he could have been since Minor C. Keith played such a prominent role in the enterprise.

[11] Texas Land and Development Company, minutes, February 25, 1919, TLDCP.

Reorganization of 1919

New York City. Probably Feeney assumed the position of secretary-treasurer only until a local person could be found. A. B. DeLoach, who had been a cashier at the First National Bank in Plainview, was offered and accepted the position in February, but was not officially elected until May 12, 1919. He probably assumed his duties before that time, however. DeLoach filled the position for a little over a year, from May 12, 1919, to August 2, 1920. He considered himself a secretary-treasurer and director of the Texas Land and Development Company "on paper only," inasmuch as many of his duties were already delegated to subordinates. He did not feel that he had enough to do to warrant his staying on the job.[12] His successor was a long-time company bookkeeper, Walter J. Klinger, who remained the company's secretary-treasurer from August 2, 1920, to February 29, 1948.

Winfield Holbrook, whom many people addressed as Captain out of respect for his rank in World War I, was the man who shouldered the massive responsibility of supervising the local operation under the Reorganization Agreement of 1919. Actually the Reorganization Agreement, which was to be the foundation of operations until the time of complete liquidation of the Texas Prairie Lands, was not in force when Holbrook came to Plainview in January 1919 to assume his duties.[13] Clyde E. Craig remained in Plainview for a time after Holbrook arrived, perhaps to acquaint Holbrook with the local operation. At any rate, the two men became friends and corresponded for many years after Craig left Plainview. This good feeling would indicate that Craig did not leave with ill will toward the company but merely considered his resignation as due course resultant from the entry of a new regime in the controlling companies. He stated, "I stayed on there in Plainview with Mr. Hubbard as long as he did, or until operations in the East were changed from Boston to New York."[14]

Probably Holbrook, who had greatly impressed the reorganization managers, was first instructed to add his suggestions for making the

---

[12] A. B. DeLoach, letter, November 25, 1958, Brunson Letters, Southwest Collection, Texas Tech University, Lubbock (hereafter cited as BL).

[13] The Reorganization Agreement was officially adopted on December 1, 1919.

[14] Clyde E. Craig, letter, September 15, 1959, BL.

Plainview operation more efficient to those already received by the reorganization managers. Upon hearing about the opening in Plainview from a fellow engineer and college friend, Holbrook had arranged a meeting with the reorganization managers in New York, and his forthright manner undoubtedly assured him the position. A man possessing "know-how" and a temperament such as his was definitely needed to straighten out the Plainview operation. His future employers would have been influenced not only by his "strict and high standards" but also by his extensive background in irrigation engineering, agricultural methods, and management. Before he volunteered for the armed services in 1917, he had worked a number of years on railroad construction and irrigation projects in Colorado, New Mexico, and Utah. He had been an engineer for the Beaver Park Irrigation project in Colorado and later an engineer for the American Sugar Beet Company's irrigation operations in western Kansas. His experience had been gained in the western part of the United States, where he had lived after his family physician in his home state of New York had advised him to go west for his health. He entered the University of Colorado as an undergraduate civil engineering student and was graduated from that institution in 1904 with a B.S. degree in civil engineering conferred *magna cum laude*.[15] His temperament and knowledge led Holbrook to go about his job systematically and carefully. It seemed that the company at last had found a man completely in tune with the operation.

A short time after he arrived in Plainview, Holbrook hired two former associates, David Dell Bowman, with whom he had worked on the Beaver Park, Colorado, operation,[16] and Fred Lowe, with whom he was associated during his employment with the Garden City Sugar and Land Company in Kansas.[17] Both men, as personal acquaintances of Captain Holbrook, no doubt had his absolute trust and were to remain with the company for twenty-one years.[18] Holbrook knew the quality of

---

[15] Based on information supplied by the son and daughter of Captain Holbrook; notes deposited with the Texas Land and Development Company papers in the Southwest Collection at Texas Tech University.

[16] David Dell Bowman, tape interview, June 27, 1958.

[17] Fred Lowe, tape interview, July 12, 1958.

[18] Bowman, tape interview, June 27, 1958.

Reorganization of 1919

their work and seemed to feel that the company needed them; moreover, it was only natural that Holbrook would wish to employ men whose work was familiar to him and who would be loyal to him. The original division of duties placed Bowman in charge of the dry-land farms,[19] formerly supervised by Fred Watson, and Lowe in charge of the irrigated farms,[20] formerly supervised by P. B. Barber.

It was almost a full year after Holbrook had been on the scene before the Reorganization Agreement, under which he was to operate, was formally completed on December 1, 1919. During the interim Holbrook, although he kept in close touch with the managers, probably proceeded on his own to correct any obvious inefficiency and to coordinate the company's farming operations.[21] In the meantime the reorganization managers were busy completing their plans. Since the reorganization was going to involve placing the responsibility for the operation in the hands of the trustees of one controlling company, the Staked Plains Trust, it was necessary to retire to the mutual satisfaction of the holders certain securities of the other two companies, Texas Prairie Lands and the Prairie Lands Trust. Before the agreement was adopted, the reorganization managers sent out a notice to the various investors informing them of the terms of the agreement as they had been worked out and accepted by "the persons most largely interested," who were in reality the principal holders of the various securities. The investors were informed in the notice that if they were to send in their valid securities by January 15, 1920, their security would be retired and they would be issued certain liquidation certificates or liquidation rights by a formula set forth in the agreement. The purpose of the reorganization was specifically stated as a plan to "facilitate the liquidation and winding up of the Texas Prairie Lands Trust, Limited, and to distribute

---

[19] *Ibid.*

[20] Lowe, tape interview, July 12, 1958.

[21] No financial records could be located for the period from September 30, 1918, to January 1, 1920, except "scraps" of the operation expenses of Texas Prairie Lands, which for all practical purposes was not carrying on any of the operation. Thus, it was hard to piece together just how extensive the farming operations were during the period in question.

the proceeds as rapidly as possible" among those who were entitled to receive them.

The basic plan underlying the agreement called for the retirement of eight securities:

(1) Texas Prairie Lands, Limited, First Mortgage Six Per Cent Bonds;
(2) Texas Prairie Lands, Limited, Prior Lien Seven Per Cent Notes;
(3) Texas Prairie Lands, Limited, interim receipts for Prior Lien Notes;
(4) Texas Prairie Lands, Limited, Profit-Sharing Certification, Class A;
(5) Texas Prairie Lands, Limited, Profit-Sharing Certificates, Class B;
(6) Texas Prairie Lands, Limited, Profit-Sharing Certificates, Class C;
(7) Texas Prairie Lands, Limited, Shares;
(8) Prairie Lands Trust, Limited, Trust Certificates.[22]

Class A Liquidation Certificates, Class B Liquidation Rights, and the thirty-five thousand shares of Staked Plains Trust were to be issued to the investors according to a specified plan.

The first mortgage bonds, issued by the Texas Prairie Lands Trust on December 12, 1912, and valued at £500,000 ($2,433,333.33), were to be retired and the security held for them by the Empire Trust Company; the thirty-five thousand shares of the Staked Plains Trust were to be divided among the bondholders at the rate of seven shares for each £100 bond. Before the proposed division of shares could be made, it was necessary to follow through on the foreclosure proceedings. As a first step, the thirty-fve thousand shares of the Staked Plains Trust, which had been held as security for the bonds, were bought at a foreclosure sale for $5,000 or $1.00 for each £100 bond, by the reorganization managers, Keith, Zehnder, and Hart, who themselves held $468,000 in bonds.[23] The Empire Trust was to distribute pro rata among the bondholders the $5,000 received from the sale.[24] The shares that were purchased were now in a position to be issued to the bondholders at the rate of seven shares for each £100 note, as provided for

[22] *Documents 1917*, Reorganization Agreement, TLDCP.
[23] See Appendix III.
[24] *Documents 1917*, pp. 367 ff., TLDCP. These are the minutes of the general meeting of the holders of the 6 per cent bonds, held June 7, 1920. At that time the proceedings carried out by the reorganization pertaining to the first mortgage bonds were confirmed.

Reorganization of 1919

in the reorganization. Not all bondholders responded to the call of the reorganization managers for the bonds. The majority did, and £490,000 of bonds were deposited. In exchange for these, 32,820 shares (no par) were issued by the Staked Plains Trust to the former bondholders. The Empire Trust Company as trustee for the bondholders held $310, the proceeds applicable to the £31,000 of bonds not deposited. The missing amount left 2,170 unissued shares in the treasury of the trust. These shares were issued from time to time, no doubt by individuals connected with the trust, and by 1932 all had been distributed.[25]

The prior lien notes issued by the Texas Prairie Lands on December 12, 1914, and valued at $500,000 and the interim receipts issued for them were retired; the security [26] held by the Old Colony Trust Company for them was vested in the Staked Plains Trust. The owners of the prior lien notes were thereupon entitled to receive Class A Liquidation Certificates of the Staked Plains Trust in an amount equal to the principal of the notes owned plus 7 per cent annual interest from July 1, 1918.

The profit-sharing certificates of Texas Prairie Lands, dated January 1, 1915, were retired, and the owners of the Class A Certificates, which were valued at $125,000, were given in exchange Class A Liquidation Certificates of the Staked Plains Trust equal to the amount of the principal. In addition 5 per cent interest per year beginning January 1, 1923, was to be paid. The profit-sharing certificates, classes B and C, were simply retired and canceled since the terms of their issue were not fulfilled.

The Staked Plains Trust received once again all property and assets of the Prairie Lands Trust, which had been created in 1916. The 4,250 trust certificates of the Prairie Lands Trust were retired, and the owners were entitled to the same amount in Class B Liquidation Rights of the Staked Plains Trust. The rights were to be redeemable at $160 each, or

[25] Staked Plains Trust, Limited, *Annual Report*, 1932, TLDCP.

[26] The security consisted of the contracts of purchase on the land sold before December 12, 1914, and on 3,361.52 acres of Texas land valued at $376,082.61, and a mortgage on the company demonstration farms. For a review of the original organization see Chapter 2.

a total principal amount of $680,000, plus interest at the rate of 7 per cent per year from January 1, 1920. Thus the holders of these rights, who had invested $425,000, in 1916 at the riskiest period in the venture in hopes of realizing a profit proportionate to their risk, were to receive $680,000 plus interest in return, or a profit of $60 for each $100 invested. The liquidation rights were divided among the owners in proportion to the amounts of the trust certificates owned by them respectively.

Under the terms of the agreement, the thirty-five thousand shares of Texas Prairie Lands were to be "surrendered and upon completion of the reorganization, cancelled and destroyed."[27] By this action the Texas Prairie Lands would be officially liquidated, and the purpose of the reorganization would be achieved. Technically the thirty-five thousand shares of Texas Prairie Lands had been valueless after 1914, when the Staked Plains Trust assumed control of the Plainview enterprise. The shares from 1912 had been in the hands of the Texas Securities Company, the Pearson syndicate organization that had been responsible for buying and then selling the Plainview land to Texas Prairie Lands. It will be recalled that the Texas Securities Company was to receive in addition to the thirty-five thousand shares, $1,800,000.00 in cash. Only $1,537,750.95 of this amount was ever paid; the company agreed, however, to write off the remaining $262,249.05 still owed in 1914. In effect the official winding up of Texas Prairie Lands by the reorganization was also to mark the end of the Texas Securities Company.[28] For all practical purposes both companies had been out of business except for the obligations incurred by Texas Prairie Lands since 1914 when the Staked Plains Trust took over the operation.

The Class A Liquidation Certificates were to be paid in full, both principal and interest, before any payments in respect to Class B Liqui-

---

[27] This point is reiterated in Hugh R. Partridge to Peyton B. Randolph, letter, April 13, 1943, RF. The Reorganization Agreement handles the matter also.

[28] The Texas Securities Company filed its last annual report to the Provincial Secretary, on December 31, 1918 (Robert James Cudney, Deputy Provincial Secretary of Ontario, letter, charter, and last annual report of Texas Securities Company, Limited, July 13, 1960, BL).

Reorganization of 1919 105

dation Rights were to be made. Class B Liquidation Rights were to be paid in full, both principal and interest, prior to the distribution of any funds to the shareholders of the Staked Plains Trust. The reorganization managers were given full legal power to carry out the terms of the Reorganization Agreement. Any owner who deposited his securities under the terms of this agreement became bound by its provisions.[29]

The reorganization managers became synonymous with the trustees of the Staked Plains Trust as one group melted into the other and the Staked Plains Trust gained official control of the operation in 1920.[30] From the time the Staked Plains Trust gained control, it became that trust's aim first to pay the holders of the Class A Liquidation Certificates; next to pay a deferred compensation to the former trustees of the two liquidated trusts and Fleming, the reorganization managers' secretary and representative;[31] and finally to pay the holders of Class B Liquidation Rights according to the agreement.[32] After accomplishing these aims, the trust would then attempt to make a profit for its own shareholders, the former holders of Texas Prairie Lands first mortgage bonds.

The Staked Plains Trust was involved in paying the obligations incurred by the reorganization for a number of years.[33] By means of several partial payments the principal amount of $625,000.00, called for under the Class A Liquidation Certificates was paid by August 31, 1930. Payment of the interest accrued, amounting to $289,175.12[34] on

---

[29] All material pertaining to the reorganization is based on the Reorganization Agreement of 1919 found in *Documents 1917*, Appendix, TLDCP.

[30] Staked Plains Trust, Limited, *Annual Report*, 1920, TLDCP.

[31] The deferred compensation amounting to $52,000 was agreed upon by the trustees of the Staked Plains Trust at a meeting on October 22, 1920. The compensation was to be paid immediately after principal and interest of Class A Liquidation Certificates were paid. The resolution is quoted by Feeney to Randolph, letter, February 16, 1938, RF. The matter of deferred compensation is more fully discussed in Chapter 7.

[32] Staked Plains Trust, Limited, *Annual Report*, 1920, TLDCP.

[33] For the story of the operation of the Staked Plains Trust and the Texas Land and Development Company during this period see Chapter 6, Chapter 7, and Chapter 8.

[34] Staked Plains Trust, Limited, *Annual Report*, 1930, TLDCP.

the Class A Liquidation Certificates, was completed March 26, 1943.[35] By October 13, 1944, all deferred compensations, $52,500.00, had been paid.[36] Payment of the principal on the Class B Liquidation Rights, $680,000.00, was completed by October 31, 1944, and the interest accrued on these rights, amounting to $728,875.00 was paid by July 2, 1947.[37] Thus it was that the terms of the Reorganization Agreement were successfully carried out by the Staked Plains Trust. After July 1947 the trust was able to operate for the benefit of its shareholders.

The reorganization had accomplished its goals. It had removed from the scene completely Texas Prairie Lands and consequently the Texas Securities Company, both of which had been "dead weight" since 1914. It had reconsolidated the operation of the Prairie Lands Trust with that of the Staked Plains Trust, thus giving the latter trust complete control over the Plainview operation. It had furnished the Staked Plains Trust with a methodical procedure for meeting payments on its obligations, all of which had been vested in the Staked Plains Trust when it issued liquidation certificates and rights and its own shares to security holders of the former company and trust. Following through with the reorganization plan, the trust had paid in full the liquidation certificates and rights plus interest thereon.

Holders of Class A Liquidation Certificates received their full original investment on prior lien notes, when they received $500,000.00 of the principal amount owed. The remaining principal amount, $125,000.00, represented what was originally a commission given to the subscribers of prior lien notes; when that amount was paid, it represented clear profit to the holders as did the interest accrued on the certificates, which amounted to $289,175.12. Thus the holders of these certificates, who had been the holders of five thousand prior lien notes valued at $100.00 each issued in 1914, were paid a gross of $914,175.12. They therefore returned a net profit of nearly eighty-three cents on each dollar invested, or $82.84 on each note.

---

[35] Partridge to Randolph, letter, June 16, 1947, RF.
[36] Staked Plains Trust, Limited, minutes, October 13, 1944 (I, 263), TLDCP.
[37] Partridge to Randolph, letter, June 16, 1947, RF.

Reorganization of 1919

The holders of Class B Liquidation Rights, who prior to the reorganization held Trust Certificates issued by the Prairie Lands Trust in 1916, profited even more. These holders had originally invested $425,000.00 in 4,250 Trust Certificates of the Prairie Lands Trust valued at $100.00 each. When these certificates had been converted to liquidation rights, a $60.00 bonus had been added to each $100.00 invested; thus the holder was to receive $160.00 plus accrued interest from January 1, 1920. The total amount of the principal, $680,000.00, plus the accrued interest, $728,875.00, was paid to the holders by July 2, 1947. The gross amount received by the investors was $1,408,975.00. The total net profit was, therefore, $983,875.00, or a net profit of $2.31 for each dollar invested, or nearly $231.50 per original certificate.

The holders of the thirty-five thousand shares of Staked Plains Trust, who before the reorganization had held Texas Prairie Lands first mortgage bonds, could not forsee in 1947 whether they would make a profit or a loss from their investment. Chances for a profit, however, were extremely doubtful. The original amount invested, £500,000, or $2,433,333.33, had been trimmed down considerably by the foreclosure proceedings initiated on behalf of the bondholders by the Empire Trust Company. At a foreclosure sale the reorganization managers had paid $5,000.00 for the thirty-five thousand shares of Staked Plains Trust, which were the security held for the bonds. That amount was in turn distributed to the bondholders at the rate of $1.00 for each £100 note.[38] Since the rate of exchange at the time the bonds were issued in 1912 had been approximately $4.87 per pound note,[39] each £100 note represented an investment of approximately $487.67. The drastic cut in the original value of the bonds from nearly $487.67 to $1.00 was, in a small way, offset by the Staked Plains Trust when it was authorized by the Reorganization Agreement to issue each bondholder seven shares (no par value) of the trust stock for each £100 note. What amount these shares would bring the holder upon final liquidation of the trust could not be estimated. As of December 31, 1947, when all other obli-

[38] *Documents 1917*, Appendix, TLDCP.
[39] This figure is rounded off, because the actual rate of exchange was $4.8666.

gations of the reorganization had been met, the book value of the shares was listed as $13.41 per share.[40] Whether there would be a marked increase in this value depended on one speculative asset that the trust held.[41] This asset was one-half of the mineral rights retained on the last 21,844.46 acres that the trust sold.[42] Should oil be discovered on that land, profits might be assured; however, that such would happen remained to be seen.[43]

The terms of the reorganization had been effectively carried out by the Staked Plains Trust from 1920 to 1947 when the last payments were made to the holders of liquidation rights. Perhaps the trustees had originally hoped for an earlier date to mark the termination of these payments. However, the trust had survived a farm depression, a major national depression, many seasons of drought, and a world war. The succeeding chapters reveal how the trust operated during that time in order to meet its obligations and how after 1947, the trust moved toward its own official liquidation.

[40] Staked Plains Trust, Limited, *Annual Report*, 1947, TLDCP.
[41] All the land had been sold by the end of 1946. See Chapter 8.
[42] Staked Plains Trust, Limited, minutes, June 1, 1945, (I, 269), TLDCP.
[43] See Chapter 8.

6. Consolidation under the Reorganization Agreement

D URING THE NINETEEN-TWENTIES the Plainview enterprise operated in an orderly fashion. The 1919 reorganization gave the Staked Plains Trust a goal toward which to work; it wished to liquidate the remaining debts as quickly as possible so that it would be free to operate for its shareholders. As general manager, Captain Holbrook was well equipped to handle the local operation with efficiency. Moreover, the trust kept a close check of the local operation because only its success would insure that obligations incurred by the terms of the Reorganization Agreement could be successfully terminated.

When the first annual postreorganization report of the trust was issued on April 21, 1921, the three trustees of the Staked Plains Trust were Minor C. Keith, Charles H. Zehnder, and Hugh R. Partridge.[1]

---

[1] Staked Plains Trust, Limited, *Annual Report*, 1920, Texas Land and Development Company Papers, Southwest Collection, Texas Tech University, Lubbock (hereafter cited as TLDCP). This was the first such report.

These three men had been appointed after a series of alterations in trustee membership had taken place in 1920. When the Staked Plains Trust originally controlled the Plainview operation, from December 1914 to December 1916, there had been five trustees. In February 1920[2] the number had been reduced to three, an action that was fully in accordance with the company's Declaration of Trust.[3] The first group of trustees after reorganization consisted of Minor C. Keith, who had been an original trustee of the company as well as a trustee of the Prairie Lands Trust; Charles H. Zehnder, who had been a trustee of the Prairie Lands Trust; and Maurice Hely-Hutchinson, an Englishman who represented the London group of investors.[4] The backers of the Staked Plains Trust had agreed to reduce the number of trustees to three as the result of a compromise that called for one member of the trusteeship to represent the Boston group; one, the Empire group (or New York group); and one, the London group. In May 1920 Keith, Zehnder, and Hely-Hutchinson signed an agreement stating that in the event of death Keith's successor would be acceptable to the Boston group; Zehnder's, to the Empire group; and Hely-Hutchinson's, to the London group.[5] By the fall of 1920 it became obvious that Hely-Hutchinson's membership in the trust presented complications. While attempting to gain approval for a Texas Land and Development Company land title for a proposed sale, a Plainview lawyer brought to the attention of the company attorney, Peyton B. Randolph, the fact that Texas had a statute forbidding the alien ownership of land, a factor Randolph had overlooked at the time Hely-Hutchinson was appointed. Randolph urged the trustees of the Staked Plains Trust to divest title out of Hely-Hutchinson's name immediately and to invest it in a citizen of the United States.[6] Hely-Hutchingson resigned on September 3,

---

[2] William F. Feeney to Peyton B. Randolph, February 18, 1920, letter Wallet 1, TLDCP.
[3] *Documents 1917*, p. 124, TLDCP.
[4] Staked Plains Trust, Limited, February 12, 1920, minutes (I, 39–40), TLDCP.
[5] Feeney to Randolph, June 28, 1929, letter, Randolph Files, Plainview (hereafter cited as RF).
[6] Peyton B. Randolph to Henry S. Fleming, letter, August 11, 1920, RF.

Consolidation under the Agreement 111

1920, and his place was taken by Hugh R. Partridge of New York.[7] Partridge was the choice of Hely-Hutchinson and in effect acted as his proxy, such a condition making him a representative of the London group. With Partridge's appointment, the trusteeship was set for some time.

There was no occasion to contest the written agreement entered into by Keith, Zehnder, and Hely-Hutchinson until December 26, 1927, when Zehnder died.[8] According to the terms of the instrument, Zehnder's successor should have been chosen by the Empire group. However, Keith, who represented the Boston group, tried to pick the new trustee. Even though he had the approval of Leroy W. Baldwin, president of the Empire Trust Company, he met too much opposition from the Empire Trust group. After a short exchange, the Empire group succeeded in electing its candidate, Henry F. Whitney, a trust officer of the Empire Trust Company. Whitney assumed his duties in March 1928.[9]

The membership of the trust was to be changed again after June 14, 1929, when Minor C. Keith died at the age of eighty-two. Keith had been a trustee of the Staked Plains Trust since its formation[10] and was the heaviest investor in the Plainview operation. It was assumed that his successor as trustee, Henry B. Price, would represent the Boston group. Evidently Price became trustee on November 8, 1929, without any of the difficulties that had attended Whitney's election.[11]

One of the first actions of Keith, Zehnder, and Partridge was to employ an official representative, Henry S. Fleming, who had acted as representative and consultant to the reorganization managers. As the liaison officer between the New York office, where he was headquartered, and the Plainview office, he was to direct the compilation of an annual report of the trust's overall operation. He no doubt relied on reports from the Plainview office when he compiled the local phase of

---

[7] Staked Plains Trust, Limited, minutes (I, 49), TLDCP.
[8] Staked Plains Trust, Limited, *Annual Report*, 1927, TLDCP.
[9] Feeney to Randolph, letter, March 16, 1929, RF.
[10] Staked Plains Trust, Limited, *Annual Report*, 1929, TLDCP.
[11] Staked Plains Trust, Limited, minutes, October 28, 1938 (I, 177), TLDCP.

the operation. Fleming held this position until 1924, when William F. Feeney, one of Fleming's personally trained men who was familiar with the Plainview operation as a result of his investigations for the reorganization managers, assumed the position.[12] Feeney remained the trustees' representative until his death on January 10, 1942, at which time he was also serving as a trustee for the company.[13]

Following the reorganization in 1919, the parent trust no longer felt that it should entirely finance the Plainview operation. Instead, through farming operations by the Texas Land and Development Company and by tenants on unsold land, through land sales, and through timely investments the trustees hoped that the company would eventually pay off all trust obligations and then possibly make a profit for the shareholders. There was to be no new development on the Plainview lands, a policy that had been established even before reorganization. The Texas Land and Development Company, with the approval of the trust, could, however, make improvements on its lands if these were considered necessary to enable the company to obtain a more desirable renter or to sell a particular piece of property. When such improvements were made, the contracts were let to local builders.[14]

Apparently the trustees relied entirely upon the judgment of their general manager, Captain Winfield Holbrook, in regard to the necessity of improving a tract of land. No instance was found where Holbrook had requested permission to improve a particular farm and had been denied the right to do so. Holbrook embodied his suggestions in letters addressed to the trustees, and his requests were acted upon at their regular meetings. In late August 1924 Holbrook requested per-

---

[12] In a letter from Fleming to Randolph, date unknown (now in Randolph Files) there was an allusion to Fleming's bitterness as a result of the change. He stated, "this is the thanks I get for straightening out the operation." No obvious reason was found for the change.

[13] Staked Plains Trust, Limited, *Annual Report*, 1942, TLDCP. One of Feeney's sons aspired to replace his father as a member of the trust (after his father's death, of course) but because of a "personality" conflict with another trustee he was never elected to that position.

[14] Staked Plains Trust, Limited, *Annual Report*, 1924, TLDCP.

Plainview Daily Herald

1. Lake Plainview Park Well, Plainview, Texas.

2. Frederick Stark Pearson.

3. Company Employees, c. 1930. *Front row left to right*: W. J. Klinger, secretary-bookkeeper; P. B. Randolph, lawyer; Mary Cox, secretary; Clarence Rogers, well repairs; Homer Rook, well repairs. *Back row left to right*: Jim Eden, teamster; John and Tobe Hammonds, pump operators; Winfield Holbrook, manager; David Dell Bowman, field superintendent; W. Fred Lowe, field superintendent.

Plainview Daily Herald; courtesy of W. F. Lowe

4. Milton Day Henderson and Joe E. Lancaster.

Plainview Daily Herald

5. Lake Plainview, c. 1914–1915.

Plainview Daily Herald

6. Lake Plainview, c. 1914–1915.   *Plainview Daily Herald*

7. Winfield Holbrook, c. 1931.

Plainview Daily Herald

8. Slaton Well. *Plainview Daily Herald*

Plainview Daily Herald
9. Deep tilling near Plainview. Some felt that the 12″ to 16″ plowing, which needed to be done only once in five years, was better than irrigation.

Consolidation under the Agreement 113

mission to improve six farms. One of his requested improvements is cited below as an example.¹⁵

File 8. This is a good section of land, about ⅓ now in cultivation. With improvements we could get a better renter and more land under cultivation. It is located six miles east of Hale Center in a good farming district.

Estimate.

4 room house	$1,400.00
Barn	500.00
Windmill	300.00
Corral	100.00
	$2,300.00

The company's farming operations for the decade started with an optimistic note. The net profit for that part of the operation for 1920 was $33,806.19. Crop yields, abetted by a rainfall of 25.88 inches for the year, were good. Prices were classified as "unusually" good for both 1920 and for the preceding year.¹⁶

During 1920 David Dell Bowman and Fred Lowe, the farm superintendents hired earlier by Captain Holbrook, organized an efficient system for supervising the farming operation; it involved overseeing the company's farming operations as well as the tenants' farming. For the first part of 1920 the two men had divided the operations so that Bowman supervised the dry-land farms, and Lowe, the irrigated farms.¹⁷ The two men soon discovered that they were "just following each other around" a great deal of the time. Often when a man had a problem on his dry-land operation, he would also have one on his irrigated lands. Thus the two men would often meet each other on the same farm. Since the original division proved inefficient, in the fall of 1920 the Plainview office decided that Bowman should supervise the farms north of State Highway 70 in Swisher County and in the north-

---

[15] Staked Plains Trust, Limited, minutes, September 4, 1924 (I, 69–73), TLDCP.
[16] Staked Plains Trust, Limited, *Annual Report*, 1920, TLDCP.
[17] Fred Lowe, tape interview, July 12, 1958.

ern part of Hale County, while Lowe was to take over the farms south of the highway in Floyd County and in the southern part of Hale County.[18] All farming carried on by the company itself was located in Lowe's territory on three or four sections, including the Demonstration Farm and the Pioneer Park Farm. These operations were actually inherited from the prereorganization period, and it was not long before the stock on them was sold and the money reinvested in thirty head of work stock, mostly mules.[19] After 1920 the management planned to rid itself of any farming by company personnel as quickly as possible.[20]

From the beginning Bowman and Lowe worked well together. Each worked his own territory; each received the same salary. If a special problem arose on which one needed the other's advice, the two men would travel together.[21] Since both men worked on a monthly salary basis, they were never known to operate within the bounds of an eight-hour day. They simply worked until the job was done. They were on call any time a tenant needed them. They often spent all their waking hours and some they should have been sleeping fulfilling their duties.[22]

Since tenant farming represented a large part of the farming operation, there were several duties connected with it. First, it was necessary for Bowman and Lowe to pick responsible tenants. Although the farm superintendent was primarily responsible for finding a new tenant when a place in his territory was vacated, he was obliged to confer with Captain Holbrook before the final decision was made. Sometimes, if the potential tenant were a complete stranger, both the farm superintendent who was seeking a new tenant and Holbrook would question him. They were primarily interested in knowing whether the man could finance himself. Often, if his former landlord were near by, either Bowman or Lowe would make a trip out to talk with him to find out whether the potential tenant was reliable and whether he was out of debt when he left his former position. It was always important to know how much land the man had farmed in previous years and how

---

[18] David Dell Bowman, tape interview, June 27, 1958.
[19] Lowe, tape interview, July 12, 1958. Both men confirmed this fact.
[20] Staked Plains Trust, Limited, *Annual Report*, 1925, TLDCP.
[21] Bowman, tape interview, June 27, 1958.
[22] Both Bowman and Lowe confirmed these facts.

large his family was. If he had two or three sons who were old enough to help, he was looked upon more favorably. Although it was not in the lease, there was usually an oral agreement determining what the tenant would raise. At first wheat, oats, barley, and grain sorghums were emphasized. Later, however, other crops, primarily cotton, took a more important place. The tenant signed a lease each year, the terms of which remained basically the same throughout the company's existence. The company received the traditional thirds and fourths; one-third of all crops except cotton and one-fourth of the cotton crop. The company agreed to pay for baling and hauling alfalfa; the tenant took care of improvements and the irrigation plant if there was one. The company kept a crew of mechanics to do maintenance work on the farms, however, and was often more lenient than its leases implied.[23]

Once the tenant signed the lease, the superintendents checked constantly to see that he was carrying out the terms of the lease and that he had what he needed to farm the land properly. The company from time to time sold equipment and seeds to tenants. The superintendent collected the payments on these sales as well as the grassland rents. Harvest time proved to be the busiest time for the superintendents; then they spent many hours in the field seeing that operations went smoothly. They supervised carrying the crops to grain elevators, gins, or other destinations. They also collected the company's share of the crop money. Although they were required to keep a duplicate receipt of any money they collected in case a question about the collection arose, they did not have to keep books on their part of the business. The deposits and other business connected with the collection were left to W. J. Klinger, the company auditor.[24] All in all their jobs were strenuous.

Although 1920 afforded the farming operation a good beginning, 1921 and 1922 were not as profitable. A loss was incurred both years, that in 1922 being the heavier. Rainfall in 1921 was 24.38 inches; the next year it fell to a low of 19.38 inches. The low came at the wrong time for the farmers, with the result that the crops were light.

[23] Bowman, tape interview, June 27, 1958.
[24] *Ibid.*

Furthermore, prices were low. Consequently, in most cases farmers were unable to meet their obligations to the company, which sustained a loss of $22,571.27.[25]

The Texas Land and Development Company was spearheading a move during the twenties to re-emphasize the value of irrigation to the farmer.[26] A good many farmers were prejudiced against irrigation because of the expense of maintaining the equipment, although the exhorbitant installation expense had been overcome. There was also a great increase in the cost of fuel oil for the irrigation engines. Even with these odds to overcome, a survey comparison made by the Texas Land and Development Company management, using wheat grown on irrigated and dry-land farms as an experiment, showed that irrigation was beneficial (see Table 3).

Table 3. Comparison of Production
Dry-Land and Irrigated Farms

	Bushels per Acre	Value at $1.30 per Bushel	Less Cost of Irrigation per Acre	Net Value per Acre
Irrigated farms	24	$31.20	$6.00	$25.20
Dry-land farms	10	13.00	0	13.00
Added Profit from Irrigation (per acre)				$12.20

Source: Staked Plains Trust, Limited, *Annual Report*, 1912, TLDCP.

Although the management compiled such convincing data, it was still "difficult to persuade the average farmer that irrigated property means the equivalent of rain whenever any part of the crop requires moisture

---

[25] Staked Plains Trust, Limited, *Annual Report*, 1922, TLDCP. There is no record available for 1921. However, each annual report summarizes the results of the operations for the previous year.

[26] The Texas Land and Development Company, especially Holbrook, was given credit by many of those interviewed for revitalizing irrigation and again demonstrating that it was profitable (David Dell Bowman, Fred Lowe, and Homer Rook, interviews, June 27, 1958, July 12, 1958, August 28, 1959).

Consolidation under the Agreement

and that weather conditions can generally be ignored." Once a farmer understood that irrigation would pay off, he profited; however, the process of convincing others was "slow."[27] Drought years like 1922 helped to win over the doubters. By 1923 the management reported a steady "appreciation" of the value of irrigation. More experience in handling the equipment also helped the farmers to prosper. A "competent pumpman" hired by the company instructed the farmer who purchased or leased company lands in beneficial ways to use irrigation. This person was also available to help the farmer with repairs.[28]

Even though 1923 proved to be a good crop year with abundant rainfall, overhead expenses caused the farming operation to show a loss of $15,765.54. Because of unusual expenses involved in the company's own interests during the early twenties, the company decided that after 1924 it would not farm any of its own land but would lease it all to tenants. This had been the aim toward which the company had vigorously worked during the early part of the decade. In 1923 the company farmed only 1,130 acres in comparison with 2,268 acres farmed in 1919.[29]

Crop yields of tenants had been good in 1923 mainly because they had accepted the company's suggestion to emphasize a diversified crop system. Had they planted the usual one crop, wheat, there would have been an even heavier loss during the year because of the rainfall distribution. Yields from other crops actually staved off bankruptcy. Cotton, maize, and kafir brought unusually good prices. The tenant farmers were also increasing the truck gardens around their premises and found that there was a great demand in the area and at distant points for the vegetables they grew.[30]

From 1924 to the end of the decade the company's tenant-farming operation successfully produced profits, although these were varied in amount. A good market and a heavy yield in wheat and cotton made 1924 the best year since 1920. A formidable profit of $30,497.20

[27] Staked Plains Trust, Limited, *Annual Report*, 1920, TLDCP.
[28] *Ibid.*, 1922.
[29] *Ibid.*, 1923.
[30] *Ibid.*, 1923.

from the farming compared well with the loss of $15,765.54 in 1923. Drought in the late winter and early spring, an early freeze, and plant lice infesting the cotton fields cut into the crop yield in 1925; nonetheless, the company realized a small profit of $1,411.88 from farming.[31] Diversified crops prevented a loss in 1926, when there was no market for cotton, which the tenants had planted extensively. There was a profit of $20,626.28 for the year's farming operation.[32] The value of irrigation was proved, perhaps more conclusively in 1927 than in any previous year; after 18 inches of rainfall in the fall of 1926, a period of drought followed the next year, when only 14.71 inches of rain fell. Only 2.5 inches fell from January through May, "resulting in next to the driest spring, that had occurred in over thirty years." Deep moisture and judicious irrigating where it was available kept the crops from failing. Two-thirds of the crop made, and the farm operations brought a profit of $31,904.47.[33] The company increased its use of irrigation in 1928 although the amount of irrigated land was small when compared to that devoted to dry-land farming. The fact that some irrigating was done prevented the company from sustaining a loss because of a severe spring drought. The profit for 1928 reached $17,609.63.[34] Although the whole Plainview farm district was suffering from lack of capital among its farmers because of an unfavorable showing of crops, the farmers were not in desperate straits in 1928 or 1929 due to "safer farming practices adopted during the late years [of the decade], and sales by farmers of eggs, poultry, and dairy products."[35] A drought season in the late spring of 1929 again cut into the yield of wheat, cotton, and grain sorghums. Only alfalfa, an entirely irrigated crop, made satisfactory yields.[36] The company still operated in the black on farming operations with an impressive net profit of $53,679.58, the highest of the decade.

Profits and losses for the decade are indicated in Table 4.

[31] *Ibid.*, 1924.
[32] *Ibid.*, 1926.
[33] *Ibid.*, 1927.
[34] *Ibid.*, 1928.
[35] *Ibid.*, 1928, 1929.
[36] *Ibid.*, 1929.

Consolidation under the Agreement

Table 4. Profits and Losses (1920–1929)

Year	Profits	Net Losses
1920	$33,806.19	
1921	No record available but loss implied by annual report in 1922	
1922		$22,571.27
1923		15,765.54
1924	30,497.20	
1925	1,411.88	
1926	20,626.28	
1927	31,904.47	
1928	17,609.63	
1929	53,679.63	
Totals	$189,535.23	$38,336.81

Source: Staked Plains Trust, Limited, *Annual Report*, 1929, TLDCP.

The last six years of the decade, each showing a net profit, gave the company the right to feel that its farming operations were successful. In addition to monetary gains, the company had succeeded in preparing more land for the tenants to use. The fact that farm machinery was taking the place of the hand- or mule-drawn plow made it easy for the tenant to farm more land more efficiently. Although the tide was swinging back to irrigation, there was still much to be done in the following decades to educate the farmer to the system. A comparison, drawn by the company, demonstrates the difference in the crop acreage between 1919, when the company initiated the reorganization, and the end of the first decade of operation under the revitalized Staked Plains Trust and the Texas Land and Development Company (Table 5).[37] It was commendable that Captain Holbrook and his staff were able to prepare enough lands for their tenants to use by 1929 so that 78.9 per cent of the unsold land held by the company was plowed and ready to use and 76.4 per cent of that amount was actually "in crop." The increased usage of the land was no doubt an important factor in the

[37] *Ibid.*

Table 5. Comparative Crop Acreage

	Crop Acreage for 1919	Crop Acreage for 1929
Wheat	5,642.70	21,956.00
Oats	1,154.00	273.00
Barley	106.00	430.00
Cotton	666.00	4,433.00
Kafir, maize	12,661.00	8,736.00
Alfalfa	625.00	610.00
Miscellaneous	517.15	124.00
	21,371.85	36,562.00
Fallow plow land	620.00	1,205.00
Grass land	25,739.13	6,392.00
Waste land	2,339.80	2,302.00
Buildings, roads	345.19	1,400.00
Total not in crop	29,044.12	11,299.08
Total acreage	50,415.97*	47,861.08*
Per cent of all land in crop	42.4	76.4
Per cent of all land under plow	43.6	78.9

Source: Staked Plains Trust, Limited, *Annual Report*, 1920, TLDCP.
* The difference in total acreage farmed by the company and its tenants is explained by the company's land sales.

company's realizing almost consistent profits from the farming operations under heavy odds, mainly brought about by weather conditions.

Farming represented only a part of the company's efforts to make money in the Plainview area. Its primary aim was ultimately to sell all its lands. Captain Holbrook was solely responsible for the local sales program, but he occasionally allowed a local realtor to complete a sale for him.[38] Although 1920 proved to be a high point in company land sales, that part of the operation was soon to be curtailed. The manage-

[38] Bowman, tape interview, June 27, 1958.

Consolidation under the Agreement

Table 6. Value of Company Property (December 31, 1919)

	Acres	Cost	Cost per Acre
Improved farms	7,461.87	$ 777,331.72	$104.17
	2,215.00	69,615.23	31.42
	41,069.40	1,290.033.85	31.41
Total	50,746.27	$2,136,980.80	
Town lots (78)		12,707.44	
Total Valuation		$2,149,688.24	

Source: Staked Plains Trust, Limited, *Annaul Report*, 1920, TLDCP.

ment made a careful examination of the property still owned by the company as of December 31, 1919, and adjusted the book value to actual costs (see Table 6).

During 1920 the company sold 7,764.56 acres, the majority of which was unimproved land. In addition it sold nine and one-half town lots. The capital gain from these sales, less commission and expenses, was $470,587.98, of which the company received $355,634.85 in vendor's lien notes. Land sales had not been particularly solicited by the company during the year, but two factors led to the unusually brisk sales. First, prices farmers received for their crops in 1919 and 1920 were good and perhaps enticed others to buy farm land. Second, many oil speculators were buying land in all regions of Texas.[39]

In 1920 an unsolicited phase of company history was also introduced. It was during the twenties and thirties that much of the original lands sold by the company between 1912 and 1916 and some land sold later had to be repossessed because the purchasers could not meet the payments on their vendor's lien notes and the accrued interest on those notes. The general policy handed down by the trustees was extremely lenient, and the company was slow to take action against delinquent accounts. Only if it were hopelessly in arrears did the company turn

[39] Staked Plains Trust, Limited, *Annual Report*, 1920, TLDCP.

over to the trust a note for legal action, and then only if it became apparent that the person could not or would not meet his obligations. Some notes were extended time and time again in order to help the person who wished to keep his land. Perhaps a failure to understand irrigation was the main reason some original purchasers could not succeed in farming the land. Others had purchased such small tracts that they did not make enough money to pay their notes as they fell due.

To foreclose on a note, suit was brought against the purchaser who could not meet his obligations and who would not return his deed to the trust. Approximately 120 cases were filed during the period, and the company did not lose a single case. After the trust's attorney won ten or fifteen of the cases, the others gave up their countersuits if they had filed one and simply released their deeds. Many countersuits had been filed on a charge of misrepresentation of the land. The plaintiffs claimed the company had assured them that they could make a fortune on the land. Purchasers also complained about the overabundance of Johnson grass on the land. Many of those who lost their property as a result of foreclosure returned to their former homes, which were located primarily in Iowa, Nebraska, Missouri, and Illinois. Very few cases were ever appealed; most were tried in the District Court and dropped. Approximately 80 per cent of the original purchasers forfeited their lands during this period.[40]

Although the full impact of the repossessions was not felt until the major depression of the thirties, the setbacks of the twenties wiped out a sizeable amount of the trust's assets. During 1920 the company repossessed 1,031.50 acres. Most of this acreage was in improved farms.[41] During 1921 it repossessed an even larger amount, 1,133.05 acres, all of which were improved.[42] From 1922 to 1928 it repossessed the following amounts each year: 1922, 622.50 acres; 1923, 976.21 acres; 1924, 635.16 acres; 1925, 1,647.22 acres; 1926, 562.00 acres; 1927, 440.00 acres; and 1928, 320.00 acres. During 1929 there were no repossessions.[43] The total number of acres repossessed during the

[40] Peyton B. Randolph to Seymour V. Connor, tape interview, April 8, 1958.
[41] Staked Plains Trust, Limited, *Annual Report*, 1920, TLDCP.
[42] *Ibid.*, 1922.
[43] *Ibid.*, 1922–1929.

Consolidation under the Agreement

decade was 6,367.64 acres, representing over $640,000. Like so many other operations hit by the farm depression of the twenties and then by the major depression of the thirties, the trust had to drift and hope for better times. During the twenties the trust was fortunate to find relief in good crop years and in its one large surge of land selling in 1920.

Although the dedicated farmer was as reluctant to give up his land as the trust was to have it back, it became obvious that the trustees' early sales policy of selling to experienced farmers who could adapt to irrigation farming had not been completely carried out. Some sales agents, it seems, had lured inexperienced men to the area by "overselling" them. These agents went so far as to make down payments for the purchasers in hopes that they would be able to collect their full commissions when the farmers paid their notes.[44] Inexperience caused the first defaults, but later it was not easy for even the best farmer to make a success of the operation, although some did.

Since the company sold nearly eight thousand acres of land in 1920 and smaller amounts during the rest of the twenties, sales did help to counterbalance repossessions for the decade. In the early twenties company sales policy demanded only a small amount of advertising in small-town papers in farming centers. The main line of effort, however, was to encourage tenants to buy the land they farmed. If, through company advice and assistance, these tenants might become successful and prosperous, they might be persuaded to invest in the land and remain on it, a result that, in the management's opinion, would build "a solid foundation" for a sales program.[45] Even without soliciting sales some meager success from this approach was forthcoming in the twenties. The breakdown shown in Table 7 represented the sales for the decade.

Few purchasers paid all their obligation to the company in cash; thus the company amassed an additional amount of vendor's lien notes to be collected. After 1920 the net profits gained from land sales were small, since repossessions and expenses incurred had to be taken into

[44] Randolph to Connor, tape interview, April 8, 1958.
[45] Staked Plains Trust, Limited, *Annual Report*, 1920, TLDCP.

Table 7. Company Sales (1920–1929)

Year	Acreage	Lots	Total Money Represented
1920	7,764.56	9.5	$470,587.98
1921	. . .	9.2	575.00
1922	. . .	. . .	. . .
1923	80.00	. . .	9,600.00
1924	750.05	7.0	16,352.66
1925	. . .	3.0	75.00
1926	160.00	. . .	5,028.64
1927	406.25	. . .	24,918.32
1928	280.00	4.0	14,714.88
1929	1,252.90	5.0	40,929.92
	10,694.03	38.0	$582,782.40

Source: Staked Plains Trust, Limited, *Annual Report*, 1920–1929, TLDCP.

account. In 1920, 1924, 1925, and 1927 the company's net profits from land sales were $212,753.49, $24,149.74, $21,455.27, and $58.23 respectively.[46] In 1922, 1923, 1928, and 1929 the company sustained net losses amounting consecutively to $45,236.64, $4,741.69, $6,243.82, $4,216.84, and $143.16.[47] There was no available record for 1921 although a loss is implied. As far as could be discerned, therefore, the net profit for the decade in land sales was $197,834.58.

One problem pertaining to clearing a title in connection with a land sale arose in 1927. With the death of one of the trustees of the Staked Plains Trust in 1927 came the problem of how to transfer the title vested in him at the time of his death to a new trustee. Such an occasion always jeopardized the titles of the land still held by the trust as well as the titles that had been conveyed in the past. The trustees' holding that the fee simple title to the land was vested in themselves complicated the situation. The trustees made this claim in order to get other attorneys to approve their titles, since the original declaration, or indenture of trust, was never made an instrument of record. In most such cases, the estate of the deceased trustee would have held his part of the

[46] *Ibid.*, 1920, 1924, 1925, 1927.
[47] *Ibid.*, 1922, 1923, 1928, 1929.

Consolidation under the Agreement

trust, and a probate would have been necessary to release it to the other trustees or to his successor. Several alternative solutions did, however, present themselves in 1927.

First, in order to prevent having to file the deceased trustee's probate and thereby encumber all titles, the declaration of trust could have been placed on record in Hale, Floyd, and Swisher counties. In pursuing this plan, however, there was always the possibility that the question of foreign or corporate ownership would arise; this result would, of course, encumber the titles, and a case could conceivably be made that the whole organization had been illegal from its inception.

Another plan was usually followed at the death of a trustee; the declaration of trust was ignored, and the two remaining trustees gave proof of the death of the trustee, appointed a new trustee, and conveyed title to him as cotrustee. This method was easiest and least costly.[48] Randolph had always been convinced that the procedure was perfectly legal, since the original titles were placed in Slaton and Randolph without any subject of trust being stated and without any beneficiary being named. Thus, the trustees held legal title and the absolute right to convey the land as though they had owned it personally. Later, Slaton, Randolph, and Baldwin conveyed the lands to Keith, Miller, Pearson, Hart, and Palmer and in so doing created a trust providing that the new trustees should have the power at any time to increase or reduce the number of trustees. This provision had been taken almost literally from the original indenture. Every subsequent conveyance to new trustees had referred to the original conveyance thus putting into force under each respective ownership the provisions of the original conveyance to Keith, Miller, Pearson, Hart, and Palmer. Randolph thought that the logical thing to do was simply to appoint a successor to the deceased and then to convey title to the successor as cotrustee.

In 1927 another reason presented itself for the original indenture's not being made a matter of record except as a last resort. The original indenture as well as the conveyance to the original five trustees of the Staked Plains Trust had provided that the trustees were to sell or

---

[48] Peyton B. Randolph to William F. Feeney, letter, December 27, 1927, RF.

dispose of the trust property within a period of thirteen years from that date. The expiration date, December 12, 1927, had, therefore, already passed. If, after that date, anyone had contested the legality of the trust's existence, the trustees would have been forced to file the original indenture, call a meeting of the shareholders, and have them extend the life of the trust in an open meeting.

Since the Texas Land and Development Company made a sale while Randolph was presenting the various plans of action to the trustees, it became an urgent necessity to arrive at some solution. Randolph's plan of having the two remaining trustees appoint a third trustee and convey title to him was ultimately adopted.[49] In no case was this policy seriously contested, and Randolph's solution proved sound.

During the decade the trust invested in other securities so that it might have a reserve of capital which could be used when the necessity arose, but which, at the same time, could be accruing interest. Some of the investments were made in Plainview, no doubt upon the advice of Captain Holbrook. When the Plainview Cotton Gin Company was built in 1920, the trust invested $1,000.00 in it.[50] In 1922 it invested $500.00 in the Bledsoe Oil and Gas Company.[51] Other investments were made in United States Treasury Notes and United States Liberty Bonds during the twenties.[52] During the decade the trust had invested $159,156.25 in various securities.[53] Only the investments in the Bledsoe Oil and Gas Company were written off as a bad debt.[54] Interest on $90,000.00 of 5.75 per cent Treasury Notes, which were purchased in 1921 and matured in 1924, accounted for $15,625.00 of the trust's profit for the decade. A dividend declared by the Plainview Cotton Gin Company in 1924 yielded the trust $345.00. That amount plus $58.00 profit realized from selling the stock in that company in late 1924 and 1925, for $575.00 and $483.00 respectively, represented a net profit on

---

[49] *Ibid.*
[50] Staked Plains Trust, Limited, *Annual Report*, 1920, TLDCP.
[51] *Ibid.*, 1922, 1923.
[52] *Ibid.*, 1922, 1923, 1924, 1926, 1927.
[53] *Ibid.*, 1920–1929, with exception of 1921, which is missing. Information for 1921 is included in the 1922 report.
[54] *Ibid.*, 1929.

Consolidation under the Agreement

the investment of $403.00. Investment in 4.25 per cent Liberty Bonds, including sales price and interest accrued, made a profit of $5,449.32 for the trust. An investment in 3.25 per cent Treasury Notes, bought in 1927 and valued at $17,000.00, brought a profit of $276.25 when they were sold in 1928. The profit represented interest accrued for the short period the trust held the notes. By the end of the decade all securities except the Bledsoe Oil and Gas Stock had been sold or had matured. Thus the trust carried none of these investments into the thirties. It had realized a net profit of $21,253.57 from its investments during the decade.[55]

An interesting event that absorbed the attention of the entire West Texas area during the early nineteen-twenties was the location of a new state college, Texas Technological College. Plainview and approximately forty other towns in West Texas competed for the location of the college. If Plainview were chosen, it could conceivably represent an investment and a land sale for the Texas Land and Development Company. These facts were brought to the attention of the trustees of the Staked Plains Trust in a letter from Captain Holbrook dated February 28, 1923.[56] He enclosed a map showing the proposed site at Plainview for the new college. He informed the trustees that the Texas legislature had appropriated $150,000 for the purchase of a site of approximately two thousand acres. The bill also provided that proximity to the residential district of the town should be considered in the location of the college.

Holbrook then explained that the Demonstration Farm of the Texas Land and Development Company was within the proposed site of the college. He further pointed out that the Plainview committee in charge of securing the proposed site hoped to purchase the full 2,000 acres, with the exception of the 130 acres for the actual campus, for a figure that was within the amount of the appropriation, which amounted to $75.00 and upward per acre. The most valuable piece chosen by the committee adjoined the city limits and had a speculative value for sub-

[55] *Ibid.*, 1920–1929.
[56] Although Holbrook sent the letter February 28, 1923, the trustees of the Staked Plains Trust did not act on the letter until their regular meeting on March 28, 1923.

division purposes of $200.00 per acre. However, the owners had agreed to reduce the price to $116.00 per acre on part and $110.00 per acre on the rest. The next most valuable land was the Demonstration Farm, which had been appraised at $87,420.00 in February 1919. Holbrook then stated that the committee on selection had asked that he forward a request to the trustees whereby they would agree that in case the college was located at Plainview and that site selected, they would deed the Demonstration Farm to the state of Texas for that purpose at $75.00 per acre. The total consideration would have been $47,064.75, payable September 1, 1923, at which time the Texas Land and Development Company would have relinquished possession of the farm. The timing of the transfer would have allowed the company to harvest its wheat, oats, barley, and the greater part of its alfalfa. The crops had an estimated value of $12,000.00.

If the trustees of the Staked Plains Trust had agreed to this proposal, they would have been making a donation of "$39,355.25," which was "somewhat more than they would be called upon to make if they were paying strictly their proportion as a proper share of the benefit to the citizens and landowners." However, Holbrook thought that on the more than forty-five thousand acres of trust land remaining to be sold in the area, the value would be enhanced by the location of the college in Plainview. He thought the "$39,355.25" gift could be considered as a donation of less than ninety cents per acre on the land they would still hold.

Holbrook concluded his letter with the opinion that if the college were located in Plainview, it would be due mainly to one fact, that irrigation could be "demonstrated" there. Since irrigated land of the Texas Land and Development Company would "receive special benefit from this demonstration and advertising," the land would "become more saleable through the location of the school" at Plainview.

After Holbrook's letter had been read to the trustees of the Staked Plains Trust, Henry S. Fleming, the trust representative, reported to the trustees the result of his meeting in Plainview with the Plainview committee on selection.[57] After the conference the Plainview committee

---

[57] The date of the meeting is unknown.

Consolidation under the Agreement

was advised, presumably by Fleming, that the lands owned by the company would not be materially benefited by the location or erection of the proposed college. According to Fleming, Plainview merchants, bankers, and real-estate agents with property adjacent to Plainview would benefit, however. He had informed the committee that while the trustees of the Staked Plains Trust desired to do "everything in their power to help the District," the burden of subscriptions should be borne by those who would receive most of the expected benefits.

Fleming then reported to the trustees that he had informed the committee that he would recommend that the trustees accept $65,530.45 for the Demonstration Farm, including the improvements. Of the proposed purchase price, the State of Texas was to pay $47,064.75 in cash and the Plainview committee was to assume the balance of $18,456.17 as "evidenced by three promissory notes, each of equal amounts, bearing interest at the rate of six per cent per annum, executed by responsible persons and guaranteed by one or more responsible banks." The notes were to bear the same date as the date of the deed conveying the land to the state and were to be payable in equal annual installments from that date. Fleming's proposal was put in the form of a resolution by Charles H. Zehnder and was carried unanimously by the trustees.[58]

The Plainview committee accepted the terms of the proposal, whereupon a contract was entered into by Keith, Zehnder, and Partridge, representing the Staked Plains Trust, and by Dennis Hefflefinger, representing the Plainview committee. The terms were identical with those listed in the proposal submitted by Fleming and adopted by the trustees. The contract was binding only if the state of Texas selected the Demonstration Farm for the site of Texas Technological College. If some other site were chosen the contract was automatically null and void with no further notice or action required by either party.[59] Since

---

[58] Staked Plains Trust, Limited, minutes, March 28, 1923 (I, 58), TLDCP. Present at the meeting were Minor C. Keith, Charles H. Zehnder, Hugh R. Partridge, trustees; Henry S. Fleming, trustee's representative; William F. Feeney, trustees' secretary; and Maurice Hely-Hutchinson, by invitation.

[59] Correspondence between Holbrook and Staked Plains Trust, Limited, trustees, Wallet 1, TLDCP.

the college was not placed in Plainview the trust took no further action.

Even though the trustees could not see their way clear to donate land for the proposed site of Texas Technological College, since in their opinion no advantage would accrue to the company, they did donate land to the Santa Fe Railway Company in 1925. Their philosophy was that such a donation was in a sense an investment.[60] The grant was in the form of a right of way for the railroad. The trustees had solicited the opinion of Peyton B. Randolph on the legality of the donation.[61] Randolph felt that the trustees could legally donate the land. To support his view he quoted several sections of the original Indenture of Trust, which had created the Staked Plains Trust on December 12, 1914. Paragraph (m) provided:

> Generally in all matters to deal with the trust premises and to manage and conduct the said undertaking as fully as if the Trustees were the absolute owners of the trust premises and to execute and do all such agreements, deeds, instruments and things as the Trustees may deem proper for any of the said purposes.

Further, under the indenture of August 7, 1920, wherein the trust premises were transferred to the trustees of the Staked Plains Trust, paragraph 1 provided:

> The grantors hereby grant, sell and convey. . . . [to the present trustees, the property held in their names] upon the Trusts and with all the powers, authority and obligations set forth in the said indenture of the 12th. of December, 1914, as fully and as completely as though they had been specifically mentioned in the said indenture as the original Trustees thereunder.

Randolph also pointed out that the donation had been made "for the sole purpose of increasing the value of the trust holdings." The donation, he thought, was a method of advertising for the estate, and for the "betterment and improvement of the trust property." He also reasoned that disregarding the fact that the trustees had absolute authority to handle the trust property in any manner they deemed proper, for the

---

[60] Staked Plains Trust, Limited, *Annual Report*, 1925, TLDCP.
[61] Feeney to Randolph, letter, May 8, 1925, RF.

Consolidation under the Agreement 131

foregoing reason they would have had the authority under the indenture of trust to make the grant.[62]

Because the trust was attempting to pay the obligations incurred by the Reorganization Agreement in 1919, it paid 90 per cent of the principal of $625,000.00, or $562,500.00, of the Class A Liquidation Certificates, at intervals during the twenties. Retiring this much of the obligation and other obligations owed by the trust prior to 1919 drained its money supply. Even though it operated at an overall net profit in sales and farming, its payments on obligations left it with less cash on hand at the end of the decade than at the beginning. The trust had $105,675.41 in cash in 1920,[63] and $60,019.08 in 1929.[64] Considering the fact that it had retired a considerable amount owed to security holders, it must be conceded that the trust was still operating with a safe margin of capital. The twenties, then, represented a successful overall operation.

[62] Randolph to Feeney, letter, May 14, 1925, RF.
[63] Staked Plains Trust, Limited, *Annual Report*, 1920, TLDCP.
[64] *Ibid.*, 1929.

7. The Depression Years

THE DEPRESSION, which struck the eastern part of the United States in 1929, did not reach the Plainview area until 1930. The company, in order to forestall financial difficulties, decided to terminate the policy of improving farms and plowing grassland for the use of additional tenants and attempted to retain the leases it already had. With careful management the company held its own up to the early part of 1931 simply by looking after its properties, keeping them leased, and collecting the rentals.[1] In fact, the directors of the Staked Plains Trust, Hugh R. Partridge, Henry B. Price, and Henry F. Whitney, no doubt following Herbert Hoover's philosophy that the Depression would be of short duration, optimistically granted all Texas Land and Development Company employees pay raises effective March 16, 1930. (The authorized increases are listed in Table 8.)

[1] Peyton B. Randolph to Charles F. Myers, letter, April 21, 1913, Randolph Files, Plainview (hereafter cited as RF).

The Depression Years 133

Table 8. Salary Schedule (1930)

Employee	Position	Rate prior to March 16, 1930	Authorized Increases
Winfield Holbrook	Gen. Mgr.	$450.00	$500.00
W. J. Klinger	Bookkeeper	260.00	275.00
Mary Cox	Stenographer	135.00	140.00
W. F. Lowe	Sup't. S. and E. Dist.	250.00	265.00
D. D. Bowman	Sup't. N. and W. Dist.	250.00	265.00
Tobe Hammond	Mechanic	200.00	210.00
Homer Rook	Mechanic	175.00	185.00

Source: Figures copied from Staked Plains Trust, Limited, minutes (I, 102), TLDCP.

Optimism quickly succumbed to realism. In August 1931 Holbrook advised the trustees that the general outlook with regard to income from crop and land sales was exceedingly discouraging. He pointed out that crop prices were the lowest in forty years, and that they were actually below the cost of production. He stated that no land sales had been made thus far in 1931 and that no land sales in the foreseeable future were likely. In view of these adverse forces Partridge, Price, and Whitney,[2] moved to reduce operating expenses. The easiest and the most obvious place to cut them was in the field of salaries. Therefore, the trustees reduced their own salaries plus those of the employees of the company (see Table 9).

[2] Partridge and Whitney remained as trustees until the trust was dissolved January 31, 1956. Price died on October 2, 1938. William F. Feeney was elected October 28, 1938, to replace Price and served until his own death in 1942 (Staked Plains Trust, Limited, minutes, October 28, 1938 [I, 178], Texas Land and Development Company Papers, Southwest Collection, Texas Tech University, Lubbock [hereafter cited as TLDCP]). He was replaced by Bradford Norman, Jr. of Portsmouth, Rhode Island (*ibid.*, November 9, 1942 [I, 230]). Norman served until his death on November 6, 1951, when he was replaced by J. West Rulon Cooper of New York City (*ibid.*, December

Table 9. Salary Schedule (1931)

Employee	Position	Rate prior to August 1931	Rate after Decrease
Hugh R. Partridge	Trustee	$150.00	$100.00
Henry B. Price	Trustee	150.00	100.00
Henry F. Whitney	Trustee	150.00	100.00
Wm. F. Feeney	Trustees' Rep.	500.00	425.00
Winfield Holbrook	Gen. Mgr.	500.00	425.00
Peyton B. Randolph	Attorney	300.00	255.00
W. J. Klinger	Bookkeeper	275.00	234.00
Mary Cox	Stenographer	140.00	124.00
W. F. Lowe	Sup't. S. and E.	265.00	225.00
D. D. Bowman	Sup't. N. and W.	265.00	225.00
J. E. Chamberlain	Janitor	30.00	28.00
R. Hammond	Mechanic	210.00	189.00
Homer Rook	Mechanic	185.00	166.00

Source: Figures copied from Staked Plains Trust, Limited, minutes, August 20, 1931 (I, 112–115), TLDCP.

When the Plainview National Bank, in which the trustees had $9,000 on deposit failed in September 1931, the Texas Land and Development Company was left in serious financial straits as far as its operational expenses were concerned. The trustees thereupon provided that a portion of their own salary, and a portion of that of their representative, Feeney, be paid in cash and the remainder be accrued. The accrued amounts were to be paid at the earliest date on which "unborrowed funds" were available.[3] Seven months later, the trustees canceled the accrued amounts on the grounds that "it was not proper to burden the Trust by continuing to accumulate unpaid salaries." At the same time, they again reduced their salaries. To further economize, salaries of all company employees were reduced effective April 16, 1932. The trustees instructed Holbrook to make a study to determine if operating expenses could be reduced by releasing one of the farm superintendents

---

10, 1951 [II, 311]). Partridge, Whitney, and Cooper were the trustees at the time of liquidation on January 31, 1956.

[3] *Ibid.*, September 16, 1931 (I, 112–115).

The Depression Years 135

and reducing the clerical and stenographic work so that it might be performed by one person.[4]

Later in 1932 the trustees met to discuss methods of reducing the expenses of the trust still more and to attempt to bring cash disbursements within cash receipts. The trustees passed a resolution providing that of their salary of $75 per month authorized on April 1, 1932, $25 should be paid in cash and $50 accrued. The trustees' representative was to receive $50 each month in cash, and $275 per month was to be accrued. The accrued amounts were to be paid at the earliest date from unborrowed funds.[5] Because of the continuing depression, these increments were canceled on January 4, 1933. At a meeting on that date, the trustees learned that "drastic measures" would have to be taken immediately in order to continue operations. Further, the trust would have to make some arrangement for borrowing money to pay real-estate taxes due to the state of Texas. Should the taxes become delinquent, their nonpayment would expose the trust property to seizure by the state. The trustees not only canceled the accrued amounts due them but also reduced their own salaries to $25 per month. The salary of the trustees' representative was cut to $50 per month.

At the January meeting in 1932, the trustees learned from Holbrook that the employees of the company "had voluntarily offered to accept further reductions in their salaries effective January 1, 1933." The trustees gratefully accepted the offer since "a further reduction in the salaries of the staff at Plainview was absolutely essential to the continuance of the operation of the Trust." The salary schedule as it was then authorized is given in Table 10. This scale marked the low-water mark for both the trustees and the Plainview employees. When the salaries are compared with those received in 1930, the reductions appear drastic (see Table 11).

In July 1934 the trustees voted raises for themselves, for their representative, and for the general manager, Winfield Holbrook. Trustee salaries were increased from $25 per month to $75 per month; Feeney's from $50 to $250 per month; and Holbrook's from $275

[4] *Ibid.*, April 1, 1932 (I, 119–122).
[5] *Ibid.*, October 14, 1932 (I, 123).

Table 10. Salary Schedule as of January 1933

Employee	Position	Rate prior to January 1933	Rate after Decrease
Holbrook	Gen. Mgr.	$325.00	$275.00
Randolph	Attorney	180.00	165.00
Klinger	Bookkeeper	192.00	166.00
Lowe	Sup't. S. and E.	185.00	160.00
Bowman	Sup't. N. and W.	185.00	160.00
Cox	Stenographer	98.00	80.00
Hammond	Mechanic	170.00	148.00
Rook	Mechanic	148.00	115.00

Source: Figures copied from Staked Plains Trust, Limited, minutes, January 4, 1933 (I, 125–127), TLDCP.

Table 11. Salary Schedule (1933–1934)

Employee	Position	1930 Rate	1933–1934 Rate	Percentage of Reduction
Partridge	Trustee	$150.00	$ 25.00	83
Price	Trustee	150.00	25.00	83
Whitney	Trustee	150.00	25.00	83
Feeney	Trustees' Rep.	500.00	50.00	90
Holbrook	Gen. Mgr.	500.00	275.00	47
Klinger	Bookkeeper	275.00	166.00	40
Cox	Stenographer	140.00	80.00	43
Lowe	Sup't. S. and E.	265.00	160.00	40
Bowman	Sup't. N. and W.	265.00	160.00	40
Chamberlain	Janitor	30.00	26.00	13
Hammond	Mechanic	210.00	148.00	30
Rook	Mechanic	185.00	115.00	38
Randolph	Attorney	300.00	165.00	45

Source: Figures copied from Staked Plains Trust, Limited, minutes, July 2, 1934 (I, 135–137), TLDCP.

to $425 per month. Holbrook's raise was given on the basis that his salary was out of proportion to the value of the services he rendered to the trust. The trustees then instructed Holbrook to conduct a study of the salaries of the Plainview staff, with the exception of the company

The Depression Years

attorney, Peyton B. Randolph, and to recommend the amount that, in his estimation, each one should be increased. These raises and proposed raises were decided upon in view of improved farming conditions in and around Plainview.[6]

Holbrook's recommendations were received and acted upon by the trustees in August 1934. His suggestions were adopted, and the salaries were retroactively effective as of July 1, 1934.[7] Salaries remained static until January 1937 when the trust authorized the last increase in pay.[8]

Salary deductions for economy reasons during the thirties did not interfere with the efficiency of the local operation. The decade, however, was filled with deterrents that even efficiency would not equitably combat. The company's farming operation was no exception. It suffered from the very first year of the decade. During 1930, farmers in the Plainview area experienced one of their worst years since World War I. To aggravate this depressed condition, a prolonged drought prevailed from the middle of June until the latter part of August and resulted in subnormal crop production. Prices received for the crops produced were the lowest in twelve years—but were not yet at their lowest ebb.

The company's tenants in 1930 had planted 20,579 acres of wheat. The wheat yield was almost normal, averaging 9.5 bushels per acre, from which the trust received an average of $2.26 per acre, representing its rental, as compared with $3.41 per acre per year for the four preceding years. The average selling price was sixty-nine cents a bushel, compared with $1.08 for the years 1926 to 1929 inclusive.

Cotton yields were only two-thirds of normal. The average yield was one-fifth of a bale per acre compared with one-third of a bale per acre for the years 1926 to 1929. The trust's income on the 5,260 acres planted in cotton for 1930 amounted to $2.04 per acre, compared with $4.93 per acre in previous years.

Grain sorghums and row crops such as kafir and maize, planted on 8,667 acres of dry land, returned the lowest crop yield on record due to an excessively hot and dry summer. Because of a shortage of feed,

[6] *Ibid.*, July 2, 1934 (I, 135–137).
[7] *Ibid.*, August 31, 1934 (I, 139–141).
[8] *Ibid.*, January 20, 1937 (I, 155–156).

however, the prices received for these crops were not exceedingly low. The Trust's return as rental from these crops averaged $1.12 per acre compared with $1.75 per acre for the preceding four years.

In terms of yield and price obtained, the most satisfactory crop raised by the company in 1930 was alfalfa. The yield for the year was 2.05 tons per acre compared with 2.08 tons per acre for the years 1926 through 1929. The trust's profit per acre as rental on 722 acres was $13.18 per acre compared with $11.07 per acre for each of the preceding four years. The trustees planned, therefore, to increase the acreage of this crop for 1931 by 300 acres. Because of poor yields and "hopelessly low prices," the trust sustained a loss of $9,672.85 for 1930, the first loss on its farming operations since 1923.[9]

Despite below average rainfall in Plainview in 1931, crop output was satisfactory. Fortunately the rainfall was distributed properly over the growing season. As a result, production of company crops for the year exceeded that of the preceding year, but prices were the lowest since the area was settled. The result was a loss of $19,940.39 on farming operations.[10]

With one exception weather conditions were normal in 1932. On June 20, 1932, a severe wind and hail storm devastated the entire Plainview area. Hail fell on one-third of the trust's property. The management estimated the damage to wheat, 18,981 acres, at 50 per cent and the damage to cotton, 4,069 acres, at 30 per cent. Prices received for crops sold were even lower in some instances than they had been the preceding year. The result was a loss for the farming operations of $25,623.55.[11]

In almost all aspects 1933 brought improved conditions for company operations. For the first time since 1929, the company realized a net profit of $34,206.53. Improved conditions were attributed to four factors: (1) greatly increased yields from the cotton crop; (2) much higher selling price for all farm produce; (3) federal govern-

---

[9] Staked Plains Trust, Limited, *Annual Report*, 1930, TLDCP.
[10] *Ibid.*, 1931.
[11] *Ibid.*, 1932.

The Depression Years

ment assistance to agriculture; and (4) a further reduction in overhead effected by lowering salaries.[12]

The company cooperated with the federal government in its Farm Relief Program as embodied in the Agricultural Adjustment Act of 1933, an action that it later regretted. The trust's land had already been rented on one-year lease terms prior to the inauguration of the government's farm relief program. The trustees of the Staked Plains Trust doubted, therefore, whether they could legally exercise any "coercion over the tenants" in respect to their cooperation with the Department of Agriculture. In order to remedy the situation, the trustees provided that all future leases should contain the following provision:

> The Trustees expressly reserve the right and authority to direct and control the acreage to be planted and the kind and character of crops to be planted under this lease, so as to be in a position to conform to any and all laws, ruling and/or regulations of the Federal Government, any official, board or commission thereof relative to crop reductions and Federal Farm Relief measures, and tenant agrees to conform and comply with any and all regulations and requirements of the Trustees or any of their agents with respect thereto.

Even though the tenants were not legally bound to cooperate with the government in its attempts to eliminate surpluses in 1933, many voluntarily did so. Approximately three thousand acres were plowed out, and the government paid $8 an acre or a total of $24,000. Of this amount, the trust was entitled to its regular landlord's share.[13]

As if the Depression were not enough, the worst drought in American history devastated many sections of the country in 1934. Although the Plainview area was hit by the drought, the company's farming operations were the most profitable since 1929. This profit was attributable to the increase of 40 per cent in the company's output of wheat, which matured early making it possible to harvest the crop before the drought reached the region. Further, the return from alfalfa, maize,

[12] *Ibid.*, 1933.
[13] Staked Plains Trust, Limited, minutes, July 3, 1933 (I, 130A–130B), TLDCP.

and other forage crops, in spite of reduced yields, doubled in price because of the scarcity of feed crops. Cotton yielded less than half of what it had the preceding year. However, its price increased by one-third, from nine cents per pound to twelve cents per pound.

Because of the drought, the company operated its irrigation wells at a higher level than they had previously been worked; repairs were correspondingly high. As a result of constant use the equipment was in better condition than it had been for many years when repairs had been deferred for the sake of economy. Participation in the federal agricultural program assisted the company in the amount of $15,418.68, and net profits from operations amounted to $51,993.39.[14]

Even though the drought did not affect the company's wheat crop in 1934, it indirectly ruined the 1935 crops. The subsoil had been so thoroughly dried out by the drought that the 1935 crop did not produce enough to warrant its harvest. The sixteen thousand acres that had been planted on dry land were a total failure. The yield on the eight hundred acres of irrigated wheat land was about half the normal return. Heavy rains fell late in May but were of little consequence for growing crops since the rainfall for the year up to that time was less than one-third of normal. Despite higher wheat prices—eighty cents in 1935 compared to sixty-nine cents per bushel in 1934—the profit from wheat sales amounted to only 12 per cent of the previous year's profit. At this time, wheat was the principal crop of the region. Oats, alfalfa, maize, and cotton did well since these important crops were grown on irrigated land. Crop prices in general were lower than in 1934, but the company was able to make a small profit of $26,155.89 for the year.

The company made a great effort in 1935 to reduce expenses of crop production, but because of the severe drought in the early part of the year, it ran its irrigation equipment almost constantly and offset the proposed reductions. The management also attempted in 1935 to find new crops that might be adaptable to the Plainview area. It planted twenty acres of sugar beets. The company sold the seeds for the crop at seven cents per pound, apparently to one or more local

---

[14] Staked Plains Trust, Limited, *Annual Report*, 1934, TLDCP.

The Depression Years

citizens. "The results" were "being carefully watched" and if the crop proved profitable, additional acres were to be planted in the fall.[15]

The drought not only brought near ruin to the farm populace but also brought the business world in and around Plainview to a virtual standstill.[16] Continuing into 1936, the drought seriously damaged dryland crops. By this time, approximately one-third of the company's land was irrigated and therefore relatively unaffected by the weather. Because of higher prices and the judicious disposal of the crops produced, the company registered a profit of $53,136.00, as compared to $26,153.89 in 1935. Wheat, which had for several years been the principal crop of the company, again proved secondary. Cotton proved to be the trust's most satisfactory crop in 1936, the yield amounting to 278,365 pounds, as compared to 162,263 pounds for 1934. The price of cotton increased from ten cents per pound to eleven cents per pound for the same periods. The sugar beet experiment continued through 1936. The experiment did not live up to the expectations of the trustees but was sufficiently satisfactory to justify their continuing the project.

During 1936 the federal government was quite interested in the poor conditions under which tenant farmers lived and worked and considered federal legislation. Commenting on this fact in the 1936 report, the trustees declared:

> We desire to point out that the extremely adverse conditions among tenant farmers which the Federal Government desires to correct do not exist on the Trust's properties. All our farms are equipped with presentable living quarters which are kept in weather tight, sanitary conditions, and with satisfactory barns, windmills, outbuildings, and fences. All pumping equipment on leased irrigated lands is, of course, maintained in good repair at our expense. Written lease agreements, are entered into annually with each tenant and crops sold for the account of tenants are settled for promptly in cash. On the whole, our tenant farmers are high type individuals, satisfied with their farms, whose confidence and good will the Trust enjoys. Proof of this is given by the very small turnover among our tenants. It is always possible, however, that radical legislators

[15] *Ibid.*, 1935.
[16] Peyton B. Randolph to William F. Feeney, letter, March 22, 1935, RF.

may introduce measures which would tend to operate to the detriment of farm relations with their tenants. Developments in Washington concerning this problem should therefore be watched closely.[17]

Several factors helped make farming operations more successful in 1937 than in any year since 1920. First, there was adequate rainfall for the first time since 1933. Second, the company had all its 46,000.15 acres of land, with the exception of a 28-acre experimental tract, rented to tenants for the year. Third, the amount of acreage under cultivation was increased. Fourth, overall crop prices were higher than they had been the previous year. Wheat regained its position as the best crop for the company. The company's net profit from farming operations was $86,904.49.[18]

In comparison to the profits made in 1937, the profits on farming operations for 1938 were greatly reduced, and the company realized $33,343.27. Again, several factors contributed to this decrease, among them another drought, an aphid plague that totally destroyed eight hundred acres of oats, barley, and alfalfa, and a 43-per-cent drop in the price of wheat. Moreover, the cotton acreage allotment was reduced from 7,782 acres to 4,564. For this the company received a federal agency payment of $3,673.87. On the basis of cotton prices, however, the company reasoned that it would have made an additional $19,500 if no allotment had been imposed. Finally, the company spent more on its irrigation equipment because of the drought.

The crop return for 1939 dropped to $17,698.48. The primary reason for the decline was the continuing drought in the area. Plainview's average rainfall for the previous forty-five years had been 21.24 inches per year. The total for 1938 was 18.89; for 1939, 14.16. Alfalfa was the only major crop that produced more revenue for the company in 1939 than it had in 1938, primarily because it was grown on irrigated land. The company, therefore, laid plans to increase its alfalfa acreage.

The decade of the thirties had been trying. The company lost money on its farming operations in 1930, 1931, and 1932. It registered

---

[17] Staked Plains Trust, Limited, *Annual Report*, 1936, TLDCP.
[18] *Ibid.*, 1937.

The Depression Years

profits for each of the remaining years in the decade, despite the drought. The company proved that irrigation farming paid, for its profits were in proportion to the amount of irrigation water used by the company and its tenants.

As the decade of the thirties opened, the company still had on hand 48,181.08 acres of land, of which amount 10,558.51 acres were improved, 2,089.00 acres were partially improved, and 35,533.57 acres were unimproved. Besides this large acreage, the company owned thirty-one town lots.[19] It valued the land, including the town lots, at $2,328,872.20.

During 1930 the Plainview management sold a total of 1,815.88 acres for a gross intake of $29,923.44, which made it the best year since 1920. The net profit on these transactions was $6,189.49.[20] No land whatsoever was sold in 1931. In fact, the company gained land since it was forced to repossess 160 acres.[21] Again, in 1932 no sales were made, but 200.92 acres were repossessed.[22]

The company made no effort to sell land in 1933 because the trustees did not think it practical "to meet the competition of lands offered for sale for the amount of mortgages" of them. However, it sold 8.22 acres of improved and 9.26 acres of unimproved land for a total of $1,161.42. Ironically, the company gave away more land than it sold; it donated 25.15 acres of improved land and 31.49 acres of unimproved land for railroad and state highway rights of way. This meant a loss to the company of $3,653.95. The trustees justified their actions on the basis that "the enhancement in value of the remaining property caused by these improvements will more than offset the cost of the land donated."[23]

There were neither sales nor repossessions during 1934 and 1935.[24]

---

[19] The *Annual Report* as of December 31, 1930, shows that the company owned forty town lots. This statement was a misprint and was corrected in the *Annual Report* of 1931 (Staked Plains Trust, Limited, *Annual Reports*, 1930, 1931, TLDCP).

[20] *Ibid.*, 1930.
[21] *Ibid.*, 1931.
[22] *Ibid.*, 1932.
[23] *Ibid.*, 1933.
[24] *Ibid.*, 1934.

The management attempted no sales in 1935 because the prevailing land prices in the Plainview area were lower than even the book values of the company land. The trustees were of the opinion, therefore, that they would render their shareholders a service by holding the land and renting it while waiting for prices to go up.[25]

The year 1936 opened with the trust still holding title to 46,652 acres of land and thirty-one town lots. During the year it made only one sale, which involved 80 acres and represented $7,000. Six farms totaling 782.40 acres plus one town lot were reconveyed.[26]

The big break in land sales seemingly came in 1937 when the company sold 1,358 acres for $42,854. It then possessed 46,000.15 acres and thirty-two town lots.[27] The break was illusory, however; for several reasons the company sold no land in 1938[28] or in 1939. First, most of the potential buyers were local farmers whose finances were depressed by the drought. Second, the drought and poor crop yields had discouraged outsiders from coming into the Plainview area to buy. Third, "the element of uncertainty which the constantly changing Federal Farm Program" had "introduced into the business of agriculture" deterred investment. The trustees were convinced, however, that "even one profitable year" for the tenants would revive interest in land buying "since the lifelong faith of the farmer in the soil is unswerving."[29]

Company land sales during the decade were disappointing. In only four years out of the ten had any land been sold: 1930, 1933, 1936, and 1937. The total acreage sold was 3,192.16 representing $80,938.86. During the decade, however, the company repossessed 1,143.32 acres plus one town lot, together worth $50,945.30. As the decade opened, the company held 48,181.08 acres plus thirty-one town lots. When the decade closed, the company still retained 46,000.15 acres and thirty-two town lots.

[25] *Ibid.*, 1935.
[26] *Ibid.*, 1936.
[27] *Ibid.*, 1937.
[28] *Ibid.*, 1938.
[29] *Ibid.*, 1939.

The Depression Years

Investments in the thirties amounted to very little. There was no carry-over from investments in the twenties, and it was not until 1933 that the trust again made investments. In that year it invested $150.00 in the South Plains Oil Refining Company.[30] In 1934 investments increased substantially; the trust invested $17,807.50 in New York City Special Corporation Bonds bearing 6 per cent interest and maturing in 1937. It also invested $5,100.00 in Federal Farm Mortgage Bonds carrying 3 per cent interest and maturing in 1949, and $300.00 in the Plainview Refining Company.[31] It made no new investments in 1935, although it purchased an additional $6,000.00 in Federal Farm Mortgage Bonds.[32] It made no investments in 1936 or 1937.[33] During the last two years of the decade the company registered investments in United States Savings Bonds: in 1938 it bought bonds worth $7,500.00 whose maturity value in 1948 was $10,000,[34] and in 1939 it purchased additional bonds valued at $7,700.00.[35] The relatively insignificant sum of $49,557.50 had been invested for the decade.

During the depression years, the Texas Land and Development Company often had difficulty collecting on notes due to it from former tenants. Usually these notes covered such items as supplies that the tenant had been advanced. For two reasons Captain Holbrook and Peyton B. Randolph, the company lawyer, established the policy of collecting these notes without legal action, if possible. First, the individual would be saved the embarrassment of being asked to appear in court, and second, the company would be saved the time and trouble of conducting a lawsuit and would stave off possible ill will to itself. However, if persuasion did not achieve the desired results, the company went to court. The following correspondence between Peyton B. Randolph and one such defendant illustrates the procedure.[36]

---

[30] *Ibid.*, 1933.
[31] *Ibid.*, 1934.
[32] *Ibid.*, 1935.
[33] *Ibid.*, 1936.
[34] *Ibid.*, 1938.
[35] *Ibid.*, 1939.
[36] Peyton B. Randolph to J. H. Pittman, letter, June 23, 1936, Wallet 1, TLDCP.

The Texas Land and Development Company

Peyton B. Randolph
Attorney at Law
Plainview, Texas
June 23, 1936

Mr. J. H. Pittman
Tulia, Texas

Dear Mr. Pittman:

Captin Holbrook of the Texas Land and Development Company has placed with me for attention a certain note in the sum of $212.71 executed by you to the said Company.

This note was due on July 1, 1932, and will bar by limitation July 1, 1936. It is absolutely necessary that some action be taken by you to keep this note from barring, and if you are unable to pay the same at this time, Captin Holbrook states that they are willing to carry you over until Fall, provided you come in at once and execute a new note. Otherwise, I shall be forced to enter suit thereon July 1 to keep the same from becoming barred.

Kindly give this your prompt attention and oblige.

Yours truly
(Signed) P. B. Randolph

Pittman, who had in the meantime moved from Tulia to San Angelo, did not receive the letter in time to take action on the note prior to legal action by the Texas Land and Development Company. However, when he did receive the letter from Randolph, he wrote his reply on the back of the letter and returned it to Randolph.[37]

San Angelo, Texas
June 30, 1936

Dear Sir,

Please send note, down here and Ill sign it and return it, Please dont addon any int, as It is going to be hard for me to ever get the principal

---

[37] J. H. Pittman to Peyton B. Randolph, letter, June 30, 1936, Wallet 1, TLDCP.

I do not outlaw my debts, I may not be able to pay them But I have not quit trying,

> Yours Truly
> (Signed) J. H. Pittman
> San Angelo Tex
> Box 975

Because the Texas Land and Development Company did not hear from Pittman prior to July 1, 1936, it filed suit against him on June 29, 1936, in the Justice Court, Precinct No. 1, in Hale County. The company contended that Pittman had executed and delivered his promissory note to them on October 12, 1931, for the sum of $125.00. The note was to carry 10 per cent interest per year. In case the note became overdue another 10 per cent interest was added to the accrued interest. The company further stated that the note provided that if the note had to be placed in the hands of an attorney for collection, the defendent was to pay an additional 10 per cent upon the principal and interest of the note as attorney's fees. Pittman had paid only $3.29 on the note, leaving a balance of $212.71.

The company alleged that the note was past due and unpaid and that the defendant, though often requested to do so, had failed and refused to pay the note or any part of it with the exception of the $3.29, which he had paid on March 17, 1933. The company asked for a judgment in its favor for the debt, principal, interest, attorney's fees, and for the cost of the suit, and "for such other relief, special and general, in law and in equity, that it may be entitled to."[38]

After filing the suit, Randolph's next move was to request the sheriff at Tulia, Texas, where it was thought Pittman lived, to issue the citation against Pittman.[39]

---

[38] Peyton B. Randolph, Brief and Notes for Case 4278, Justice of the Peace Court, Precinct No. 1, Hale County, Texas, Wallet 1, TLDCP.

[39] Peyton B. Randolph to J. B. Gayler, letter, n.d., Wallet 1, TLDCP.

Mr. J. B. Gayler, Sheriff
Swisher County
Tulia, Texas

Dear Sir:

Please find herewith an original and copy of the citation in the case of Texas Land and Development Company vs J. H. Pittman to be served on Mr. Pittman, who, I understand, resides in or near your city. Kindly secure service of this and advise me as to the amount of your fees, and I will remit to cover.

Yours truly,
(Signed) P. B. Randolph

While Randolph was attempting to serve the court citation on Pittman, he received the letter quoted earlier and promptly answered it.[40]

Dear Sir:

The Texas Land and Development Company has referred to me your letter of the 30th ult replying to my letter to you on June 23. Owing to the fact that we did not hear from you, I was forced to institute suit on the note in order to keep limitation from running thereon, but Captain Holbrook states that he is willing to dismiss the suit, waive the interest and take a new note for the principal and costs of suit incurred to this date, as requested by you, in order to help you along as far as possible.

I have prepared a new note, including only the principal without the interest or attorney's fees and herewith enclose the same. Please sign this note and return to me at once, and I will have the suit dismissed.

Yours truly,
(Signed) Peyton B. Randolph

Pittman signed and returned the note. The renewal date for the note was July 9, 1936. The Texas Land and Development Company paid the court costs the following day and the court dismissed the suit.[41]

Another matter required Randolph's counsel during the nineteen-

---

[40] Randolph to Pittman, letter, July 3, 1936, Wallet 1, TLDCP.

[41] Peyton B. Randolph, notation in regard to the Pittman case, Wallet 1, TLDCP.

The Depression Years

thirties. Randolph was called upon from time to time during the trust's existence by some of the lawyers who examined the trust's land titles for prospective purchasers to explain the complicated series of trustees who held title to the land over the years, so that the lawyer might determine if the title were actually valid. After he clarified the position of the trust in regard to ownership by explaining that the trustees were given the "absolute right" to assign land to either buyers or to other trustees,[42] the validity of the title was accepted in all but one known case. In 1937 Kenneth Bain, a Floydada lawyer, contended that the conveyance to the trustees, Keith, Miller, Pearson, Hart, and Palmer, in 1914 provided that the Staked Plains Trust was to extend for thirteen years from that date, and that after the expiration of the thirteen-year period, the trustees had no power to convey the property. After the expiration date, he claimed, the trustees could merely hold the titles for the beneficiaries. Randolph and the trustees of the Staked Plains Trust interpreted the function of the trusteeship differently. They contended that the charter of the Staked Plains Trust did not imply that the trustees would act as beneficiaries after thirteen years. Instead the trustees were to maintain "absolute ownership of the land until it was sold."[43] It was pointed out that the purpose of the clause that extended the life of the trust for thirteen years after its formation in 1914 was to prevent the investors from foreclosing on the trust until it had a chance to sell its lands. In view of the fact that at one time or another the Federal Land Bank, the Joint Stock Land Banks, various life insurance companies, and the attorneys of Plainview, examined and approved the trust's titles, there should be no doubt as to their validity.

---

[42] Peyton B. Randolph to Kenneth Bain, letter, October 7, 1937, RF.

[43] A confirmation of this opinion is found in a report sent to the shareholders of the Staked Plains Trust before a special meeting on September 21, 1949. The report further contended that since the point had been brought up more than once (only once adversely), it might be a safeguard to the holders of the titles to amend the charter officially by substituting *fifty years* for *thirteen years*, and thereby to extend the trust's life to 1964. The recommendation was officially accepted by the shareholders at their meeting in September 1949 (Staked Plains Trust, Limited, minutes, September 21, 1949 [II, 297–303], TLDCP).

Although Randolph's counsel concerning the trust's titles to its lands was perhaps more consequential, in 1938 the trustees asked him for advice when they attempted to settle an entirely different type of problem. Shortly after the reorganization of 1919, the trustees agreed to a plan whereby the trustees of the Staked Plains Trust who served before the reorganization of 1919 would receive compensation for their services. By the agreement Henry S. Fleming, who was the Reorganization Manager's Representative, was also to receive compensation. The agreement stipulated that the trustees—Keith, Zehnder, Palmer, Ward E. Pearson, Hart, and Miller—were to receive amounts ranging from $10,000 to $2,500 according to the following schedule: Minor C. Keith, $10,000; Charles H. Zehnder, $10,000; Bradley W. Palmer, $10,000; Ward E. Pearson, $5,000; Francis R. Hart, $5,000; Harry I. Miller, $2,500.[44] Fleming was to receive $10,000 for his services. None of the payments was to be made until the principal and interest of Class A Liquidation Certificates had been paid in full.

The trustees in 1938 considered the possibility of altering the above resolutions in view of the fact that most of the obligees were dead. They were of the opinion that the estates of the obligees might settle for a compromise amount, rather than the original amount, if the obligations were paid in 1938, instead of waiting until all the interest on the Class A Liquidation Certificates had been paid. Of the $15,000 owed to Keith and Pearson, approximately 50 per cent had already been assigned to E. E. Marshall of Philadelphia. Marshall had been attempting to obtain oil leases on the Texas property from the trustees. The trustees desired to grant him a lease in return for his canceling the $7,500 due to him from the trust. However, the trustees were not certain of the legality of their proposed move. They therefore solicited the opinion of Randolph, who felt that the Reorganization Agreement of 1919 did not in any way abrogate or alter the terms of the Indenture and Declaration of Trust entered into December 12, 1914, between the trustees of the Staked Plains Trust and the holders of the trust's shares. He called the trustees' attention to Paragraph 2, sections

---

[44] Figures copied from William F. Feeney to Peyton B. Randolph, letter, February 16, 1938, RF.

The Depression Years 151

(k) and (m).⁴⁵ Section (k) empowered the trustees "to settle all accounts and to compound compromise abandon or adjust by arbitration or otherwise any actions, suits, proceedings, disputes, claims, demands, and things relating to the trust premises. . . ." Section (m) gave the trustees the right "in all matters to deal with the trust premises" as if the premises were their own.⁴⁶ Randolph thought, however, that the trustees should make no agreement with Marshall unless they were in a position to make some sort of compromise offer to all of the other obligees or their estates.⁴⁷

To make doubly sure that they might legally compromise on the indebtedness to the various obligees or to their estates, the Staked Plains trustees obtained the opinion of the law firm of Olin, Clark, and Phelps of New York City in regard to the matter. That firm rendered an opinion almost identical to Randolph's and on the same basis.⁴⁸ After considering the two opinions, the Staked Plains trustees laid plans to attempt to compromise with the obligees for twenty-five cents on the dollar.⁴⁹ Apparently the proposal miscarried. The basis for this assumption is found in a report from one of the Staked Plains trustees to his colleagues on October 13, 1944, which stated that the $2,500 had been paid to the estate of Harry I. Miller covering his deferred compensation as a former trustee, "thus completing these payments."⁵⁰ Since $2,500 represented the full amount owed Miller, it is logical to assume that the others were paid in full also. This seems true because Randolph as the company lawyer in Texas had consistently insisted that the obligees must be treated uniformly.

Even though the trust benefited from a rather large profit on the Texas Land and Development Company's farming operations during the decade of the thirties, its overall operations were almost constantly

⁴⁵ Randolph to Feeney, letter, February 26, 1938, RF.
⁴⁶ *Documents 1917*, 121–122, TLDCP.
⁴⁷ Randolph to Feeney, letter, February 26, 1938, RF.
⁴⁸ Olin, Clark, and Phelps (attorneys) to Whitney, Partridge, and Feeney (trustees), letter, inclosed in a letter from Feeney to Randolph, March 11, 1939, RF.
⁴⁹ Feeney to Randolph, letter, March 11, 1939, RF.
⁵⁰ Staked Plains Trust, Limited, minutes, October 13, 1944 (I, 263), TLDCP.

in the red. The trust unfortunately had to stand a substantial loss from repossessions and poor land sales. The trust registered net profits for only three years out of the decade; $1,510.85 in 1933; $1,533.09 in 1934; and $10,635.20 in 1937. The total profit amounted to $13,679.14. The trust registered deficits for the remaining years: $34,745.82 in 1930; $61,565.08 in 1931; $55,977.44 in 1932; $46,181.36 in 1935; $28,044.22 in 1936; $36,124.56 in 1938; and $37,813.18 in 1939. The total loss was $300,451.56. Deducting the small profits registered in 1933, 1934, and 1937 from the loss, the company withstood a net loss of $286,722.42 for the decade.

8. Retiring the Debt

THE DECADES of the forties and fifties moved the Texas Land and Development Company to its dissolution. During the nineteen-forties the company sold all the land and finally terminated the tenant-farming operation. During the same period the Staked Plains Trust successfully retired its indebtedness to the holders of liquidation securities as provided for in the Reorganization Agreement of 1919. Thereafter the Staked Plains Trust had no reason to continue to operate, since it had no lands and the purpose of its existence had been fulfilled. Consequently liquidation proceedings, which involved dividing the remaining assets among the shareholders, were begun in the late forties. The trust, however, did not succeed in closing its books until January 31, 1956.[1] Two matters had to be resolved before the trust could convert its assets into cash, distribute these assets, and go out of

---

[1] Staked Plains Trust, Limited, *Final Report*, 1955, Texas Land and Development Company Papers, Southwest Collection, Texas Tech University, Lubbock (hereafter cited as TLDCP).

existence. The first was disposing of one-half of the mineral rights, which the trust had retained when it sold its last 21,844.46 acres of land.[2] These rights had to be converted into cash after the trust obtained the approval of the shareholders. The second matter concerned income tax returns that had not been filed to the satisfaction of the Bureau of Internal Revenue.

In order to maintain a cash reserve, the trust continued to invest in negotiable securities during the forties and fifties. The trust carried over from the thirties a relatively small investment reserve of $31,380.00; but the volume increased rapidly as the decade wore on. Table 12 shows the amount in the investment reserve for each year that one was maintained.

Table 12. Funds in the Investment Reserve (1940–1953)

Year	Amount
1940	$ 45,233.79
1941	57,211.56
1942	71,523.00
1943	107,347.50
1944	98,270.00
1945	139,660.00
1946	136.520.00
1947	133,790.00
1948	126,080.00
1949	77,980.00
1950	69,480.00
1951	41,720.00
1952	42,980.00
1953	19,420.00

Source: Figures copied from Staked Plains Trust, Limited, *Annual Report*, 1940–1953, TLDCP.

By March 1954 the trust, in preparation for liquidation, had divested itself of its investments and retained as its sole asset $64,548.70 in cash.[3]

[2] Staked Plains Trust, Limited, minutes, August 10, 1948, TLDCP.
[3] *Ibid.*, 1954.

Retiring the Debt 155

Although the company had hoped to usher in a momentous land-selling campaign in the forties, sales in 1940 were disappointing. The company disposed of only 69.58 acres, for a total compensation of $4,950, and reduced its land holdings to 45,930.57 acres and thirty-two town lots.[4] Sales in 1941 were also small; the management sold only 680 acres representing $21,600.[5]

Because farming in the Plainview district became more profitable, perhaps as a result of a need for farm products during World War II, 1942 marked the beginning of a land-buying boom in the area. In 1942 the company sold 1,982.03 acres for a total consideration of $62,324.00. These sales were the best since 1920 when nearly 8,000 acres had been sold.[6] In 1943 the sales program reached a new high; 13,331.44 acres of farm land and eleven town lots were successfully transferred to fifty-six new owners, bringing in a total of $511,006.44. It was significant that the company received $327,873.24 in cash because many buyers refinanced with the Federal Land Bank.[7] Land sales in 1944 favored the company's improved lands since equipment was difficult to obtain during the war years, but prices on unimproved lands also increased several dollars per acre. The total acreage sold for the year was 7,812.99. Again many of the purchasers arranged their own financing and paid the trust in cash.[8] The poor results of the year's farming operation did not seem to affect land sales in 1945, when the company sold 5,811.44 acres. Land prices were somewhat better than they had been the previous year. The most desirable unimproved lands brought as much as $40.00 per acre. Improved farms, because of a continued demand for equipment and materials, were sold for prices substantially above the depreciated cost carried on the company's books.[9] The climax and conclusion of land sales came in 1946 when the company sold its remaining 16,263.20 acres and twenty-one town lots. Prices were about the same as they had been the preceding year, and

[4] *Ibid.*, 1940.
[5] *Ibid.*, 1941.
[6] *Ibid.*, 1942.
[7] *Ibid.*, 1943.
[8] *Ibid.*, 1944.
[9] *Ibid.*, 1945.

most of the buyers paid in cash. Because a high percentage of sales had been settled in cash during the period, the company held a relatively small number of vendor's lien notes, representing deferred payments of $427,798.00 to be collected.[10]

These notes were quickly paid out during the boom era of the late forties. After a profitable crop season in 1947, the notes were substantially reduced to $139,870 by December 31 of that year.[11] Only $55,830 remained outstanding as of December 31, 1948.[12] The following year the sum was reduced to $5,380,[13] and by the end of 1950 the notes had been paid in full.[14]

The policy of persuading tenants to purchase the land they worked, which the company had initiated in the early twenties, did not succeed until the land-buying boom in the forties when many purchasers were company tenants. The other purchasers were also local people who already had farming interests in the area.[15] The company's desire to sell its land fortunately coincided with a period of prosperity that allowed local people to buy it. The land was sold cheaply, if one considers today's value of the same land, and one person, in reflecting the company's land-selling policy during the forties, leveled the criticism that the company "gave its land away."[16] It should be remembered, however, that in most cases the company received as much as or more than the average price of land sold statewide during the same period.[17] It would have been difficult to foresee the manner in which the value of the land would soar in succeeding years.

As long as there was land to farm, the company continued to lease it to tenants on a yearly basis. In 1940 crop production gained a slight edge over the preceding year; the four major crops—wheat, cotton, alfalfa, and sorghums—produced from 34 per cent to 108 per cent

[10] *Ibid.*, 1946.
[11] *Ibid.*, 1947.
[12] *Ibid.*, 1948.
[13] *Ibid.*, 1949.
[14] *Ibid.*, 1950.
[15] Peyton B. Randolph to Seymour V. Connor, tape interview, April 8, 1958.
[16] *Ibid.*
[17] Staked Plains Trust, Limited, *Annual Report*, 1943, TLDCP.

Retiring the Debt

more revenue. Even with a low rainfall of 15.43 inches, the company managed to make a small profit of $42,730.62 from its share of the farming operations.[18]

The year 1941 was unusual for the South Plains because forty-three inches of rain drenched the southeastern area of the company's property. For the first time since the company had operated in the area it suffered from too much moisture instead of from too little. The rain greatly damaged wheat and alfalfa. The wheat loss was partially offset by an increase to ninety cents per bushel in comparison with the previous year's price of seventy cents. The alfalfa crop was plagued by lower prices and by the fact that only 60 per cent of the anticipated crop was harvested. Because of subsoil moisture, the fall crops, cotton and grain sorghums, benefited from the rain and increased their yields. The overall farming operation made a profit of $41,001.05 for the year.[19]

In 1942 the profits from company tenant farming reached their peak. The company's tenants received higher prices for all their crops and had the advantage of the average rainfall as well as of the subsurface moisture resultant from the previous year's overabundance of rain. One major deterrent, a manpower shortage, kept the farmers from gathering all their crops after they reached maturity. Laborers either had been called into the armed services or had been attracted to highly paid defense jobs. Relief for the farm problem did not seem to be forthcoming for the next year. Despite this drawback, the company realized a net profit of $95,351.30 for the year's farming operations.[20]

Even with less rainfall, a labor shortage, and a lack of parts to repair irrigation equipment, the company greatly exceeded its profits for 1942 in 1943. High prices, especially in grain sorghums, were responsible for a profit of $127,933.82. A comparison of the average prices received on the sale of the company's major crops during 1942 and 1943 is found in Table 13.

Although prices were higher on grain sorghums in 1944, the sale of a sizeable amount of company land during 1943 took out of operation

---

[18] *Ibid.*, 1940.
[19] *Ibid.*, 1941.
[20] *Ibid.*, 1942.

Table 13. Comparison of Average Prices (1942 and 1943)

Crop	1943	1942
Wheat (per bu.)	$ 1.19	$ 1.02
Cotton (per lb.)	.18	.15
Alfalfa (per ton)	22.63	14.04
Threshed sorghum grain (per cwt.)	1.82	1.10

Source: Staked Plains Trust, Limited, *Annual Report*, 1943, TLDCP.

a number of acres that had previously been farmed by tenants. Thus net profit from farm operations, although substantial in 1944, reached only $63,862.38.[21] Because even more of the company's land was sold in 1945 and because there was a severe drought that year, the company's farming operations made a profit of only $20,706.65.[22] The succeeding year marked the end of the company's farming operations because most of the land was sold by harvest time and all was sold by the end of the year. The land that was still in the hands of the company's tenants during 1946 yielded a profit for the company of $5,889.45. Farmers in the area generally experienced a "satisfactory year" because use of irrigation facilities increased and because crop prices reached a new high.[23]

As company farming operations began to decrease in 1942, it became apparent that if the boom lasted the company would sell its land quickly. In that year Dave Bowman, one of the farm superintendents, terminated his work with the company. He had already become interested in farming on his own and in a nursery business he and his brother operated together. In fact, some time before he resigned, he was admonished by Holbrook not to spend too much time at the nursery since he was supposed to be giving his full time to the company. He complied with Holbrook's wishes until his retirement from company employment in 1942.[24] When the last sales of company land were made in 1946, Fred Lowe, the other farm superintendent, also resigned.

[21] *Ibid.*, 1945.
[22] *Ibid.*, 1945.
[23] *Ibid.*, 1946.
[24] David Dell Bowman, tape interview, July 27, 1958.

Retiring the Debt 159

Lowe had already acquired some land in the Plainview area which his sons farmed. After his retirement in 1946, he spent some time supervising his own land, although primarily he enjoyed the leisure of retirement.[25]

Soon after the company sold its land it became clear that the company office in Plainview was overstaffed. After August 1, 1947, only Holbrook as vice-president and general manager, Klinger as secretary-treasurer, and Randolph as assistant secretary-treasurer and company attorney, remained as employees.[26] Klinger resigned on February 29, 1948; Randolph and Holbrook then assumed Klinger's duties, Randolph becoming secretary, and Holbrook, treasurer.[27] Sometime between February 9, 1948, and June 14, 1954, Hugh R. Partridge, a trustee of the Staked Plains Trust, of which he was also secretary, succeeded Randolph in his secretarial duties,[28] although Partridge did not live in Plainview. Holbrook retained his position as vice-president and treasurer until July 14, 1954, when the Texas Land and Development Company was officially dissolved.[29]

After 1919 the president of the Texas Land and Development Company was primarily a figurehead. As has been pointed out earlier, the first person to assume that duty after reorganization was Henry M. Keith, who retained the presidency until his death on April 2, 1926.[30] He was succeeded by William F. Feeney, a trustee of Staked Plains Trust; Feeney remained until his death on January 10, 1942.[31] Then Henry F. Whitney added the duties of president of the company to his duties as president of the Staked Plains Trust and continued to serve in that capacity until the company was dissolved on June 14, 1954.[32]

[25] Fred Lowe, tape interview, July 12, 1958.
[26] Texas Land and Development Company, time book, December 15, 1935–December 31, 1953, TLDCP.
[27] Texas Land and Development Company, minutes, February 9, 1948, TLDCP.
[28] The last minutes, June 14, 1954, are signed only by Partridge as secretary.
[29] Texas Land and Development Company, minutes, June 14, 1954, TLDCP.
[30] *Ibid.*, April 2, 1926.
[31] *Ibid.*, April 2, 1926, May 14, 1942.
[32] *Ibid.*, May 14, 1942, June 14, 1954.

After dissolution of the Texas Land and Development Company and until the Staked Plains Trust could terminate the business of the trust, Holbrook remained on call to take care of any managerial or financial problem that might involve the trust locally. He agreed to function without pay although the trust provided that there would be a small payment to him when it was officially liquidated should the distribution of a final payment to the shareholders and other expenses allow it.[33] The Plainview office at the corner of Seventh and Broadway was closed some time before the dissolution of the company, and all business was thereafter conducted from Captain Holbrook's home at 309 East Fourth Street, Plainview.[34]

From the time the company sold the last piece of land in December 1946 to the final liquidation of the trust, several matters had to be handled. Local land purchasers made payments on their notes until the debts were paid in 1950,[35] and the business of closing the books, having them audited, and filing the last income tax returns occupied some time. Since the trust had retained, for a twenty-year period, one-half of the mineral rights on the last 21,844.46 acres it sold,[36] it became one of Holbrook's duties in winding up trust business to find buyers for the rights. Successfully selling the rights would convert one of the trust's paper assets to cash that would ultimately be distributed to shareholders.

To understand the philosophy behind the trust's decision to retain mineral rights, a review of oil developments in the area is useful. As early as 1926 oil had been discovered in areas not too far removed from Plainview. After 1926 the trustees watched oil developments with a great deal of interest. At first oil fields were not very near trust property, since the largest single oil field in West Texas was in the Amarillo area, approximately 100 miles northeast of the trust's holdings. The San Angelo oil field was 190 miles due south of their holdings, and the

---

[33] Staked Plains Trust, Limited, *Annual Report*, 1953, TLDCP. He was given a token payment of $350 when the trust officially liquidated (Staked Plains Trust, Limited, *Final Report*, 1955, TLDCP).

[34] Hugh R. Partridge to Winfield Holbrook, letter, May 7, 1954, unnumbered Wallet, TLDCP.

[35] Staked Plains Trust, Limited, *Annual Report*, 1950, TLDCP.

[36] Staked Plains Trust, Limited, minutes, June 1, 1945 (I, 269), TLDCP.

Retiring the Debt 161

Artesia, New Mexico, oil field was 190 miles southwest. The interest of the trustees is more understandable if one considers that the trust was attempting to pay off the enormous obligations incurred by the terms of the Reorganization Agreement of 1919. Needless to say, the trustees hoped that oil operations would reach their area.[37]

Apparently it was Maurice Hely-Hutchinson, the former trustee of the Staked Plains Trust, who had first brought the oil prospects to the attention of the trustees. Hely-Hutchinson had been led to believe that the "whole state of Texas" was underlaid by "a vast oil area." His attitude led the trustees to the hope and even to the expectation that oil might be found on trust property.[38]

No important oil development was reported near trust property until 1938, if a negative report can be called important. Two test wells had been sunk within twenty-five miles of Plainview. Both were dry to six thousand feet at which depth they were abandoned.[39] Prospects for mineral revenue for the trust, therefore, were quite discouraging. Through 1938 the company had let no oil or gas leases.

By 1939 "oil and gas prospecting, which for years" had "been carried on extensively in other parts of Texas," had "finally reached Plainview." Because of this prospecting interest, the trust in 1939 leased to the Amerada Petroleum Corporation 1,933 acres of its land for $2 per acre for the first year with the option to renew the lease for the next four years at fifty cents per acre. The trustees assured the trustholders that these leases would not interfere materially with farming operations. In case of an oil discovery the trust was to receive the customary one-eighth royalty. None of the leases carried a mandatory drilling clause. As test wells were sunk nearby, the trustees began to feel that the next few years would determine "fairly conclusively" whether there was oil on its property.[40] The trustees renewed leases let in 1939 for 1940,[41] and in March 1940 they leased an additional

---

[37] Staked Plains Trust, Limited, *Annual Report*, 1926, TLDCP.

[38] William F. Feeney to Peyton B. Randolph, letter, July 16, 1927, Randolph Files, Plainview (hereafter cited as RF).

[39] Staked Plains Trust, Limited, *Annual Report*, 1937, TLDCP.

[40] *Ibid.*, 1939.

[41] *Ibid.*, 1940.

3,083.4 acres of land to Sinclair Prairie Oil Company for $1 per acre. The leases were for a ten-year period with a $1 per acre renewal or rental clause.[42] By 1941 drilling operations came within eight miles of trust lands. The nearest producing well, however, was still sixty miles to the southeast.[43]

Even though the trust had granted oil and gas leases on a total of 8,246.4 acres of its land in 1941, it had a somewhat discouraging year in regard to oil prospects. The nearest drilling operation in relation to the trust property had receded to thirteen and one-half miles. Further, the producing well sixty miles southeast of the trust property was abandoned. The opening of a producing well forty-five miles southeast of the trust property was the only hopeful event of the year.[44]

The trust let no new leases in either 1942 or 1943, although in both years it renewed those already let on 8,246.4 acres.[45] A producing well brought in within twenty-three miles of trust land lent an optimistic note to the year. The new well, which was located in the southeastern part of Lamb County, produced 350 barrels of oil a day. Although the lease on the original 1,933-acre oil and gas grant was not renewed in 1944, the trust renewed all other leases previously sold and made an additional lease of 320 acres to the Humble Oil and Refining Company in January 1945.[46]

The trust set forth no official policy regarding mineral rights on land it sold until one of the trustees, Henry F. Whitney, broached the subject in 1944.[47] Official action was taken by the trustees on June 26, 1945, when they agreed to retain one-half of the mineral rights on all the trust's remaining 21,884.46 acres.[48]

Hale County's first producing oil well, known as Stanolind's No. 1 Lee Irish, came in in April 1946. The well was located twenty miles

---

[42] Peyton B. Randolph to William F. Feeney, letter, February 19, 1940, Wallet 1, TLDCP.
[43] Staked Plains Trust, Limited, *Annual Report*, 1940, TLDCP.
[44] *Ibid.*, 1941.
[45] *Ibid.*, 1942, 1943.
[46] *Ibid.*, 1943.
[47] Partridge to Randolph, letter, January 11, 1944, RF.
[48] Staked Plains Trust, Limited, *Annual Report*, 1945, TLDCP.

southwest of the nearest land formerly owned by the trust. Stanolind, in December 1946, brought in another well within six miles of former trust property on which the trust had retained one-half of the mineral rights.[49]

Because oil developments nearby proved to be shortlived and because no further adjacent oil developments were favorable, the trustees at a special meeting of shareholders, on September 21, 1949, requested that the shareholders decide, among other items of business, what to do with the retained mineral rights now that all trust land had been sold. Shareholders representing 29,435 of the 35,000 shares of Staked Plains Trust were either present in person or represented by proxy. The shareholders were requested to vote either to retain the mineral rights until January 1, 1955, or for any other period they might decide upon, or to sell the rights and proceed as rapidly as possible with the final liquidation of the trust. Of the shares represented, 16,595 voted in favor of selling the rights as soon as possible, 11,445 voted to hold, and 1,400 abstained.

The implications of the vote, favoring the sale of the mineral rights, were far-reaching since the vote also indicated that the trust was to be dissolved as quickly as possible. Thus the trustees presented to the shareholders, who approved them, articles of liquidation, which had been drawn up in case the vote should favor selling the rights. As of June 30, 1949, the trust's assets exclusive of mineral rights totaled $259,874.[50] Of that amount, $99,858 were in cash, $113,386 were in government bonds, and $46,630 were in vendor's lien notes.

The meeting adjourned after passing a resolution outlining the manner in which trust assets would be liquidated.

WHEREAS, the Trust has fulfilled the purpose for which it was organized;

THEREFORE BE IT HEREBY RESOLVED, that the Trustees be and are hereby directed to convert the said mineral rights, U. S. Government Bonds and Vendor's Lien Notes into cash, and after reserving sufficient cash to satisfy the Trust's Federal income tax liability (the Trustees to transfer

---

[49] *Ibid.*, 1946, TLDCP.
[50] No exact value could be placed on the mineral rights.

such cash to a deposit account established for such purposes), to distribute the balance of the cash funds to the shareholders in complete redemption and cancellation of the shares of the Trust.[51]

The trust directed Holbrook to market the rights locally, since it was expected that the landholders who already owned the other half of the rights would buy most of them. In 1949 the trust sold 320 rights for $1,600.00. The trustees expected to sell the remainder in 1950,[52] but only sold 1,550.54 for $11,629.05.[53] In 1951 they sold 5,184.83 rights mostly for $7.50 each but a few for $9.20 each;[54] the total income from these rights was $47,686.22. The trust disposed of 4,079.84 mineral rights in 1952 for $25,506.30[55] and was left with 10,749.25 rights. Every effort was made to dispose of these rights in 1953. The trustees advertised in Texas newspapers and listed their rights with several brokers. Through the efforts of one broker, the Burdell Oil Company offered $13,500.00 for the remaining rights. Since this was the best offer the trust received, it was accepted. The low price was due to several factors, but primarily to the discouraging oil developments in the area and to the fact that of the original twenty-year life of the rights, only eleven and twelve years remained.[56] The total profit realized from selling the rights was $99,921.57.

Since the trust had successfully sold its mineral rights by 1953, it had only one other matter to settle before it could carry through its liquidation process. That matter, having to do with income tax, was to delay the liquidation process further. The trust had encountered disagreements with the Bureau of Internal Revenue over its bookkeeping system since 1939. In that year the trust began a major squabble with the bureau. The bureau had challenged the trust's tax return for 1937. The Internal Revenue agent handling the company return, ruled that the trust's yearly charge for interest on Class B Liquidation Rights was

[51] Staked Plains Trust, Limited, minutes, August 10, 1949 (II, insert between 303–304); minutes, September 21, 1949 (II, 297–303), TLDCP.
[52] Staked Plains Trust, *Annual Report*, 1949, TLDCP.
[53] *Ibid.*, 1950.
[54] *Ibid.*, 1951.
[55] *Ibid.*, 1952.
[56] *Ibid.*, 1953.

Retiring the Debt 165

to be disallowed as a deduction from taxable income. He disallowed the deduction on the basis that the charge was on preferred stocks rather than on an indebtedness. The trustees, of course, claimed the opposite. They argued that the interest deduction on Class B Liquidation Rights was an indebtedness and therefore deductible.

As a result of the agent's ruling, the trust was assessed an additional $15,708.99 for 1937. The trust appealed the decision to the Technical Staff of the Bureau of Internal Revenue.[57] The staff ruled adversely for the trust in 1941, whereupon the trust appealed the decision to the Board of Tax Appeals.[58] The Board of Tax Appeals heard the case in Dallas on December 2, 1942,[59] and held adversely for the trust on the basis that Class B Liquidation Rights constituted preferred stock rather than an indebtedness, that the accrued interest was actually accumulated dividends, and that the trust could not deduct the accrued interest on its income tax returns. The trust next appealed the decision to the Fifth Circuit Court of Appeals.[60] In the meantime the Bureau of Internal Revenue had assessed additional taxes for the years 1940, 1941, 1942, and 1943.[61] The Circuit Court upheld the decision of the Tax Court (the new name for the Board of Tax Appeals) in June 1944, "in a short opinion."

The trustees, as a result of the Circuit Court opinion, were forced to pay a total of $40,088.32 additional taxes for the years 1937, 1940, 1941, and 1942; the 1943 tax was also pushed up to $42,318.08.[62] The trustees made no appeal to the United States Supreme Court, since in their opinion, it "would have been futile." After 1944 the trust was released from additional taxes on the accrued interest on Class B Liquidation Rights because interest ceased to accrue on them as of October 31, 1944, when the rights were paid in full.[63]

---

[57] *Ibid.*, 1940.
[58] *Ibid.*, 1941.
[59] *Ibid.*, 1942.
[60] *Ibid.*, 1943.
[61] *Ibid.*, 1943.
[62] Apparently the tax returns made by the trust for 1938 and 1939 were satisfactory to the Bureau of Internal Revenue.
[63] Staked Plains Trust, Limited, *Annual Report*, 1944, TLDCP.

The disagreement over the taxes on the liquidation rights was scarcely concluded when another question pertaining to income tax arose, this time over the book value of the trust's property. The Staked Plains Trust, since its reorganization in 1919, had carried its lands on its books at $31.5567 per acre. The Bureau of Internal Revenue contended that the figure of $24.98 per acre should have been used. If the bureau's figure were used and accepted by the trust as accurate, then the trust had not reported all its profits on land sales made for 1942, 1943, and 1944, the big selling years. On the basis of its belief, the bureau had assessed an additional $71,633.83 in taxes for the three years mentioned. In 1946 the trust and the bureau effected a compromise whereby the land would be listed at $27.50 per acre. This meant that the trust had to pay an additional $48,936.29 in taxes plus $5,355.96 interest. The compromise represented a considerable scaling down of the original $71,633.83, and resulted in a substantial saving.[64]

The Treasury Department audited and accepted income tax returns for 1945 through 1949 without alteration.[65] The trust was again to encounter difficulty from 1949 to 1953, the period in which it sold mineral rights. The Bureau of Internal Revenue contended that the profit realized from the sale of the mineral rights should have been reported as "ordinary income," not as "capital gain." If the bureau were correct, the trust owed approximately $7,200.00 additional tax plus the interest.[66] A compromise cut the payment due to $3,278.06 additional tax and $688.17 interest. The trustees were of the opinion that this was as "favorable a settlement" as could have been effected. Since the settlement cleared the way for complete liquidation, the trustees were quick to move toward that end.[67]

Even before the shareholders had agreed to liquidation of the trust in their meeting in September 1949 when they voted to sell their mineral rights and liquidate as quickly as possible, the trust had successfully retired the indebtedness it had incurred by the terms of the Reorganization Agreement of 1919. This retirement had been completed when

[64] *Ibid.*, 1946.
[65] *Ibid.*, 1950.
[66] *Ibid.*, 1954.
[67] *Ibid.*, 1955.

Retiring the Debt

the last payment of interest due on Class B Liquidation Rights had been made on January 30, 1947.[68] As a result, the Staked Plains Trust had finally freed itself from former indebtedness and could operate for the benefit of its shareholders. The following April 9, 1948, the trust declared a dividend of $6.00 per share.[69] In December, after the shareholders meeting in 1949, an initial "distribution in liquidation" was made to the shareholders amounting to $5.00 per share. At that time the trust planned to make a "second and final distribution after all assets" had "been turned into cash and after the Trust's liability for Federal income taxes" had "been determined."[70] The second distribution, made in 1951, amounted to $2.50 per share.[71] It was not until the sale of mineral rights was completed in 1953 and the income tax problems connected with their sale were settled in 1955 that the trust made its final payment to its shareholders. The payment amounted to $1.66 per share and was to be made on December 12, 1955, upon "surrender for cancellation of certificates for shares" to the Old Colony Trust of Boston, which was acting as agent for the trust.[72] In all, each share of Staked Plains Trust stock had earned $6.00 in dividends and $9.16 in liquidation distributions, representing a total of $15.16 per share or $530,600.00 for the total thirty-five thousand shares. Seven shares of Staked Plains Trust stock for each £100 bond (exchange value at time of issue $486.67) had been issued to the original holders of first mortgage bonds. Each seven-share unit paid $106.12. This amount plus the $1.00, received for each £100 bond after reorganization, or $107.12, represented the total amount received for each £100 bond of the original issue. Thus the investors of the first mortgage bonds sustained a loss of $379.55 per £100 bond. The total of $535,600.00 was paid to the bondholders. Since they had originally invested £500,000 (or $2,433,333.33), their loss was $1,897,773.33; their loss per £100 bond, $379.55, and their loss per share, $54.22. At the time the final report of the Staked Plains Trust was made on November 29,

[68] *Ibid.*, 1947.
[69] *Ibid.*, 1947.
[70] *Ibid.*, 1949.
[71] *Ibid.*, 1951.
[72] *Ibid.*, 1955.

1955, it was stated that "the transfer books for the shares" would "close permanently on January 31, 1956." With the closing of the books came also the official end of the Plainview enterprise. In its earlier days it had brought wealth and prosperity to Plainview and had helped furnish the area with its "Gilded Age"; in its succeeding years it had given the area agricultural and irrigational leadership.

9. Appraisal

THE TEXAS LAND and Development Company, as operating agent for the Plainview enterprise, was charged with a tremendous task. To develop and sell 61,360 acres of land in an allotted five-year period would require a steady flow of capital, an "around the clock" work schedule, and favorable times that would yield a ready market for the land. The first two requirements could possibly have been provided had the third one been forthcoming. In 1912 it was impossible to foresee that M. D. Henderson's scheme for selling land in a developed state would be hampered by almost insurmountable odds, which would prolong the life of the enterprise almost four decades past the originally projected five-year period. That World War I would curtail the financial backers, F. S. Pearson and his associates, in their efforts to acquire the necessary capital for the operation became increasingly obvious when troubles in Europe spread around the world. During the early days of the war in Europe, development continued at an uninterrupted pace since the backers, by a series of financial maneuvers, were able to provide funds. Development ceased entirely, however, after 1917, when the United States entered the war. Sales, which had enjoyed only sporadic success from 1913 to 1916, had to be discontinued also. The company planned to complete development on the approximately ten thousand acres that it had sold, even though inflated prices made the expense exorbitant. When the original sales and development program waned, the company turned toward tenant farming as a stop-gap measure to provide some operating capital until it could sell its lands. In 1919 the enterprise was completely reorganized; its business was put into the hands of a trust; and it looked forward to selling its land, terminating obligations to its investors, and going out of business.

Despite innumerable vicissitudes, the Texas Land and Development Company had tremendous stability, as witnessed by its survival of the farm depression and drought seasons in the twenties and of the even more terrible conditions of depression and droughts in the thirties. During those years the company was forced to take drastic cuts in operational expenses, but it managed to survive. Although the operation often lost money, its capital reserve was never depleted. During the period, the company relied almost entirely upon tenant farming, abetted in part by irrigation, to keep the operation going. Wartime prosperity of the forties, which continued into the postwar period, gave the trust the needed impetus to terminate its obligations. It sold all the land, most of it in a raw or semicultivated state. Although the company never revived the original development plans, it did meet its obligations, until the trust was liquidated in 1956. The legacy left to the area could not, however, be wiped out by a mere liquidation.

Throughout the years that the Texas Land and Development Company operated in Plainview, area citizens gave it their warm support. When Pearson's syndicate purchased the land in 1912, the area was suffering from a depression that had been felt in other parts of the United States since 1907 but had been staved off locally by a land boom precipitated by the coming of the railroad in 1907. A delayed depression did reach the area after two successive drought years, and since dry-land farming dominated the area, these years proved disastrous. The depression was short-lived, after the "syndicate" spent more than $1,500,000 on the purchase of area land, much of which went

Appraisal

directly to local farmers from whom the "syndicate" purchased the land. With the sudden circulation of cash in the area and a chance for employment on work crews that were immediately set to work developing company land, the area once again flourished. The company spent additional capital in the area for some of the materials it planned to use. Within a few short years the enterprise had spent approximately $3,000,000, $2,000,000 or more of which circulated in the Plainview area.

The enterprise contributed far more than financial stability to the area. Its pioneer work in irrigation was noteworthy. As part of the development process, it planned to install an irrigation system on each tract of land. It contracted expert engineering consultants and pump men to do the work. Not only did these men take care of the irrigation needs of the company's tenants and purchasers, but also they gave free advice to many other area farmers. Much more important than that, the company operation added immeasurably to the small start that area farmers had already made toward using irrigation. More than one person has stated that irrigation operations of the Texas Land and Development Company speeded up the acceptance and usage of extensive irrigation in the area. During the latter years of World War I, when the company struggled for existence, the irrigation equipment already installed was, in many instances, not used because it was too costly to operate. However, during the twenties and thirties, when times were still bad, Winfield Holbrook and his staff, and George Green, who had discovered that smaller and less expensive car engines would run a well efficiently, were credited with reviving irrigation in the area, thus lessening the effect of droughts and depressions. Many area people contended that it was mainly through the efforts of the Texas Land and Development Company that the area so quickly established itself as a prosperous irrigation district.

Experimentation conducted on company demonstration farms furnished area farmers with valuable information since the company's agricultural experts were anxious to share their knowledge. Numerous educational articles appeared in the local papers in which Texas Land and Development Company personnel gave advice about successful farming methods and about crops grown favorably under irrigated conditions. It was to the advantage of the company and of the area farmers that these experiments were openly discussed, because prosperity in the area would enhance the local market for the company's land. Now that irrigated farming dominates the Plainview area, it is interesting to note that many of the experimental crops grown by company farmers have been "rediscovered" as profitable crops. In the past few years, truck crops, in particular, are being given more attention and are being grown more extensively. Cotton, wheat, and grain sorghums, still the staples of the area, have flourished under irrigation. From all indications it would be safe to conclude that the programs of the Texas Land and Development Company paved the way for the substantially sound agricultural conditions that exist in the area today.

Many people in the area, quickly recognizing the advantages the company offered, accepted the suggestions of the outsiders. As a matter of fact, in the first months of the company's operation, the Plainview Chamber of Commerce extended an official welcome and honored employees and friends of the company at an annual dinner. Judge Joe E. Lancaster, a former real-estate partner of M. D. Henderson, responded to a toast, "The Attituae [sic] of Plainview to the Pearson Interests." He stated that initially he had been a 'doubting Thomas,' but he now admitted that the more he saw of the syndicate's plans and work, the more convinced he was that the contributions of the syndicate to the shallow water belt would be "tremendous." He contended that "everyone should help the syndicate in its great work of development" and pledged that the attitude of Plainview toward the enterprise was one of loyalty and good will.[1] The spirit of welcome extended in 1912 seemed to prevail thereafter. The favorable reception was especially noticeable in editorial comments written in the early years by a local editor, Buford R. Brown.[2] In one such editorial entitled "Be an Engine," Brown urged all Hale County citizens to follow the lead of the Texas Land and Development Company and be progressive. In part he wrote:

[1] *Plainview News*, December 20, 1912.
[2] Brown later became one of the first instructors in the newly organized department of journalism at The University of Texas.

Appraisal 173

Are you moving? And when you go is it forward? Do you carry anything? . . .

Here on the South Plains developments are taking place of which few of us are cognizant. Men of vision tell us that we have here the most magnificent resources in soil and water that man has ever been privileged to enjoy. These are men whose judgement has won them fortunes in the battle of life. And they are backing their statements about the South Plains with money.

Do you realize that anything unusual is taking place in Hale County? Have you observed that the Texas Land and Development Company is spending $3,500,000.00 developing irigated [sic] farms—that nearly $2,000,000.00 if [sic] this amount has already been spent here? This means much for prosperity.[3]

One might wonder how an out-of-state company, especially one backed by "Wall Street Capitalists" and foreign investors, would receive such a hearty welcome in the area. Although the enterprise offered financial security to the area at a time when it was needed, it would not necessarily follow that the area citizens would immediately accept imported company personnel into their inner circle of civic and social life. Nor would it be expected that the community should, as a matter of course, develop a feeling of closeness to the Texas Land and Development Company that even now after its dissolution seems to linger. Good public relations were at least partly responsible for the friendly feeling; the company was noted for sharing its discoveries with others and for giving freely its help and advice to those who sought it. More than that it seemed to have respect for the customs of the area. For example, a company representative was careful to explain in a newspaper article that it was necessary to run pumps on Sunday for a short time in order to save the company trees.[4] Consideration of a then local custom of not working on the Sabbath would have gone unexplained by less thoughtful groups. The company was also noted for being extremely fair with its tenants. Although they were required to keep any equipment installed on the leased tract in good repair, the company

[3] *Hale County Herald*, May 9, 1913.
[4] *Ibid.*, May 8, 1913.

maintained a repair crew to assist them. The farm superintendents were also always available to advise and assist. The "benevolent" attitude of the company toward its tenants gave them a notable advantage over other lessees in the area.

Pearson's attitude toward the area helped cement good public relations. When he visited the area, he took an interest in civic affairs and offered advice regarding city engineering problems, especially street construction. Henderson, Pearson's local counterpart, was equally interested in civic problems and rendered extensive service to the community with his chamber of commerce work. The tradition of civic and social leadership seems to have been instilled in a majority of company personnel and in their families during the life of the enterprise. Most of the men were active members of fraternal organizations and contributed their special talents to the chamber of commerce and the Hale County Fair Association. Notable among this group was W. H. Mason, who served as company auditor for three years. During his stay in Plainview he sang one of the male leads in "Martha," when the opera was presented by the Plainview Choral Group.

Mason and many others became active church leaders. Mason used his singing talents by instituting an "informal choir school" at St. Mark's Episcopal Church. His short association with Plainview, especially with the church, must have been memorable to him, for at his death, he left a sizeable legacy to the Plainview church.[5]

The wives of company personnel carried on charity work and social leadership. Mrs. Clyde E. Craig, whose husband was a wartime general manager, was active in Red Cross work. It was, no doubt, through her efforts that the Texas Land and Development Company offered a load of alfalfa for auction, the proceeds of which would go to the local Red Cross chapter.[6] Many of the ladies were prominent in women's club work. At one time Mrs. J. W. Longstreth was president of the County Federated Women's Club. Among others prominent in club work and

[5] Diocese of Northwest Texas (Episcopal), *The Adventure*, XXXVII, no. 4 (September 1959), copy in Brunson Letters, Southwest Collection, Texas Tech University, Lubbock (courtesy of Mrs. S. V. Connor).

[6] *Plainview Evening Herald*, September 11, 1917.

Appraisal 175

in the society columns were Mrs. R. S. Charles, Mrs. J. W. Grant, Mrs. J. W. Pipkin, Mrs. Peyton Randolph, Mrs. H. I. Miller (when she came to Plainview with her husband), and Mrs. W. H. Mason.

Three of the company's long-time employees deserve special mention for their contributions to the community and to the area. Mary L. Cox, the company stenographer for over twenty years, is remembered as *the* Hale County Historian. Many consider her *History of Hale County Texas*, published in 1937, as the definitive work on the subject. As a member of the Business and Professional Women's Club she had promoted an interest in local history by encouraging the club to sponsor Plainview's annual "Pioneer Round-Up," and by preparing numerous scrapbooks containing original source material that is being used in the instruction of local history in the Plainview schools.

Walter J. Klinger, who was associated with the company from 1915 until his retirement in 1948, first as bookkeeper and then as secretary-treasurer, was well known for his civic work. His earliest civic contribution, helping to establish a professional fire department for the city in 1910, led him to serve as its chief for one year. Much of his energy was directed toward the youth of the area. As park commissioner, he started and equipped the City Park; through the Kiwanis Club, he helped organize and operate a Youth Center; in Boy Scout work, he served as president of the Central Plains Council in 1930; and he also helped organize the Young Men's Christian Association and served on its first board of directors.

Perhaps most outstanding as a civic and area leader was Winfield Holbrook, the company's general manager from 1919 to liquidation. At different times during his years in Plainview he was a member of the Board of City Development, the city council, and the Plainview School Board. He served as president of the Plainview Chamber of Commerce and was twice elected mayor of the city. Because of his intense interest in an adequate water supply for both rural and city use, he was an active member and director of the Texas Board of Water Engineers and, at the time of his death on August 25, 1956, was one of Plainview's directors of the Canadian River Municipal Water Authority. Because of his interest in history he maintained membership in and, at the time of his death, was a director of the Panhandle-Plains Historical Society. As an authority on geology, he worked with universities and colleges in conducting field trips to the area in an effort to promote a better knowledge of the geological structure of the region. Such employees certainly aided the Texas Land and Development Company in commanding the respect and good will of area citizens.

Not all its activities, however, can be recorded on the favorable side of the company's record. Most of the adverse criticism must be aimed at its operation before reorganization in 1919. In those early years, when the company was doing so much to furnish financial stability for the area as a whole and agricultural "know-how" for the farmer, some phases of its internal operation suffered. Experimentation, although valuable for what it would reveal about crops that could or could not be grown in the area, proved costly and delayed the development of a standard system of growing staple crops, which former experiments had proved to be profitable. Although to have continued with traditional methods would have negated the purpose of experimentation, the experimental program was of questionable value to the overall development and operation of the company.

At times the company seems to have spent carelessly and extravagantly. Some of its laxity can be attributed to inexperience with farming in West Texas but was due more to the prevailing attitude among some of the early personnel that "we have the money to spend; let's spend it." The blame for this attitude was primarily the fault of the wealthy eastern backers, who displayed their wealth with seemingly casual abandon when in Plainview. It was not unusual for F. S. Pearson, H. I. Miller, or C. J. Hubbard, as representative members of the early group, to arrive in Plainview in an elaborately furnished private railroad car where they entertained local citizens freely. A chauffeured car at company expense was always available for their use. H. I. Miller maintained a home in Plainview that was used only during his occasional business trips to Plainview and was maintained by a Negro caretaker named Alexander.

The operation of the Plainview office during the early period seems to have been unnecessarily expensive. Company employees were paid,

Appraisal 177

on the whole, more than other local employees. Accustomed to a large-scale operation in a metropolitan area, the backers set up a far more complicated office system than was needed. The office was overstaffed at one time to a point that A. B. DeLoach, an officer and director who was hired as treasurer, felt obliged to resign for lack of anything to do. DeLoach claimed that most of his duties were delegated to subordinates.

The early land-selling policy, likewise, should be criticized. The company agents misled early purchasers about what to expect and gave them an overly optimistic picture of farming possibilities. Although the company instructed the sales agents to find buyers who could adjust to irrigation farming, it seemed to be the rule to "promise a potential buyer anything verbally" to get him to make the down payment, not considering in the least how he would acclimate to the area and to the conditions of the contract. The agents were assisted in the selling campaign by Henderson's brochure, which, although seemingly compiled with honest convictions, exaggerated the possibilities for making money quickly. His predicted net profit for a year of farming, estimated before any of the actual development took place, represented a conjectural case instead of a realistic one, and it tended to oversell. It was not surprising that many of the early purchasers' land had to be repossessed.

In 1919 an over-all reorganization corrected most of the weak points of the enterprise. An efficient local operating policy was put into the hands of Winfield Holbrook, who personified firm convictions and "know-how." That the company initiated a stricter policy when it did, one would suspect, saved it from complete ruin. Surely a continuation of former policies would have wiped out the operation in the twenties and thirties. When the local situation is viewed critically, it is apparent that Holbrook and his steadying influence must be credited for much that saved the enterprise.

The same reorganization benefited the investors. The series of bonds, notes, and certificates held by investors might have been worthless had wise measures not been taken. Although investment in the Plainview operation may have been considered "pocket change" to men of means, it is never the aim of an investor to lose money. For example, the heaviest individual investor, Minor Cooper Keith, had invested approximately $285,590.54 in the enterprise: £25,000 (or $121,667.50) in Texas Prairie Lands mortgage bonds in 1912; $25,000.00 in Texas Prairie Lands prior lien notes in 1914; and $91,923.04 in Prairie Lands Trust certificates in 1916. To Keith, the man who founded the United Fruit Company, this amount may have seemed small, but a profit on a small investment meant more operating capital for him. He did not, however, sustain a loss from his investment, thanks to the efficiently handled reorganization. Although he lost approximately $118,687.50 net from his initial investment of mortgage bonds, he made a net profit of nearly $20,750.00 from the prior lien notes and one of nearly $212,342.00 from the trust certificates. Thus his net profit was approximately $114,404.50. His net gain, a long time in coming, was mostly realized by his estate after his death in 1929. Keith was more fortunate than many of the investors in that he invested most heavily in the best profit-making issue. Those who invested heavily in first mortgage bonds and then lost faith in the enterprise or were not in a position to continue investing were the heavy losers. For example, the original backer, F. S. Pearson, who did not live to invest past the 1912 issue, ironically left his estate an unprofitable legacy.

The over-all enterprise, hampered by a complicated internal financial structure and overwhelming external factors, sustained a capital loss of approximately $504,683.00. Profits made by the original holders of Prior Lien Notes (Class A Liquidation Certificates plus interest) and Trust Certificates (Class B Liquidation Certificates plus interest) amounted to approximately $414,175.00 and $958,875.00 respectively. These profits could not counterbalance the loss sustained by the holders of First Mortgage Bonds (shareholders of the Staked Plains Trust after reorganization) of nearly $1,877,733.33. Individual investors lost or profited according to their original holdings.[7]

Except for two major factors, the over-all loss sustained by the holders of the original securities and the failure of the company to carry out its original prospectus of a complete development program on

[7] See Appendix III.

Appraisal 179

all its lands, the company succeeded in producing benefits for nearly all connected with it—the tenants, the purchasers, the employees, the area, and some of the investors. The Plainview enterprise can be considered a good example of the American system of free enterprise capitalism at work.

APPENDIX I

BIOGRAPHIES

Many people, some who were already citizens of Plainview, others who were to settle in Plainview and be counted among its active citizens, others who visited the city from time to time on company business, and still others who invested in the enterprise but never saw the site of operations, were connected with the Texas Land and Development Company and its parent organizations. Since it was not feasible to give biographical information concerning many of these people in the body of this study, it seemed in order to have a biographical appendix in which some of those who fell into one of the above-mentioned categories could be listed. To list everyone, however, was an impossible task because most of the original people connected with the various companies from 1912 to 1919 are deceased and contact could not be made with their survivors. In many cases it was difficult to obtain adequate information, and in other cases it was impossible to obtain uniform information.

ALEXANDER, D. L.
  Company supervisor. Supervised building of houses and improving of land for the Texas Land and Development Company around 1916.
  (Source: William J. Williams, tape interview, August 22, 1959).

ALLEN, OSCAR LEROY
  Company warehouse manager. Born White County, Arkansas, May 26, 1881; attended high school and business school; moved to Plainview, 1913; married Pearl K. Allen; employed as construction worker by Texas Land and Development Company, January 1913; served company later as office worker, warehouse manager, farm manager until 1918; farmed independently; worked for government farm programs; died June 1951.
  (Source: Mrs. Pearl K. Allen, letter, September 16, 1959, Brunson Letters).

AYRES, WALTER S.

Company vice-president and sales manager. Born last part of 1860 or first part of 1861; married Effie Brindley, July 16, 1890; one daughter, Isabel; known generally as a "land man"; headquartered in Chicago, Illinois; worked through Passenger Department of the Rock Island Railroad, principally in Texas and Oklahoma; became one of the first land men to bring potential purchasers to "Gulf Coast Country" of Texas, 1904; made vice-president in charge of all land sales of Gulf Coast Irrigation Company, 1906; joined the Medina Dam Project, San Antonio, Texas, around 1911; served as vice-president and sales manager of Texas Land and Development Company with offices in Chicago, Illinois, August 14, 1913, to October 7, 1916; served as regional director of land activities in South for federal government around 1917 with headquarters in New Orleans, Louisiana; joined Bogalusa Lumber Company, a project of Dr. F. S. Pearson's (q.v.), after World War I; engaged in land development and sales in and around New Orleans; died *circa* 1936.

(Source: Marietta Workman, Washington County, Iowa, District Court Clerk, letters, January 25, February 2, 1960, Brunson Letters.)

BALDWIN, LEROY W.

Texas Prairie Lands, Limited, trustee. Appointed joint trustee of Texas Prairie Lands, Limited, December 1912; associated with Empire Trust Company of New York City; later became president of the Empire Trust Company.

(Sources: *Documents 1917*, Texas Land and Development Company Papers; William F. Feeney to Peyton B. Randolph, letter, March 16, 1928, Randolph Files, Plainview.)

BARBER, P. B.

Company superintendent of irrigated farms around 1917. Directed experiments for company farms; terminated employment with the Texas Land and Development Company March 18, 1918; worked on irrigation project, Las Cruces, New Mexico, prior to joining company; deceased.

(Sources: *Plainview Evening Herald*, March 18, 1917; William F. Feeney to Henry S. Fleming, letter, November 25, 1918, Bain Files, Plainview; Winfield Holbrook to Clyde E. Craig, letter, October 28, 1950, Brunson Letters.)

BLACK, ZENAS E.

Company publicity man. Employed by Texas Land and Development

Company, 1912; stayed until closing of Chicago office, 1916; was active in Plainview civic projects; was secretary of Plainview Chamber of Commerce.

(Sources: *Hale County Herald*, August 26, 1913; *Plainview Evening Herald*, September 12, 1916; other reports from Plainview newspapers.)

BOWMAN, DAVID DELL

Company superintendent of farms. Born Burns City, Indiana, 1880; was manager of lumber yard, Gibson Lumber Company, Pinrose, Florence, and Beaver Park, Colorado; met Captain Winfield Holbrook (q.v.), Beaver Park, Colorado, *circa* 1909; worked for Garret Cain Construction Company, Fox and Smith Construction Company, and O'Garra-Cain Construction Company, Colorado; was bookkeeper, Continental Tie and Lumber Company, Cimeron, New Mexico; later returned to Gibson Lumber Company, Pinrose, Colorado; joined the Texas Land and Development Company as superintendent first of dry-land farms but after fall of 1920 of all company farms north of Texas Highway 70, 1919 to 1942; after 1942 was part owner of nursery in Plainview; deceased.

(Source: David Dell Bowman, tape interview, June 27, 1958.)

BRASK, KARL

Company foreman of paint crew. Swedish; was member of original crew.

(Source: Hanley Wasson, tape interview, August 19, 1959.)

CABOT, N. W.

Company director. Appointed director of Texas Land and Development Company, October 3, 1916, to February 25, 1919; was member of Boston law firm.

(Source: Texas Land and Development Company, minutes, October 3, 1916, February 25, 1919, Texas Land and Development Company Papers; Peyton B. Randolph, oral interview, August 5, 1959.)

CHARLES, ROBERT S.

Company director, vice-president, and acting general manager. Born Richmond, Indiana, June 20, 1876; graduated from Richmond High School; received A.B. degree, Earlham College (Quaker by birthright), 1898; received postgraduate degree, University of Pennsylvania, 1903; married; two sons: Robert, president of Layne and Bowler Pump Company, Los Angeles, California; and John, head of International Water

Corporation office, Pittsburgh, Pennsylvania; presently resides in Richmond, Indiana.

Was teacher and principal of a township high school in Indiana, 1898–1900; spent summers with engineering surveying party for location of new railroad through Richmond, Indiana, from Cincinnati, Ohio, to Chicago, Illinois, now part of Chesapeake and Ohio Railroad; began career as civil engineer on railroad location, construction, and maintenance, 1900; spent next six years with various railroad engineering offices; became division engineer, 1906; later placed on special projects, reconnaissance surveys and other assignments, Chicago and Eastern Railroad and the Rock Island-Frisco system; sent on railroad reconnaissance survey for extension of the Frisco Railroad from Quanah, Texas, through Plainview, Texas, to El Paso, Texas, 1912; plan deemed not feasible; joined Texas Land and Development Company, 1912; applied engineering talents to ground-water problems and production for irrigation farming; served as vice-president, October 29, 1912, to December 7, 1912; acting general manager, August 14, 1913, to November 1, 1915; director, October 21, 1912 to October 5, 1915, of Texas Land and Development Company; rejoined the Wabash Railroad, 1915–1917; became field manager for M. E. Layne, Memphis, Tennessee, 1917; remained with Layne until semiretirement, 1948.

In 1922 Mr. Charles organized Layne New York Company in eastern United States; expanded company into France, England, North Africa, Canada, and other French-speaking countries; company known as International Water Corporation and included International Water Supply, Limited, of Canada.

(Sources: Texas Land and Development Company, minutes, October 12, 1912, October 29, 1929, December 7, 1912, August 14, 1913, October 5, 1915, November 1, 1915, Texas Land and Development Company Papers; R. S. Charles, letter, November 1, 1958, Brunson Letters.)

CONOVER, R. B.

Company director. Served as director of Texas Land and Development Company, October 5, 1915, to June 7, 1916.

(Sources: Texas Land and Development Company, minutes, October 5, 1915, June 7, 1916, Texas Land and Development Company Papers.)

COOPER, J. WEST RULON

Staked Plains Trust, Limited, trustee. Served as trustee of Staked Plains, Limited, December 10, 1951, to January 31, 1956, when the company officially liquidated.

(Sources: Staked Plains Trust, Limited, *Annual Report*, 1951, Texas Land and Development Company Papers; Staked Plains Trust, Limited, *Final Report*, 1955, Texas Land and Development Company Papers.)

COX, MARY L.

Company stenographer. Born March 24, 1885, Beatrice, Nebraska; moved to Texas with parents in 1907. After business course at Wayland College became court stenographer. Worked for Judge W. B. Lewis, the Third National Bank, the Santa Fe Railroad, Crosby County Draft Board in World War I, and Patterson and Groves Insurance Company. Employed by the Texas Land and Development Company as stenographer 1920–1948. Published *History of Hale County Texas* in 1939; contributed to *Handbook of Texas*; active Panhandle-Plains Historical Society, Business and Professional Women's Club; founder of Pioneer Round-Up, an annual gathering of area pioneers; deceased.

(Source: Mrs. A. B. Cox, letter, July 13, 1960, Brunson Letters.)

CRAIG, CLYDE EMERSON

Company vice-president and general manager. Born in small country home near Quincy, Michigan, March 13, 1878; graduated from Three Rivers High School, St. Joseph County, Michigan, 1895; attended summer school at small college, St. Joseph, Michigan, 1895; attended Sage's Business College, Three Rivers, Michigan, 1897; married Grace Pixley of Lyford, Texas; daughter, Mrs. R. H. Edgerton, Corpus Christi, Texas; presently resides in Lyford, Texas.

Taught school in Michigan, 1896–1897; worked in real-estate office for few months, Kalamazoo, Michigan; worked for Sheffield Car Company until December 31, 1903; joined Law Department of Rock Island Railroad, Chicago, Illinois, until fall of 1907; joined the Gulf Coast Irrigation Company as a secretary-manager, Lyford, Texas, 1907; became president of Gulf Coast Irrigation Company, 1910–1945; became general manager and vice-president of Texas Land and Development Company, February 1917 to February 25, 1919; became president of First National Bank of Raymondville, Texas, and president of Valley Loan and Trust Company, 1932–1939; was vice-president of Santa Rosa, Inc.; organized Carricitos Oil Corporation, 1931; now retired.

(Sources: Texas Land and Development Company, minutes, February 7, 1917, February 25, 1919, Texas Land and Development Company Papers; Clyde E. Craig, letter, September 15, 1959, Brunson Letters, and card, January 3, 1970, in possession of author.)

CRAIG, SAMUEL O.

Company painter. Born Watertown, South Dakota, August 7, 1891; worked for Thompson and Carter Painting Company, Plainview, October 12 to December 1913; worked for Texas Land and Development Company, January to April 1914; presently resides in Munday, Texas.

(Source: Samuel O. Craig, oral interview, June 15, 1958.)

DALY, U. DE B.

Company secretary-treasurer. Employed as secretary-treasurer of Texas Land and Development Company, December 7, 1912, to February 19, 1915; represented Empire Trust of New York.

(Sources: Texas Land and Development Company, minutes, December 7, 1912, February 19, 1915, Texas Land and Development Company Papers; Peyton B. Randolph, oral interview, August 5, 1959, notes in Brunson Letters.)

DELOACH, A. B.

Company director and secretary-treasurer. Born Longview, Texas, January 29, 1876; graduated from high school; attended Ft. Worth University for two years; took correspondence course in common law, University of Texas; passed bar examination.

Was bank cashier, Texarkana, Texas; elected mayor of Texarkana, 1908, served two terms; moved to South Texas; became sales manager of the Texas City Company, Texas City, Texas; became assistant cashier, Texas City National Bank, 1915; employed by Lumbermen's National Bank, Houston, Texas, 1918; joined the staff of Dallas Federal Reserve Bank, 1918; accepted position as cashier in Plainview National Bank, Plainview, Texas, 1918; served as secretary-treasurer and director of Texas Land and Development Company, May 12, 1919, to August 2, 1920; entered partnership in grain business; did part-time bookkeeping and auditing; became bookkeeper, Wayland Baptist College, Plainview, Texas, later became business manager until 1947; retired and presently resides in Bentonville, Arkansas.

(Sources: Texas Land and Development Company, minutes, May 12, 1919, August 2, 1920, Texas Land and Development Company Papers; A. B. DeLoach, letter, December 17, 1958, Brunson Letters.)

DOUBLEDAY, GEORGE BARTON

Company secretary-treasurer. Born on sheep ranch, Belton, Texas, May 6, 1871; high school education and studied banking under John G. Harris,

Biographies 187

Dublin, Texas; married De Alva Miller, 1896; five children plus two adopted; member of Amarillo Country Club, Douglas Arizona Development Club, Mason (York Rite), Shrine, and Knights Templer; Presbyterian.

Worked in Hico bank and lumber yard; moved to Tulia, Texas, in 1906 to form a land company; moved to Hurley, Texas, to promote land development; moved to Plainview *circa* 1913; associated with Third National Bank of Plainview and in real-estate business; secretary and treasurer of Texas Land and Development Company, July 11, 1916, to December 6, 1916; remainder of career in banking and real estate; president of Chamber of Commerce, Douglas, Arizona; died December 31, 1933, Douglas, Arizona.

(Sources: Texas Land and Development Company, minutes, July 11, 1916, December 6, 1916, Texas Land and Development Company Papers; Mrs. Sam F. Richardson, daughter of Doubleday, letters, September 9 and October 10, 1959, Brunson Letters.)

DOWDEN, E.

Company superintendent of dry-land farms. Employed as superintendent of dry-land farming of Texas Land and Development Company, later served as sales manager around 1915; was active in civic affairs, Plainview.

(Sources: *Plainview Evening Herald*, April 20, 1915; reports from Plainview newspapers.)

DUBLIN, R. C.

Company well driller. Was expert well driller; worked for Texas Land and Development Company under Robert S. Charles (q.v.) beginning 1912 and for several years thereafter.

(Sources: R. S. Charles, letter, November 1, 1958, Brunson Letters; Homer Rook, tape interview, August 28, 1959.)

FEENEY, WILLIAM F.

Company secretary-treasurer. Employed as secretary-treasurer of Texas Land and Development Company, February 25, 1919, to May 12, 1919; became trustees' representative 1924; director of Staked Plains Trust, Limited, 1938 to 1942; was from New York City; died in 1942.

(Sources: Texas Land and Development Company, minutes, February 25, 1919, May 12, 1919, Texas Land and Development Company Papers; T. C. Shephard, oral interview, August 19, 1959, notes in Brunson Letters; Winfield Holbrook to Clyde E. Craig, letter, October 28, 1950, Brunson Letters; Staked Plains Trust, Limited, *Annual Report*, 1941, Texas Land and Development Company Papers.)

FIFE, WILLIAM S.

Company chief of engineering. Born Allegheny, Pennsylvania, March 16, 1882; was civil engineer; served as chief of the engineering department of Texas Land and Development Company, 1915 to March 1916; left Plainview, 1917; went to Logansport, Indiana.

(Sources: Elks' Records, Plainview; *Plainview Evening Herald*, March 14, 1916; Hanley Wasson, tape interview, August 19, 1959.)

FLEMING, HENRY S.

Texas Prairie Lands, Limited, secretary. Functioned as secretary of Texas Prairie Lands, Limited, beginning December 1, 1919; secretary to reorganization managers; representative for trustees of Staked Plains Trust, Limited, until 1924.

(Source: *Documents 1917*, Texas Land and Development Company Papers.)

FORBES, F. MURRAY

Company director. Served as director of Texas Land and Development Company, October 3, 1916, to February 25, 1919; was member of Boston law firm.

(Sources: Texas Land and Development Company, minutes, October 3, 1916, February 25, 1919, Texas Land and Development Company Papers; Peyton B. Randolph, oral interview, August 5, 1959, notes in Brunson Letters.)

FRY, C. W.

Company director. Served as director of Texas Land and Development Company, July 11, 1916, to October 3, 1916.

(Sources: Texas Land and Development Company, minutes, July 11, 1916, October 3, 1916, Texas Land and Development Company Papers.)

GRANT, JAMES WALKER

Company director. Born Showns, Tennessee, December 13, 1879; attended public schools in Showns; attended the University of Tennessee; received dental degree; married Mae Irwin Massey; daughter, Ina; belonged to Elk's Club, was Exalted Ruler; moved to Plainview, Texas, 1905.

Helped form Texas Land and Development Company with Milton Day

Biographies 189

Henderson (q.v.); served as director of Texas Land and Development Company, October 21, 1912, to December 7, 1912; left Plainview, 1921; had interest in Burke Burnette Oil Company, Wichita Falls, Texas; moved to Huntington Park, California, 1923; opened real-estate office and Grant and Hughes Investment Company; died in Los Angeles, California, 1931.

(Sources: Texas Land and Development Company, minutes, October 21, 1912, December 7, 1912, Texas Land and Development Company Papers; Mrs. W. D. Pulling, Grant's stepdaughter and only child, letter, October 16, 1959, Brunson Letters.)

HAMMOND, TOBE

Company master mechanic. Born Carter, Illinois, September 22, 1875; graduated from high school in Carter; worked for R. S. Charles (q.v.) in Illinois; joined Texas Land and Development Company as master mechanic, 1912; remained until 1946; retired in Plainview; deceased.

(Source: W. H. Hammond, Tobe's son, letter, September 4, 1959, Brunson Letters.)

HART, FRANCIS R.

Staked Plains Trust, Limited, trustee. Appointed trustee of Staked Plains Trust, Limited, December 12, 1914; was a resident of Milton, Massachusetts.

(Source: *Documents 1917*, pp. 179, 181, Texas Land and Development Company Papers.)

HELY-HUTCHINSON, MAURICE

Staked Plains Trust, Limited, trustee. Appointed trustee of Staked Plains Trust, Limited, February 12, 1920, to September 3, 1920.

(Sources: Staked Plains Trust, Limited, minutes, February 12, 1920, [I, 34, 40, 49], Texas Land and Development Company Papers.)

HENDERSON, MILTON DAY

Company director, president, vice-president, and general manager. Born Alis, Ohio, December 22, 1858; married; three children, Helen, Louise, and Karl; came from Kansas to Plainview; was land promoter and developer; had real-estate office; was active in many civic projects in Plainview; was member of BPOE; interested Dr. F. S. Pearson (q.v.) in forming Texas Land and Development Company; became company director, October 29, 1912, to August 14, 1913; president, October 29, 1912, to December 7, 1912; vice-president and general manager, December 7, 1912, to August 14, 1913; died March 29, 1924, Kansas City, Missouri.

(Sources: Texas Land and Development Company, minutes, October 29, 1912, December 7, 1912, August 14, 1913, Texas Land and Development Company Papers; Peyton B. Randolph to Dr. Seymour V. Connor, tape interview, April 8, 1958; R. S. Charles, letter, November 1, 1958, Brunson Letters; Mrs. W. D. Pulling, letter, October 29, 1959, Brunson Letters; *Plainview News*, December 20, 1912; Elk's Records, Plainview, Texas.)

HESS, JOE

Company sales manager. Employed as sales manager of Texas Land and Development Company, 1912 to 1915.

(Source: *Plainview Evening Herald*, May 21, 1915.)

HIRT, JULES

Company engineering consultant. Was engineer; headed the Pearson Engineering Corporation of New York; served as consultant to Texas Land and Development Company in selection and purchase of mechanical equipment, 1912 or 1913.

(Source: R. S. Charles, letter, November 1, 1958, Brunson Letters.)

HOLBROOK, WINFIELD

Company director, vice-president, and general manager. Born Watertown, New York, June 18, 1880; graduated from Waterloo High School; received degree in civil engineering, *magna cum laude*, University of Colorado, 1904; was member of Tau Beta Pi, honorary civil engineering fraternity; married Gertrude Allen Teague of Denver, Colorado, 1909; she died, 1910; married Agnes Punnel of Penrose, Colorado, 1913, two children, Raymond Braden and Elizabeth; Agnes Holbrook died, 1946; married Mrs. Amelia Bacon of Wichita, Kansas, 1954; moved to Plainview, 1919; was one of organizing members of Board of City Development; served on city council, 1923–1927; returned later for another two terms on council; served as president of Chamber of Commerce; was member of School Board; elected mayor, 1950, served two terms; was Mason, member of American Legion, and Kiwanan; was member of Unitarian Church although attended Presbyterian Church; was member and director of Texas Board of Water Engineers; was one of Plainview directors on Canadian River Municipal Water Authority; established branch of the Texas Section of American Society of Civil Engineering, 1952, and was director, 1953–1954; served on Panhandle-Plains Historical Society board.

Was field engineer performing surveys for railroads and reservoirs in

Biographies

Middle West, 1904–1909; was engineer for Beaver Park Land and Water Company, Penrose, Colorado, 1909–1913; entered private practice, 1913; became chief engineer for Garden City Sugar Beet Company, Deerfield, Kansas, 1916; entered Army Engineers' Corps as Captain, 1917, stationed at Fort Belvoir, Virginia, later at Camp Humphreys, Virginia; learned of Texas Land and Development Company while in Virginia; served as director and vice-president, February 25, 1919, to June 14, 1954; general manager, February 25, 1919, to February 9, 1948; treasurer, February 29, 1948, to June 14, 1954; considered an authority on Texas geology; worked with universities and colleges in conducting field trips, died August 25, 1956.

(Sources: Texas Land and Development Company, minutes, February 25, 1919, February 9, 1948, February 29, 1948, June 14, 1954, Texas Land and Development Company Papers; Information supplied by Holbrook's daughter, Mrs. L. R. Bain, Plainview, Texas.)

HUBBARD, CHARLES J.

Company director and president. Appointed director and president of Texas Land and Development Company, October 3, 1916, to February 25, 1919; was member of the Old Colony Trust, Boston.

(Sources: Texas Land and Development Company, minutes, October 3, 1916, February 25, 1919, Texas Land and Development Company Papers; R. S. Charles, letter, July 19, 1958, Brunson Letters.)

JONES, J. C.

Company carpenter crew foreman. Was member of original construction crew of Texas Land and Development Company, 1912; deceased.

(Source: Hanley Wasson, tape interview, August 19, 1959.)

KEITH, HENRY M.

Company director and president. Functioned as director and president of Texas Land and Development Company, February 25, 1919, to April 2, 1926; deceased.

(Source: Texas Land and Development Company, minutes, February 25, 1919, April 2, 1926, Texas Land and Development Company Papers.)

KEITH, MINOR COOPER

Staked Plains Trust, Limited, and Texas Prairie Lands, Limited, trustee, chairman of Reorganization Managers. Born January 19, 1848; attended private school; decided not to attend college; Episcopalian.

At sixteen worked in men's furnishing store, New York; quit to become lumber surveyor; at seventeen owned lumber business, Brooklyn; remained in this business four years; went to Padre Island, Texas, which was owned by his father, 1869; stayed for two years, raised cattle and hogs; became identified with railway construction, Costa Rica, 1872; organized United Fruit Company, 1899; was vice-president of Premier Gold Mining Company; president of Atlanta and St. Andrews Bay Railway Company, St. Andrews Bay Lumber Company, Guatemala Central Railroad Company, International Railway of Central America; director of Empire Trust Company; invested in Texas Land and Development Company through Empire Trust Company; appointed trustee of Staked Plains Trust, Limited, 1919–1929, and Texas Prairie Lands, Limited, 1916–1919; was chairman of Reorganization Managers, December, 1919; died June 14, 1929.

(Sources: *Who Was Who in America*, 1897–1942, I, 660; Samuel Crowther, *The Romance and Rise of the American Tropics*, p. 144; Peyton B. Randolph to Dr. Seymour V. Connor, tape interview, April 8, 1958; *Documents 1917,* Appendix, Texas Land and Development Company Papers.)

KLINGER, WALTER J.

Company secretary-treasurer. Born Shamokin, Pennsylvania, November 15, 1882; attended Northumberland County, Pennsylvania, schools; moved to Plainview, 1907; married Elizabeth West; no children; chief, Plainview Fire Department, 1909; business manager, high school band, 1920's; president Central Plains Council, Boy Scouts, 1930; first board of directors, Plainview YMCA; director of Young Business League; Exalted Ruler, Plainview Elk's Lodge; Mason; Shriner; Plainview Park Commissioner; clerk for Santa Fe Railroad after moving to Plainview (1907); promoted to agent, 1911; associated with P. E. Blasingame in B and K Confectionary, 1913; served as secretary-treasurer of Texas Land and Development Company, February 1915 to February 29, 1946; served seven months as sergeant, Company L, 4th Texas Infantry, 1916; died January 28, 1957.

(Sources: *Plainview Evening Herald*, January 28, 1957; Texas Land and Development Company, minutes, August 2, 1920, February 29, 1946, Texas Land and Development Company Papers.)

KRUEGER, A. M.

Company horticulturist. Joined Texas Land and Development Company as horticulturist, 1913.

(Source: *Hale County Herald*, August 12, 1913.)

Biographies 193

KUNESH, JOE

Company civil engineer. Graduated from University of Wisconsin; associated with Texas Land and Development Company as civil engineer around 1914 or 1915; left Plainview 1915; accepted position with Government Reclamation Service.

(Sources: *Plainview Evening Herald*, May 28, 1915; Keith Catto to Mrs. L. R. Bain, tape interview, May 31, 1958, Bain Files, Plainview.)

LONGSTRETH, JOHN WALTER

Company general manager. Born Williamsburgh or Hutchinson, Kansas; graduated Ames, Iowa, Agricultural College; married Mabel Purcell, 1897; no children; Presbyterian; Republican.

Worked with father on orchard demonstration farms; served Finney County, Kansas, farm agencies; moved to Plainview, 1915; became general manager of Texas Land and Development Company, November 1, 1915, and remained until October 7, 1916; moved to Yuma, Arizona, 1916; became County Agriculture Agent; worked on Citrus Project, Yuma; died April 28, 1949.

(Sources: Texas Land and Development Company, minutes, November 1, 1915, October 7, 1916, Texas Land and Development Company Papers; Virginia P. Hicks, letter, January 18, 1960, Brunson Letters.)

LORING, J. A.

Company master mechanic. Employed as master mechanic for Texas Land and Development Company, 1912.

(Source: A. B. De Loach, letter, November 25, 1958, Brunson Letters.)

LOWE, WILLIAM FREDERICK

Company superintendent of farms. Born Cass County, Iowa, 1881; moved to Kansas, 1912; worked for Garden City Sugar and Land Company, Garden City, Kansas, 1912–1919; met Winfield Holbrook (q.v.); moved to Plainview, April 1919; joined Texas Land and Development Company as superintendent of irrigated farm lands, 1919–1946; retired; lives in Plainview.

(Source: William F. Lowe, tape interview, July 12, 1958.)

MASON, W. H.

Company treasurer. Was from New York; civic-minded in Plainview; helped build up Episcopal Church's membership; sang basso in first Plainview opera, "Martha"; assistant secretary of Texas Land and Development Company, December 7, 1912, to December 18, 1915; treasurer, February

19, 1915, to December 18, 1915; after 1915 became Comptroller for J. C. Penney Department Stores; died before World War II.

(Sources: Texas Land and Development Company, minutes, December 7, 1912, February 19, 1915, December 18, 1915, Texas Land and Development Company Papers; Fred Watson, tape interview, July 12, 1958; *Plainview Evening Herald*, December 22, 1915, March 12, 1915; R. S. Charles, letter, July 19, 1958, Brunson Letters.)

MILLER, HARRY IRVING

Company director and president. Born Cleveland, Ohio; attended Russell's Military College, New Haven, Connecticut; Mount St. Mary's College, Emmetsburg, Maryland; Cornell University; received LL.D. from Mount St. Mary's College, 1909; May Burbank, first wife; Florence Neff, second wife; one son, Harry Irving, Jr.; instigator of reconnaissance survey in which R. S. Charles (q.v.) participated; was member of Old Colony Trust, Boston; was active investor and organizer of Texas Land and Development Company; directed early operations of the company; proposed lake be made in Plainview near railroad station; later brought in wildlife for project.

Was inspector of masonry and later assistant engineer of Pennsylvania lines, 1882–1885; engineer Pennsylvania lines, Indianapolis to Columbus and Richmond to Logansport, 1885–1888; division superintendent of Pennsylvania lines, Richmond, Indiana, 1888–1890, Louisville, Kentucky, 1890–1894; superintendent of Vandalia line, 1894–1901, later general manager, June 10, 1901, to December 15, 1903; general manager of Rock Island System, December 1903 to March 1905; vice-president, March 1, 1905, to November 15, 1906; president of the same line November 15, 1906, to November 30, 1909; receiver of Buffalo and Susquehanna Railroad, May 1910 to December 1915; vice-president Mexico N. W. Railways; president Madeira Company, Limited, September 1911 to December 1916; vice-president and general manager, Automatic Straight Air Brake Company; director and president of Texas Land and Development Company, December 7, 1912, to October 7, 1916; died April 22, 1930.

(Sources: Texas Land and Development Company, minutes, December 7, 1912, October 7, 1916, Texas Land and Development Company Papers; *Who Was Who in America* 1899–1942, I, 841; R. S. Charles, letter, September 14, 1959, Brunson Letters.)

MISE, MELVIN

Company truck driver. Born Lee County, Virginia, March 24, 1890;

Biographies

moved to Plainview, 1902; educated in Plainview public schools; joined Texas Land and Development Company as truck driver around 1916; since leaving the company has been in automobile business in Plainview.

(Source: Melvin Mise, tape interview, August 20, 1959.)

MOTLEY, J. LOTHROP

Company director and secretary. Was member of Old Colony Trust; became secretary of Texas Land and Development Company, February 6, 1916, until February 25, 1919; elected director, October 3, 1916, remained until February 25, 1919.

(Sources: Texas Land and Development Company, minutes, February 6, 1916, October 3, 1916, February 25, 1919; Peyton B. Randolph, oral interview, August 5, 1959, notes in Brunson Letters.)

MYERS, CHARLES FREDERICK

Company director and general manager. Born Allegheny, Pennsylvania, January 23, 1862; attended public schools in Ohio and small college nearby for two years; married Marguerite Raguet; no children; was Mason; affiliated with Methodist Church but attended Episcopal Church.

Became railroad dispatcher for Pennsylvania Railroad, 1902; worked in Chicago, Illinois, for CRT&P Railroad, 1904; sent to Davenport, Iowa, as chief clerk to division superintendent, 1907; later became superintendent of transportation and car accountant for Mexico Northwestern Railway Company; joined Texas Land and Development Company as general manager, October 7, 1916, remained until February 7, 1917; director, December 18, 1915, to July 11, 1916; reappointed director, October 3, 1916, remained until February 7, 1917; became general manager of Guantanamo and Western Railroad Company, Cuba, 1919; later became vice-president of International Railways of Central America, 1919; died June 1, 1946, in Atherton, California.

(Sources: Texas Land and Development Company, minutes, December 18, 1915, October 3, 1916, October 7, 1916, July 11, 1916, February 7, 1917, Texas Land and Development Company Papers; *Plainview Evening Herald*, December 11, 1915; Charles F. Myers to Peyton B. Randolph, letter, April 11, 1931, Randolph Files; Charles F. Myers to Peyton B. Randolph, letter, August 25, 1919, Randolph Files; Marguerite Raguet Myers, letter, November 19, 1959, Brunson Letters.)

NORMAN, BRADFORD, JR.

Staked Plains Trust, Limited, trustee. Was vice-president of Commercial

National Bank and Trust Company of New York; was elected trustee of Staked Plains Trust, Limited, November 9, 1942; died November 6, 1951.

(Sources: Staked Plains Trust, Limited, *Annual Report*, 1942, 1951, Texas Land and Development Company Papers.)

PALMER, BRADLEY W., JR.

Staked Plains Trust, Limited, trustee. Appointed trustee of Staked Plains Trust, Limited, December 12, 1914, remained until January 1920; was from Boston, Massachusetts.

(Source: *Documents 1917*, pp. 179, 181, Texas Land and Development Company Papers.)

PARTRIDGE, HUGH R.

Company director and secretary. Elected trustee of Staked Plains Trust, Limited, on September 3, 1920, remained until liquidation; was secretary of Texas Land and Development Company from unknown date in the late forties to June 14, 1954; appointed director of company, February 9, 1948, remained until June 14, 1954; later lawyer for H. H. Pike and Company, Inc.; deceased.

(Sources: Texas Land and Development Company, minutes, February 9, 1948, June 14, 1954, Texas Land and Development Company Papers; Staked Plains Trust, Limited, *Final Report*, 1955, Texas Land and Development Company Papers; Hugh R. Partridge, letter, September 8, 1959, Brunson Letters.)

PEARSON, FREDERICK STARK

Company director. Born Lowell, Massachusetts, July 3, 1861; attracted attention of teachers at Tufts College, which he entered in 1879; transferred to Massachusetts Institute of Technology for course in chemistry, 1880; returned to Tufts College, graduated, 1883; given three-year appointment as Walker Instructor in Mathematics and opportunity for further studies; married Mabel Ward; both drowned in sinking of *Lusitania* May 7, 1915; survived by two sons, Ward Edgerly and Fred, both engineers, and by daughter, Natalie, wife of Reginald Nicholson, manager of the *Times* (London); interest gained in irrigation project in Plainview by M. D. Henderson (q.v.); was through Pearson's foresight and energy that Texas Land and Development Company became a reality; started project in 1912; was interested in civic improvements for Plainview; often made suggestions when he visited Plainview.

Helped to develop a large number of power plants throughout the world; belonged to a large number of technical societies and clubs; became a trustee of Tufts College, 1900; was awarded the degree of Doctor of Science, 1900, and Doctor of Laws, 1905, by Tufts College.

(Sources: M. O. Chenoweth to Dr. Seymour V. Connor, letter, December 2, 1958, Texas Land and Development Company Papers; Texas Land and Development Company, minutes, October 21, 1912, October 5, 1915, Texas Land and Development Company Papers; *Hale County Herald*, April 17, 1913; R. S. Charles, letter, November 1, 1958, Brunson Letters.)

PEARSON, WARD EDGERLY

Company director. Born Boston, Massachusetts, November 8, 1887; attended Hotchkiss School, Lakeville, Connecticut, and Yale University, New Haven, Connecticut; married Helen Elise Weed; two sons; was assistant treasurer of Empire Trust Company, New York; became associated (through father, F. S. Pearson [q.v.]) with Texas Land and Development Company as director, October 5, 1915, to February 25, 1919; later involved in real estate in New York; died February 8, 1939, in London, England.

(Sources: Texas Land and Development Company, minutes, October 5, 1915, February 25, 1919, Texas Land and Development Company Papers; Mrs. Ward E. Pearson, letter, October 6, 1959, Brunson Letters.)

PERDUE, GEORGE TOLBERT

Company treasurer and assistant secretary. Born Erath County, Texas; attended Plainview public schools; moved to Plainview, 1902; married, 1912; worked for Guaranty State Bank, Tyler, Texas, 1912–1914; moved back to Plainview; worked at Third National Bank, 1914; accepted position as assistant secretary and treasurer with Texas Land and Development Company, December 6, 1916, to August 1918; called into service in World War I, 1918; after war was chief clerk and traveling auditor for American Smelting and Refining Company; returned to Plainview as public accountant; resides in Plainview.

(Source: George T. Perdue, tape interview, July 14, 1958.)

PHENIS, GUY HOWARD

Company cook for construction and drilling crews. Born Emporia, Kansas; attended grammar school and part of high school, Guthrie, Oklahoma; moved to Canadian, Texas; owned café; moved to Plainview, 1910; was head cook at Ware Hotel for two years; worked for ten months as cook for construction and drilling crews for Texas Land and Development

Company around 1912; worked for city bakery, Plainview, fourteen years; later owner of bakery, Lockney, Texas, until 1947; resides in Lockney.
(Source: Guy H. Phenis, letter, September 6, 1959, Brunson Letters.)

PIPKIN, JAMES WALKUP

Company director and general manager (acting). Born Bristol, Texas, July 10, 1895; attended grammar school and high school, Canyon, Texas; attended Metropolitan Business College, Dallas, Texas; married Carolyn Jordan, 1906; moved to Plainview, 1907; was member of BPOE and Exalted Ruler; member of Masonic Lodge, Royal Arch and Master Mason; helped organize the Elks' Lodge in Huntington Park, California; Methodist.

Was accountant for father's general merchandise store, Canyon, Texas; worked as surveyor in Yuma, Arizona; established men's furnishings store, Plainview, 1907; joined Texas Land and Development Company as superintendent of dry-land farms to 1916; was director and acting general manager, July 11, 1916, to October 3, 1916; became manager of livestock ranch west of Plainview; moved to California, August 1918; died September 20, 1921, in Los Angeles, California.

(Sources: Texas Land and Development Company, minutes, July 11, 1916, October 3, 1916, Texas Land and Development Company Papers; Mrs. Carolyn Pipkin, letter, September 16, 1959, Brunson Letters.)

PRICE, HENRY B.

Staked Plains Trust, Limited, trustee. Elected trustee of Staked Plains, Trust Limited, November 8, 1929; died October 2, 1938.

(Source: Staked Plains Trust, minutes, October 28, 1938, [I, 177], Texas Land and Development Company Papers.)

RANDOLPH, HALBERT CYRUS

Company director and legal counselor; Texas Prairie Lands, Limited, trustee. Born September 22, 1861, Austin, Texas; son of Cyrus Halbert Randolph, legislator and treasurer of state of Texas, 1858–1865; graduated from Bickler Military Academy, Austin, Texas; enrolled in first class of law, University of Texas, graduated with highest honors; married; son, Peyton B. (q.v.); moved to Plainview, 1900; envisioned fertile fields in Plainview area; aided in bringing in syndicate to develop area; represented a definite figure in legal, educational, and Masonic orders of his day; was Prohibitionist and Democrat.

First practiced in Coleman City, Texas; moved law practice to Plainview 1900–1921; became trustee of Texas Prairie Lands, Limited, 1912; became director of Texas Land and Development Company, August 14, 1913, to October 3, 1916; appointed member of Commission Appeals, Supreme Court, by Governor Neff, Austin, Texas, 1921; returned to Panhandle to serve as Associate Justice on Court of Civil Appeals, Seventh District of Texas, Amarillo; died April 19, 1932, in Amarillo, Texas.

(Sources: Texas Land and Development Company, minutes, August 14, 1913, October 3, 1916, Texas Land and Development Company Papers; Mrs. Peyton B. Randolph, letter, March 20, 1960, Brunson Letters; *Plainview Evening Herald*, April 19, 1932.)

RANDOLPH, PEYTON BEAUMONT

Company legal counselor, assistant secretary-treasurer, secretary. Born May 24, 1888, Coleman, Texas; attended private school (his aunt's, Anna Randolph); Howard Payne College, Brownwood, Texas; graduated from Austin Male Academy, Austin, Texas, 1907; attended University Law School, Austin, three years; married George Alice May, July 23, 1912, Plainview; one daughter, Margaret Ann Randolph Smith; served in William J. Burns Law Office, Fort Worth, Texas, 1907; later joined father, H. C. Randolph (q.v.), forming firm of Randolph and Randolph, Plainview; was legal counsel for Texas Land and Development Company, 1912 to liquidation; served as assistant secretary-treasurer, August 8, 1940, to February 29, 1948; served as secretary, 1948; memberships in County, District, State, and American Bar Associations; member of the American Judicature Society; served fourteen years as vice-president and president of Texas Judicial Council; rewrote Texas Statutes on Business and Corporations as member of State Bar Committee; represented the Judicial Council on State Bar Committee that rewrote the Probate Laws of Texas; served in St. Mary's Episcopal Church, Plainview, as Junior and Senior Warden; Chamber of Commerce; charitable organizations; Plainview School Board; deceased.

(Sources: Texas Land and Development Company, minutes, August 8, 1940, February 9, 1948, February 29, 1948; Mrs. P. B. Randolph, letter, March 20, 1960, Brunson Letters.)

ROGERS, CLARENCE

Company trouble shooter. Born Plainview, Texas, August 8, 1909; attended Plainview schools; worked as mechanic for father prior to joining Texas Land and Development Company; trained as mechanic by his father and his uncle, Homer Rook (q.v.); worked for Texas Land and Development Company 1925–1932 as mechanic; since leaving Texas Land and

Development Company in 1932 has worked for Shook Battery Company and Phillips Battery Company; served in World War II; returned to Phillips Battery Company after the war; in 1948 established the Rogers Brake and Electric Company in cooperation with his brothers; presently resides in Plainview.

(Source: Clarence Rogers, tape interview, August 21, 1959, Southwest Collection.)

ROOK, HOMER

Company maintenance engineer. Born July 5, 1894, Crockett, Texas; attended public schools and Seth Ward Methodist College, Plainview; joined Texas Land and Development Company as maintenance engineer for pumping plants, 1913–1918; farmed in Plainview; then went to California; returned to Plainview in 1926; worked for company again until 1943; presently resides in Plainview.

(Source: Homer Rook, tape interview, August 28, 1959.)

SLATON, JOHN HENRY

Texas Prairie Lands, Limited, trustee; original company land titles in his name. Born February 12, 1867, Nenden, Louisiana; married Sallie B. Dyer; three children, Mrs. Bob Hooper (Plainview), Dyer Slaton (Plainview), Nancy Carter (deceased); first irrigation well in Plainview area dug on his property.

Drove cattle across site of Plainview when sixteen; worked for XIT and Yellow House; established First National Bank, Plainview; gave Will Rogers first job in Amarillo, cattle drive from Amarillo to Kansas; did not remember this incident but Will Rogers did; Rogers sent Slaton tickets to a performance in Amarillo; trustee, Texas Prairie Lands, Limited, 1912; died June 6, 1926.

(Sources: Peyton B. Randolph to Dr. Seymour V. Connor, tape interview, April 8, 1958; Mr. and Mrs. Bob Hooper, daughter and son-in-law of John Henry Slaton, oral interview, July 5, 1960; R. S. Charles, letter, July 19, 1958, Brunson Letters; *Hale County Herald*, April 24, 1913.)

TREUB, A. M.

Company director. Was member of Old Colony Trust of Boston; was secretary of Texas Prairie Lands, Limited; was director of Texas Land and Development Company, December 7, 1912 to October 3, 1916.

(Sources: Peyton B. Randolph, oral interview, August 5, 1959; Brunson Letters; *Documents 1917*, p. 83, Texas Land and Development Company

Biographies

Papers; Texas Land and Development Company, minutes, December 7, 1912, October 3, 1916, Texas Land and Development Company Papers.)

WASSON, HANLEY

Company superintendent of all construction. Born Smithville, Arkansas, August 11, 1885; moved to Plainview, 1898; graduated from Plainview high school; began occupation as carpenter around 1905; finished first building in Slaton, Texas, under the employment of M. D. Henderson (q.v.); later hired to work for Texas Land and Development Company, September 1, 1912, to 1917; was superintendent of all construction; then farmed in Plainview where he now lives.

(Source: Hanley Wasson, tape interview, August 19, 1959.)

WATSON, FRED

Company superintendent of dry-land farms. Born near Lexington, Tennessee, 1869; moved to Texas, 1881; moved to Plainview, 1907; worked in lumber; was law enforcement officer; worked as field superintendent of dry-land farms of Texas Land and Development Company, August 1914 to September 1919; farmed in Plainview; deceased.

(Source: Fred Watson, tape interview, July 12, 1958.)

WHITNEY, HENRY F.

Company director. Was member of Empire Trust Company; trustee of Staked Plains Trust, Limited, March 1928 to January 31, 1956, liquidation; elected director of Texas Land and Development Company, May 14, 1942, to June 14, 1954.

(Sources: Peyton B. Randolph, oral interview, August 5, 1959, Brunson Letters; Staked Plains Trust, Limited, *Final Report*, 1955, Texas Land and Development Company Papers; Texas Land and Development Company, minutes, May 14, 1942, June 14, 1954, Texas Land and Development Company Papers; Peyton B. Randolph to William F. Feeney, letter, March 19, 1928, Randolph Files, Plainview.)

WILLIAMS, WILLIAM J.

Company chief engineer. Born Johnson County, Texas; mother taught to read, write, and work long division; self-educated thereafter; only one year of formal education; taught school; was surveyor; received employment as chief engineer with Texas Land and Development Company through H. C. Randolph (q.v.), March 1916–1917; became county surveyor; since 1919 has been a state surveyor; now lives in Plainview.

(Source: W. J. Williams, tape interview, August 22, 1959.)

ZEHNDER, CHARLES H.

Prairie Lands Trust, Limited, and Staked Plains Trust, Limited, trustee. Was trustee of Prairie Lands Trust, Limited, December 1, 1916, to December 1, 1919; was trustee of Staked Plains Trust, Limited, February 12, 1920, to December 26, 1927, when he died.

(Sources: *Documents 1917*, p. 233, and Reorganization Agreement, Appendix, Texas Land and Development Company Papers; Staked Plains Trust, Limited, minutes, February 12, 1920, [I, 39–40], Texas Land and Development Company Papers; Staked Plains Trust, Limited, *Annual Report*, 1927, Texas Land and Development Company Papers.)

APPENDIX II

OFFICERS OF THE TEXAS LAND AND DEVELOPMENT COMPANY

Below is a list of the Texas Land and Development Company officers, including presidents, vice-presidents, general managers, secretaries, treasurers, and directors. The first date following the officer's name indicates the official date on which he was employed; the second, the official date on which his services with the company were terminated. The official dates and the actual dates of employment and termination of services were not necessarily the same. Because there are no minutes for the year 1918 the list is probably not complete.

Presidents of the Texas Land and Development Company

Milton Day Henderson . . . . October 29, 1912–December 7, 1912
(resigned)
Harry Irving Miller . . . . . December 7, 1912–October 7, 1916
(voted out)
Charles J. Hubbard . . . . . October 7, 1916–February 25, 1919
(voted out)
Henry M. Keith . . . . . . February 25, 1919–April 2, 1926
(deceased)

Company Officers

William F. Feeney . . . . . April 2, 1926–January 10, 1942
  (deceased)
Henry F. Whitney . . . . . . May 14, 1942–June 14, 1954
  (corporation dissolved)

General Managers of the Texas Land and Development Company

Milton Day Henderson . . . . December 7, 1912–August 14, 1913
  (resigned)
Robert S. Charles . . . . . . August 14, 1915–November 1, 1915
  (voted out)
John W. Longstreth . . . . . November 1, 1915–October 7, 1916
  (voted out)
Charles F. Myers . . . . . . October 7, 1916–February 7, 1917
  (resigned)
Clyde E. Craig . . . . February 7, 1917–February 25, 1919
  (voted out)
Winfield Holbrook . . . . . February 25, 1919–February 9, 1948
  (no mention of a general manager after February 9, 1948)

Vice-Presidents of the Texas Land and Development Company

Robert S. Charles . . . . . . October 29, 1912–December 7, 1912
  (resigned)
Milton Day Henderson . . . . December 7, 1912–August 14, 1913
  (resigned)
Walter S. Ayres . . . . August 14, 1913–October 7, 1916
  (voted out)
Charles F. Myers . . . . . . October 7, 1916–February 7, 1917
  (resigned)
Clyde E. Craig . . . . February 7, 1917–February 25, 1919
  (voted out)
Winfield Holbrook . . . . . February 25, 1919–June 14, 1954
  (corporation dissolved)

Secretary-Treasurers of the Texas Land and Development Company

W. H. Mason . . . . October 29, 1912–December 7, 1912
  (resigned)

Appendix II

SECRETARIES

A. M. Treub . . . . December 7, 1912–October 7, 1916
Ass't. Secy. W. H. Mason . . . December 7, 1912–December 18, 1915 (resigned)
Ass't. Secy. Charles F. Myers . . December 18, 1915–July 11, 1916 (resigned)
Ass't. Secy. George B. Doubleday . . . . . July 11, 1916–December 6, 1916 (resigned)
J. Lothrop Motley . . . . . . October 7, 1916–February 25, 1919
Ass't. Secy. George T. Perdue . . . . December 6, 1916–February 25, 1919

TREASURERS

U. de B. Daly . . . . December 7, 1912–February 19, 1915 (resigned)
W. H. Mason . . . . February 19, 1915–December 18, 1915 (resigned)
Charles F. Myers . . . . . . December 18, 1915–July 11, 1916 (resigned)
George B. Doubleday . . . . July 11, 1916, and October 7, 1916, to December 6, 1916 (resigned)
George T. Perdue . . . . . . December 6, 1916–February 25, 1919

SECRETARY-TREASURERS *(after February 25, 1919)*

William F. Feeney . . . . . February 25, 1919–May 12, 1919 (resigned)
A. B. DeLoach . . . . May 12, 1919–August 2, 1920 (resigned)
W. J. Klinger . . . . August 2, 1920–February 29, 1948 (retired)

SECRETARIES *(after February 29, 1948)*

(Note that records are incomplete here)
Peyton B. Randolph . . . . . February 9, 1948–?
Hugh R. Partridge . . . . . . ?–June 14, 1954

TREASURER *(after February 29, 1948)*

Winfield Holbrook . . . . . February 29, 1948–June 14, 1954

Company Officers 205

Directors of the Texas Land and Development Company

Robert S. Charles . . . . . . October 21, 1912–October 5, 1915
 (voted out)
Milton Day Henderson . . . . October 21, 1912–August 14, 1913
 (resigned)
W. H. Mason . . . . October 21, 1912–December 18, 1915
 (resigned)
James Walker Grant . . . . . October 21, 1912–December 7, 1912
 (resigned)
Frederick Stark Pearson . . . . December 7, 1912–May 7, 1915
 (deceased)
Harry Irving Miller . . . . . December 7, 1912–October 3, 1916
 (voted out)
A. M. Treub . . . . December 7, 1912–October 3, 1916
 (voted out)
Halbert C. Randolph . . . . . August 14, 1913–October 3, 1916
 (voted out)
Ward E. Pearson. . . . . . . October 5, 1915–February 25, 1919
 (voted out)
R. B. Conover . . . . October 5, 1915–June 7, 1916
 (resigned)
Charles F. Myers . . . . . . December 18, 1915–July 11, 1916
 (resigned)
R. Kenny . . . . June 7, 1916–July 11, 1916
 (resigned)
C. W. Fry . . . . June 11, 1916–October 3, 1916
 (voted out)
James W. Pipkin . . . . . . June 11, 1916–October 3, 1916
 (voted out)
N. W. Cabot . . . . October 3, 1916–February 25, 1919
 (voted out)
F. Murray Forbes . . . . . . October 3, 1916–February 25, 1919
 (voted out)
Charles J. Hubbard . . . . . October 3, 1916–February 25, 1919
 (voted out)
J. Lothrop Motley . . . . . . October 3, 1916–February 25, 1919
 (voted out)

Charles F. Myers ...... October 3, 1916–February 7, 1917
(second term) (resigned)
Clyde E. Craig .... February 7, 1917–February 25, 1919
(voted out)
Henry M. Keith .... February 25, 1919–April 2, 1926
(deceased)
Winfield Holbrook ..... February 25, 1919–June 14, 1954
(corporation dissolved)
William F. Feeney ..... February 25, 1919–May 12, 1919
(resigned)
A. B. DeLoach .... May 12, 1919–August 2, 1920
(resigned)
Walter J. Klinger ..... August 2, 1920–February 9, 1948
(voted out)
William F. Feeney ..... April 2, 1926–January 10, 1942
(second term) (deceased)
Henry F. Whitney ..... May 14, 1942–June 14, 1954
(corporation dissolved)
Hugh R. Partridge ..... February 9, 1948–June 14, 1954
(corporation dissolved)

APPENDIX III

INVESTORS BEFORE 1919

Below is a list of the holders of securities issued by the Texas Prairie Lands, Limited, in 1912, 1914, and 1915, and by its subsidiary, the Prairie Lands Trust, Limited, in 1916. Holders of these securities, when they were called in during the reorganization of 1919, were issued certain liquidation securties according to the following plan:

Original Holding	*Date Issued*	*New Holding*
Texas Prairie Lands, Limited, First Mortgage Bonds	1912	7 shares Staked Plains Trust per £100 note

Investors before 1919

Texas Prairie Lands, Limited, Prior Lien Notes	1914	Class A Liquidation Certificates
Texas Prairie Lands, Limited, Class A Profit-Sharing Certificates	1915	Class A Liquidation Certificates
Texas Prairie Lands, Limited, Class B Profit-Sharing Certificates	1915	Canceled
Texas Prairie Lands, Limited, Class C Profit-Sharing Certificates	1915	Canceled
Prairie Lands Trust, Limited, Trust Certificates	1916	Class B Liquidation Certificates

HOLDERS OF SECURITIES

Names	First Mortgage Bonds	Prior Lien Notes	Class A	Class B	Class C	Prairie Lands Trust Limited
			Profit-Sharing Certificates			
American Investment Trust Co.	...	$25,000	$6,250	...	$18,750	...
Anglo-Austrian Bank	£10,000	...	...	...	...	...
Baldwin, L. W.	2,500	6,250	1,562.50	...	4,687.50	$17,692.32
Bank of Scotland	20,000	...	...	...	...	...
Benson, R. & Co.	20,000	19,500	4,875	...	14,625	...
Bonn & Co.	10,000	9,800	2,450	...	7,350	...
Bradley, R. M.	...	...	1,000	$1,000	...	...
British Investment Trust Ltd.	20,000	20,000	5,000	...	15,000	...
British Linen Bank	3,000	...	...	...	...	...
Brown, M. J.	11,000	27,500	6,875	...	20,625	43,846.14
Brown, R. C.	5,000	...	...	...	...	...
Cabot, H. B.	...	25,000	6,250	6,250	...	...
Cabot, H. B., Trustee	...	25,000	6,250	6,250	...	...
Cabot, Lyman, Putnam & Bradley, Trustees	...	2,000	...	...	...	...
Cabot, Norman W.	...	5,000	1,250	1,250	...	...
Caisse-Hypothécaire Sud-Américaine	20,000	...	...	...	...	...
Caledonian Trust Co. Ltd.	3,000	3,000	750	...	2,250	...

Appendix III

Names	First Mortgage Bonds	Prior Lien Notes	Class A	Class B	Class C	Prairie Lands Trust Limited
			Profit-Sharing Certificates			
Canadian Bank of Commerce	£17,000	...	...	...	...	...
Canadian Bank of Commerce (a/c Dr. Pearson)	14,000	...	...	...	...	...
Carey, William	...	$10,000	...	...	...	...
Carlisle & Waller	25,000	...	...	...	...	...
Chamberlin, T.	...	5,000	$1,250	$1,250	...	...
Clydesdale Bank	12,000	...	...	...	...	...
Cox Bros. Ltd.	2,000	...	...	...	...	...
Cox, E. (truseees of)	...	2,000	500	...	$1,500	...
Crawford, Alice I.	...	4,000	...	...	...	...
Dominion Securities Corp.	30,000	...	...	...	...	...
Dunn, Fisher & Co.	10,000	...	...	...	...	...
Dunn, Fisher & Co. (a/c Demme)	4,000	...	...	...	...	...
Dunn, J. H.	10,000	...	...	...	...	$15,384.60
Empire Trust Co.	20,000	...	...	...	...	...
English, W. H.	2,500	6,250	1,562.50	...	4,687.50	17,692.32
Fearing, Mrs. H.	...	5,000	1,250	1,250	...	...
First Scottish-American Trust Co. Ltd.	3,000	3,000	750	...	2,250	...
Fleming, R., & Co.	70,000	...	...	...	...	...
Forbes, Isabel C.	...	10,000	2,500	2,500	...	...
Frost's R., Sons	...	5,000	...	...	...	...
Gilroy, Alexander	2,000	2,000	500	...	1,500	...
Goldsmith, Kahn & Teitsch	25,000	...	...	...	...	...
Gow, Walter	5,000	...	...	...	...	...
Gross, Mrs.	2,000	...	...	...	...	...
Grundwig, C. J.	5,000	...	...	...	...	...
Hambro, C. J., & Son	25,000	...	...	...	...	...
Hardenbeigh, C. M.	...	2,000	...	...	...	...
Harrsen, Harro	5,000	...	...	...	...	...
Hartwell, H.	...	500	125	...	375	...

Investors before 1919

Names	First Mortgage Bonds	Prior Lien Notes	Class A	Class B	Class C	Prairie Lands Trust Limited
			____Profit-Sharing Certificates____			
Haserick, F. W. & H. W.	...	$1,000	...	...	...	...
Hecksher, A.	...	...	...	...	...	$50,000.00
Hill, Barlow & Homans	...	30,000	$7,500	$7,500	...	...
Hirt, L. J.	£4,000	10,000	5,200	...	$7,200	...
Hubbard, Alice D.	...	5,000	1,250	1,250	...	...
Hubbard, H. Malcolm	3,000	2,000	500	...	1,500	...
Investment Trust Corp. Ltd.	20,000	20,000	5,000	...	15,000	...
Jones, H. V. F.	2,000	...	...	...	...	...
Keith, M. C.	25,000	25,000	6,250	...	18,750	91,923.04
Kleinwort Sons & Co.	10,000	9,800	2,450	...	7,350	...
Lane, Sir Hugh	20,000	...	...	...	...	...
Law Debenture Corp.	10,000	...	...	...	...	...
Leary, G.	...	...	...	...	...	25,000.00
MacKenzie, Alex.	10,000	...	...	...	...	...
Mercantile Inv. & General Trust Co. Ltd.	...	9,800	2,450	...	7,350	...
Messel, L., & Co.	30,000	...	...	...	...	...
Miller, H. I.	...	...	2,500	...	7,500	...
Minot, Sedgwick	...	2,000	...	...	...	...
Morgan, Grenfell & Co.	25,000	25,000	6,250	...	18,750	...
National Bank of Scotland	20,000	...	...	...	...	...
Neuman, Luebeck & Co.	25,000	...	...	...	...	...
Northern American Trust Co. Ltd.	5,000	5,000	1,250	...	3,750	...
Palmer, B. W.	10,000	10,000	5,750	...	...	15,384.62
Palmer, B. W., Trustee	...	...	...	...	...	50,000.00
Parshall, H. F.	2,000	2,000	500	...	1,500	...
Pearson, F. S., Exrs. of, & J. H. Dunn	5,000	...	...	...	...	...

Names	First Mortgage Bonds	Prior Lien Notes	Class A	Class B	Class C	Prairie Lands Trust Limited
			Profit-Sharing Certificates			
Porter, T.	£4,000	...	...	...	...	...
Preston, A. W.	5,000	$25,000	$6,250	...	$18,750	$25,000.00
Prince, F. H., & Co.	10,000	25,000	6,250	...	18,750	30,769.24
Reeves, Whitburn & C.	10,000	...	...	...	...	...
Revelstoke, Lord	...	9,800	2,450	...	7,350	...
Ridgeway, Thomas, Trustee	...	10,000	...	...	...	...
St. Leger Trust	20,000	...	...	...	...	...
St. Oswald, Lord	10,000	9,800	2,450	...	7,350	...
Scott, Hugh D.	...	...	2,500	$2,500	...	...
Scottish Western Investment Co. Ltd.	7,000	7,000	1,750	...	5,250	...
Schermerhorn, S. G.	...	...	...	...	...	10,000.00
Second Scottish American Trust Co. Ltd.	4,000	4,000	1,000	...	3,000	...
Seligman Brothers	10,000	5,000	1,250	...	3,750	...
Smiles, W.	3,000	...	...	...	...	...
Stockton, P.	...	5,000	1,250	1,250	...	...
Talmadge, H. P.	2,000	5,000	1,250	...	3,750	16,153.86
Third Scottish American Trust Co. Ltd.	4,000	4,000	1,000	...	3,000	...
Trowbridge, E. D.	2,000	...	...	...	...	...
Universal Securities Trust Co. Ltd.	3,000	...	...	...	...	...
Walmsley, W. M.	5,000	...	...	...	...	...
Walter, Jacob, & Co.	8,000	...	...	...	...	...
Warren, Frances K.	...	5,000	1,250	1,250	...	...
Wesselhoeft, W. F.	...	1,000	...	...	...	...
Whitburn, C. W. S.	10,000	...	...	...	...	...
Williams Deacons Bank	20,000	...	...	...	...	...
Zehnder, C. H.	2,000	5,000	1,250	...	3,750	16,153.86
	£763,000	$500,000	$125,000	$33,500	$257,250	$425,000.00

APPENDIX IV

THE LAND AND ITS PEOPLE

The Texas Land and Development Company, as operating agent for the Plainview enterprise, was responsible for selling over sixty thousand acres of land in Hale, Floyd, and Swisher counties. A brief history of each sale's transaction is presented here, in so far as the records are available. Records pertaining to the early sales were somewhat more detailed than the records of the later ones, as there was often correspondence between the company and the purchaser concerning the improvements to be placed on the land. Correspondence was also plentiful between the company and the early purchasers who were unable to meet payments on their property, often causing them to reconvey to the company. It was evident that most of the purchasers who defaulted had sincerely tried to pay their obligations to the company. There was equal evidence that the company was very benevolent in allowing extensions on payments and, at times, refunds, although it was not legally bound to do so. Records of land sales in the later years, which represented the bulk of sales, were not as detailed as earlier records, because the land was not developed and there was seldom a problem involved in payment.

All pertinent information regarding the sale of the land has been included in the table that follows. Many of the files were incomplete and furnished only the barest facts. Any vacant space in the table indicates that information was not available.

Purchaser	Residence*	Acres Purchased (Date)	County	Amount of Purchase (in Dollars)	Down Payment (in Dollars)	Amount Due with Delivery of Deed (in Dollars)	Annual Payments Remaining and/or Special Arrangements	Purchaser of Notes Still Financed by TL&D (Date)	Next Disposition (Date)	Date TL&D Fully Paid	Dev. and/or File No.
Alewine, V.	Hedley	96.8 (1-3-44)	Hale	6,600	500	2,100	10				Dev. 3-7, File 105
Alford, Morris W.†	Grapevine	80 (9-15-45)	Floyd	10,200	500	2,700	10	Great Southern Life Insurance Co. (1-13-47)		1-13-47	Dev. 6, 94, File 77
Anderson, Carl B.	Wausa, Neb.	80‡ (12-10-15)	Hale	10,000	100		$900 by 1-10-16 $250 by 1-10-17 12		Reconveyed (c. 1918)		Dev. 3-5, File 78
Anderson, Joe	Lockney	402.5 (8-4-20)	Floyd	25,156.25	1,250	3,756.25	10		Canceled due to company error		Files 110, 47
Anderson, Joe	Lockney	160 (9-7-20)	Floyd	10,000	500	2,250	10	Part to Ira Simpson; part to E. M. Randolph (c. 1921)	40 acres to C. O. Simpson (1926) Reconveyed (11-3-27)	5-28-27	Files 110, 47
Anderson, Joe	Lockney	240 (9-7-20)	Floyd	15,000	750	2,250	10		Reconveyed (1926)		Files 110, 47
Anderson, Joe	Lockney	160 (11-1-45)	Floyd	5,760	500	Balance					File 33
Anderson, Sever	Wynot, Neb.	74.52 (11-5-15)	Hale	9,315	100				Canceled for nonpayment (7-29-16)		Dev. 3-24
Ashburn, D. W.†	Louviers, Colo.	320	Hale							4-24-48	File 13-B
Ashburn, D. W.†	Louviers, Colo.	640	Hale								File 56
Axtell, Harrison F.	Kress	160 (6-26-46)	Swisher	6,400	500	2,500	10			12-7-49	Files 95, 96
Barbian, Peter	Kress	.420 (5-5-43)	Swisher	13,440	300	6,700	Remainder in 60 days	Federal Land Bank		7-3-43	Files 20, 15
Barton, Clayton	Flomot	220 (11-24-42)	Hale	12,060	600	3,960	10				File 133
Bass, E. O.	Kress	160 (1-29-30)	Swisher	6,400	500		10				File 131
Beebee, C. L. and Fannie†		86 (6-5-44)	Floyd	5,500	2,500		10				File 136
Bell, C. C.	Hale Center	160 (12-8-45)	Hale	8,640	200	1,240	10	Traveler's Insurance Co. (9-10-46)		9-10-46	Dev. 64, File 25-B

Name	Location	Acres (date)	County					Notes	Date	File
Belt, J.R., Jr.‡	Lockney	80 (9-6-43)	Floyd	6,000	500	1,780	6		11-23-44	File 128
Berlin, J.F.	Abernathy	160 (2-15-43)	Hale	4,480	500	2,380		Remainder to be paid by 4-23-43	2-17-43	File 10-B
Berner, Bernhard C. H.	Kress	320 (5-23-30)	Swisher	12,000		1,000	10	Canceled for nonpayment (1931)		File 37-A
Billings, Archie	Erie, Penn.	240‡ (8-9-15)	Floyd	20,900	400		8	$2,212.50 by 10-16-15 $2,612.50 by 10-16-16		Dev. 24, Files 348, 76, 112
Boden, John‡	Duluth, Minn.	160 (c. 10-20-16)	Swisher					Reconveyed or repossessed Reconveyed (1920)		Dev. 3-1
Boedeker, T. H.	Lockney	320 (7-28-20)	Floyd	20,250	1,000	5,250	10			File 125
Borum, Roy E.	Kress	320 (11-6-45)	Swisher	11,680	200	6,480	10	Fed. Land Bank (1946)	3-16-46	File 20
Borum, Roy E.	Kress	320 (6-29-46)	Swisher	13,200	500	7,700	10	Tulia Farm Loan Assoc. (1946 or 1947)	1-13-47	Files 121, 122
Bostic, Tom	Plainview	320 (5-7-43)	Hale	8,000	300	3,700		Remainder to be paid by 7-7-43		File 29
Bowman, Harley D.†	Lockney	120 (11-15-45)	Floyd	7,100	500	1,000	10	Franklin Life Insurance Co. (May 1947)	1947	Dev. 80, Files 47, 60
Bowman, J.R.	Norborne, Mo.	80‡ (5-1-15)	Floyd	10,000	1,500		8	$1,000 by end of first year;		Dev. 80, Files 60, 67, 76
Bowman, J.R.	Lockney	80 (8-25-20)	Floyd	4,800	250	950	10	Reconveyed (12-31-26)		Dev. 80, File 47-A
Bradley, H. C.	Plainview	160 (9-12-30)	Hale	11,200			10	Reconveyed (5-25-25)		File 25-A
Branham, G. H., Jr.	Plainview	160 (3-28-29)	Hale	6,400	200	1,000	10			File 99
Brown, A. W.	Scarsdale, N.Y.	1,280‡ (11-26-45)	Hale	51,200	5,000	12,200	10	Note sold through Dallas Exchange (c. 1947)	2-5-47	Dev. 41, 42, 43
Brown, A. W.	Scarsdale, N.Y.	600 (12-3-45)	Hale	30,000	3,000	6,000	10		1-31-47	Files 138, 152
Bruns, Leslie	Clovis, N.M.	80 (11-12-43)	Floyd	6,000	500	1,000	10	Traveler's Insurance Co. (10-1-48)	10-1-48	File 77

† The person or persons were not the original purchasers of part or all of this land.
* All places listed are located in Texas unless otherwise specified.
‡ This was to be a standard development by the company and/or by some special arrangement.

Purchaser	Residence*	Acres Purchased (Date)	County	Amount of Purchase (in Dollars)	Down Payment (in Dollars)	Amount Due with Delivery of Deed (in Dollars)	Annual Payments Remaining and/or Special Arrangements	Purchaser of Notes Still Financed by TI & D (Date)	Next Disposition (Date)	Date TI & D Fully Paid	Dev. and/or File No.
Buchanan, A. M. and J. E.	Plainview	640 (8-27-37)	Hale	16,000	200	Remainder				c.9-15-37	File 8
Burch, Lela A.	Plainview	320 (11-10-42)	Hale	10,400	1,000	Remainder					File 40
Burnett, R. O.‡	Plainview	320 (6-12-46)	Hale	13,500	500	Remainder					File 86
Campbell, J. H. and A. V.	Lockney	80 (4-6-44)	Floyd	5,650	500	Remainder				4-7-44	Dev. 51, File 85
Carlson, C. Axel	Minneapolis, Minn.	80‡ (4-22-16)	Swisher	10,400	100		$1,200 by 12-1-16 12		Reconveyed (3-18-19)		Dev. 3-29
Carthel, W. A.	Lockney	80 (1-11-28)	Floyd	6,400	500		10.				Dev. 20, File 115
Castleberry, C. C.‡	Plainview	320 (9-10-45)	Hale	13,490	9,600			Fed. Land Bank (1946)		1946	File 39
Castleberry, C. H.	Plainview	80§ (12-3-43)	Hale	2,800	200	600	10	Fed. Land Bank (3-18-44)		3-18-44	File 102
Cates, E. O.	Quanah	640 (6-10-44)	Hale	23,680	500	Remainder				7-11-44	File 103
Cates, E. O.	Plainview	160 (6-29-46)	Swisher	6,000	500	Remainder					Dev. 3-44, File 122
Chaddick, J. S.	Plainview	160§ (8-5-20)	Hale	9,920	500	1,980	10		Reconveyed (12-19-25)		File 86
Clark, R. H.	Kress	160 (6-26-46)	Swisher	6,400	500	1,500	10			12-24-46	File 96
Cogdell, A. B.	Wellington	200 (2-21-28)	Hale	15,000	500	9,500	10			4-12-29	File 138
Collins, E. M.	Floydada	320 (2-5-43)	Floyd	8,800	500	Remainder				3-10-43	File 140-D
Collins, L. R.	Lockney	160 (11-6-43)	Floyd	8,480	500	1,600	10			6-27-46	File 115
Colson, W. D.	Lockney	70.5 (4-24-44)	Floyd	5,500	500	Remainder				5-2-44	File 47
Colson, W. D.	Lockney	4.67	Floyd								File 61
Compton, Floyd‡	Lockney	160‡ (11-24-25)	Hale and Floyd	8,800	200	800	10			12-30-46	Dev. 63, File 25-C

Name	Location	Acres (Date)					Notes	Date	File
Cooper, J. H.‡	Lockney	160 (7-25-45)	Floyd	5,600	500	Remainder			8-20-45	File 59
Cooper, W. W. and J. J. Graham	Lockney and Lubbock respectively	40 (12-2-36)	Floyd	3,000	100	1,400		Winfield Holbrook	12-26-36	Dev. 46, File 79
Cornett, J. B.	Benjamin	480 (11-19-43)	Hale	16,800	1,000		10		2-3-49	File 10-A
Courtney, M. E.	Plainview	813 (1-26-46)	Hale	30,000	500	Remainder			2-15-46	Files 137, 71, 57
Cowan, H. M.	Covington	80 (12-24-43)	Floyd	5,300	500	2,500	10			Dev. 32, File 60
Cox, R. C.† (see Lee Schrivner)										Dev. 4.4, File 45
Culp, Nealy W.†	Plainview	160 (6-25-46)	Swisher	9,600	500	2,400	10			Dev. 3-1
Culpepper, W. F. (see J. E. Tivis)										File 107
Cunningham, W. N.	Ventura, Calif.	150 (11-27-23)	Hale	26,250	6,550		10			File 26
Dalton, A. P.	Plainview	160 (10-11-45)	Hale	6,000	200	Remainder			7-10-47	File 84
Davis, Willis W.	Sweetwater	640 (2-26-43)	Hale	21,200	1,200	5,600		Canceled due to company error		File 44-A
Davis, Willis W.	Sweetwater	590.1 (3-31-43)	Hale	12,965	6,800				5-31-43	File 44-A
Degarmo, H. B.	Plainview	80 (6-12-44)	Floyd	4,800	500	1,000	10	First National Bank, Lockney (12-5-46)	12-5-46	File 114
Dennis, Orian	Anton	120§ (11-16-45)	Floyd	4,200	500	800	10		11-18-47	File 19-B
Denver Alfalfa Milling and Products Co.		2.81 (6-5-44)	Floyd	250					6-10-44	File 136
Dew, Allen and J. R.	Brownfield	80 (10-25-22)	Floyd	9,600	500	1,900	10			File 77
Dew, Allen†	Lockney	80	Floyd							Dev. 80, File 47-A

† The person or persons were not the original purchasers of part or all of this land.
* All places listed are located in Texas unless otherwise specified.
‡ This was to be a standard development by the company and/or by some special arrangement.
§ There were some developments on this property.

Purchaser	Residence*	Acres Purchased (Date)	County	Amount of Purchase (in Dollars)	Down Payment (in Dollars)	Amount Due with Delivery of Deed (in Dollars)	Annual Payments Remaining and/or Special Arrangements	Purchaser of Notes Still Financed by TL&D (Date)	Next Disposition (Date)	Date TL & D Fully Paid	Dev. and/or File No.
Dickey, Mrs. Alice Anna	Floydada	320 (4-8-43)	Floyd	8,800	1,000	Remainder					File 140-E
Dillard, V. N.	Lockney	160 (8-2-20)	Floyd	8,800	500	2,000	10	N. H. Greer			File 63
Dilling, John	Erie, Penn.	80† (6-19-15)	Floyd	10,300	100		$1,187.50 by 8-1-15 $1,287.50 by 8-1-16 8		Reconveyed (1-21-19)		Dev. 6, Files 74, 79
DuBose, John F.	Plainview	80 (12-9-43)	Hale	6,000	500	1,000	10				Dev. 3-9, File 150
DuBose, John F.	Plainview	160 (4-26-44)	Hale	5,600	200	1,400	10				File 150
Dunn, M. T.†	Plainview	160§ (9-25-45)	Floyd and Hale	8,800	200	2,600	10	H. C. Gentry (5-29-46)		5-29-46	Dev. 67, File 25
Duvall, L. F.†	Lockney	240 (11-23-45)	Floyd	11,760	500	3,460	10			12-9-50	Dev. 24, Files 348, 76, 112
Dyer, Delbert B.	Norman, Okla.	160 (5-13-44)	Hale	8,800	500	2,200	10				Dev. 3-5, File 105
Dyer, Melvin R.	Cleveland, Okla.	314 (4-9-43)	Hale	10,519	1,000	Remainder			Canceled due to company error (c. 5-20-43)		File 55
Dyer, Melvin R.	Cleveland, Okla.	295.5 (c. 5-20-43)	Hale	9,899	1,000	Remainder					File 55
Dyer, Melvin R.	Cleveland, Okla.	320 (4-20-43)	Hale	11,200	2,200	1,000	10	Sold through Dallas Exchange (6-1-43)		6-1-43	File 43
Estridge, W. A.	Aldrich, Mo.	80† (5-19-16)	Hale	10,400	250		$400 by 8-1-16 $650 at 6% by 1-1-17 12		Reconveyed (4-13-32)		Dev. 101, File 77
Eastridge, W. A.	Plainview	160 (9-1-20)	Hale	12,160	500	2,560	10				Dev. 97, 99, File 9
Edwards, B. F.	Kress	158 (7-14-37)	Swisher	5,100	1,100						File 91
Ehresman, H. A. and Don P.	Plainview	11 town lots (12-16-46)	Hale	9,000	500	8,500				12-21-46	
Estep, V. L.	Turney, Mo.	120‡ (12-31-15)	Hale and Floyd	13,480	1,685		10		Reconveyed (8-24-20)		Dev. 63

Name	Location	Acres (Date)	County					Date	File
Evans, Melvin	Plainview	200 (5-28-41)	Hale	6,000	200	1,500	10		Files 28-A, 28-B
Everett, R. T.	Hedley	160 (11-22-43)	Hale	9,600	500	2,500	10	12-7-44	File 46
Francis, Mrs. Edith Mae	Kress	160 (7-1-44)	Swisher	5,760	200	3,960	8	7-15-45	File 31
Francis, Roger Melvin	Kress	480 (7-1-44)	Swisher	17,600	600	7,400	10	11-6-47	File 31
Francis, Roger Melvin†	Kress	320 (12-17-45)	Swisher	11,680	500	3,080	10		File 37-A
Frogge, L. M.	Plainview	320 (8-6-45)	Hale and Floyd	12,800	500	Remainder			Files 67, 68
Gaither, John B.	Plainview	238 (10-1-42)	Hale	6,050	250	1,300	Remainder by 10-4-43		Files 28-A, 28-B
Gaither, J. B.	Plainview	240 (1-19-43)	Hale	9,300	300	2,200	8		File 28-A
Garden, E. R.‡	Plainview	160 (1946 or 1947)	Swisher					4-13-47	File 36-A
Garrett, C. E.	Plainview	240 (11-4-43)	Hale	9,000	500	3,000	10		Files 108, 120
Garrett, R. F.	Memphis	80 (11-2-43)	Floyd	6,000	1,000	Remainder			File 136
George, G. C.	Corpus Christi	120 (7-12-43)	Hale	4,020	200	820	10		File 28-B
Gienn, Curt	Plainview	160 (7-2-46)	Hale					9-30-30	File 130
Gillies, J. A.†		160	Hale and Floyd	6,000	500	2,500	10		File 102
Goen, Minnie†		20	Floyd					7-18-34	Files 110, 47
Golden, S. R.‡	Plainview	240 (7-6-46)	Hale and Swisher	11,600	500	1,500	10	12-13-47	Dev. 3-27, 3-28, 3-46
Golden, Felix M.	Tulia	160§ (12-6-45)	Hale	8,800	500	3,500	10	9-28-47	Dev. 3-5, 3-38

† The person or persons were not the original purchasers of part or all of this land.
* All places listed are located in Texas unless otherwise specified.
‡ This was to be a standard development by the company and/or by some special arrangement.
§ There were some developments on this property.

Purchaser	Residence*	Acres Purchased (Date)	County	Amount of Purchase (in Dollars)	Down Payment (in Dollars)	Amount Due with Delivery of Deed (in Dollars)	Annual Payments Remaining and/or Special Arrangements	Purchaser of Notes Still Financed by TL & D (Date)	Next Disposition (Date)	Date TL & D Fully Paid	Dev. and/or File No.
Greer, N. E.	Lockney	160§ (7-31-20)	Floyd	9,900	500	2,200	10			1-1-26	File 59
Guest, J. L.†	Plainview	160 (11-28-45)	Hale and Floyd	5,840	500	1,350	10			12-12-49	File 130
Gunther, J. W.	Plainview	320 (8-8-45)	Hale	11,200	500	2,300	10	Sold through Dallas Exchange (12-?-46)		12-?-46	File 34-B
Guthrie, E.	Lockney	160 (7-29-20)	Floyd	9,200	500	1,800	10		To A. R. Meriwether		File 140
Guthrie, E.	Lockney	160 (8-18-20)	Floyd	9,150	500	1,800	10		Reconveyed (6-5-30)		File 59
Hallmark, E. L.	Plainview	160 (6-14-44)	Hale	6,080	1,580		10	Fed. Land Bank		9-4-45	File 10-B
Hallmark, J. A.	Knox City	160 (1-8-43)	Hale	4,400	300	1,000	Remainder in 60 days				File 10-B
Hallmark, J. A.	Knox City	160 (6-6-44)	Hale	6,400	400	1,200	10				File 41
Hallmark, Velma Ray	Lubbock	640 (10-25-45)	Swisher	23,360	500	5,560	10	Traveler's Insurance Co. (3-10-47)		3-10-47	Files 125, 16-D
Hampton, B. F.†	Lockney	354 (8-7-20)	Floyd	20,320	1,000	6,080	10		Reconveyed (11-28-25)		Dev. 72, File 19-A
Hampton, J. E.†	Lockney	240 (1921)	Floyd						Reconveyed (7 or 8-26)		Files 110, 47
Handley, Hammon L.	Lockney	160	Floyd								File 59
Hardaway, John†	Plainview	80 (7-31-28)	Floyd	7,200	500	Remainder				9-11-28	File 11
Harding, J. W.	Plainview	15.8 (5-12-44)	Hale	500	100	Remainder				5-17-44	File 101
Harper, Henry	Plainview	312 (4-20-43)	Hale	11,300	300	3,000	10				File 101
Harris, C. F.†	Lockney	160 (1937)	Floyd	5,000	2,500				Canceled (2-18-38)		File 59
Harris, C. F.†	Plainview	255.99§ (6-24-46)	Floyd	7,600	500	1,800	10	Farm Security Administration		10-2-46	Dev. 3-48, File 106
Harris, E. A.†	Hereford	113.22 (6-18-45)	Hale	11,200	500	Remainder					File 150

Name	Town	Acres (Date)	County				Notes	%	Date	File
Hart, Ross, and J. C. Wilmoth	Plainview	320 (12-29-29)		12,800	600	1,960		10		File 75
Harwit, Ben†	Midland	1,280 (1950)								Dev. 41, 42, 43
Haws, C. H.	Shamrock	160 (1-4-30)	Hale	5,760	500			10		File 51
Helm, J. E.	Plainview	160 (9-16-46)	Swisher	6,400	200	1,800		10		File 36-A
Henley, H. E.	Plainview	160	Swisher							File 36-A
Henry, M. C.	Petersburg	60 (12-14-20)	Floyd	7,700	400	1,530		10		Dev. 79, File 136
Hering, W. D.	Plainview	77.91 (4-5-43)	Hale	3,038.49	300	738.49		10		File 66
Hester, J. P.	Knox City	160§ (7-31-44)	Hale	6,400	500	Remainder			8-16-44	File 23
Hester, J. P.	Knox City	160§ (7-31-44)	Hale	7,200	500	1,300		10	7-9-47	File 23
Hill, Clarence	Hedley	120 (4-20-43)	Hale	6,700	300	1,600		10		Dev. 3-53, File 2
Hill, Clarence	Plainview	116.82 (2-16-45)	Hale	9,700	500	3,500		10		Dev. 3-43, Files 106, 131
Holcomb, Finas A.†	Plainview	320 (6-21-46)	Hale	13,000	200	3,800	Remainder in 90 days		7-5-46	File 100
Hollums, John A.	Floydada	160 (5-18-43)	Floyd	3,904.20	200	704.20	Remainder in 60 days from contract date		6-28-43	File 140-E
Horn, Ray E.	Pampa	320 (4-15-46)	Swisher	11,840	500	3,340	J. W. Chapman and Sons, Lubbock (2-21-46)	10	12-17-49	File 37-A
Howard, Alfred L.	Plainview	80 (6-19-46)	Hale	2,940	200	740		10	12-2-49	File 97
Huff, E. A.	Plainview	400 (3-24-43)	Hale	15,800	1,000	5,000		10		Files 51, 66
Hughes, G. C., and Paul V. Pierson	Plainview	320 (7-30-20)	Hale and Floyd	20,000	1,000	5,240	One-half reconveyed (8-4-23)	10	9-30-30	File 130
Hunt, F. B.	Kress	320 (4-14-41)	Hale	10,560	500	500		11	2-12-44	File 118

† The person or persons were not the original purchasers of part or all of this land.
* All places listed are located in Texas unless otherwise specified.
§ There were some developments on this property.

Purchaser	Residence*	Acres Purchased (Date)	County	Amount of Purchase (in Dollars)	Down Payment (in Dollars)	Amount Due with Delivery of Deed (in Dollars)	Annual Payments Remaining and/or Special Arrangements	Purchaser of Notes Still Financed by TL & D (Date)	Next Disposition (Date)	Date TL & D Fully Paid	Dev. and/or File No.
Hunter, Joe L.	Pampa	160 (5-4-44)	Swisher	5,760	500	1,260	10			9-30-46	File 6
Jackson, J. E.	Higginsville, Mo.	80 (3-8-15)	Floyd	10,000	500		$750 by 4-1-16 $1,250 by 4-1-17 8		Reconveyed (8-14-19)		Dev. 28, File 18-A
Jacobs, John Bert‡	Plainview	160 (6-26-46)	Hale	10,400	500	1,500	10	Hale County State Bank, Plainview (10-24-49)		10-24-49	Dev. 2-3, File 22-A
Johnson, Edgar J.	Wausa, Neb.	120‡ (1-7-16)	Hale and Swisher	11,500	500		$937.50 by 4-1-16 12		Reconveyed (1-29-19)		Dev. 3-27, File 78
Johnson, J. V.	Kress	320 (3-4-46)	Hale	11,680	3,380		10			9-10-47	File 43
Johnson, S. John	Princeton, Ill.	160‡ (11-6-15)	Swisher	17,600	250		$850 by 3-1-16 $1,100 by 11-6-16 10		Reconveyed (9-?-19)		Dev. 3-1, File 106
Johnston, Ellbert‡	Estelline	160 (1946 or 1947)	Swisher							4-13-47	File 36-A
Jones, Roe	Floydada	320 (2-5-43)	Floyd	9,600	500	Remainder				3-10-43	File 140-D
Karrh, Joe J.	Hale Center	160 (10-18-46)	Swisher	6,480						10-18-46	File 36-B
Karrh, Winnie and Annie	Plainview	138.2	Swisher	5,400	500	1,500	10	Traveler's Insurance Co. (5-4-48)		5-4-48	File 36-C
Keniston, R. E.	Plainview	80 (12-24-36)	Hale	6,000	100	200	10				File 25
Kern, Paul V.†	Nazereth	159 (between 1920 and 1923)	Floyd						Reconveyed (9-28-23)		File 61
Kimble, Dr. Wilson	Floydada	480 (2-5-43)	Floyd	12,500	500	12,000				3-10-43	File 140-E
Kindwall, Frank A.†	Wynot, Neb.	74.52 (5-1-16)	Hale	9,315	100				Repossessed (5-24-32)		Dev. 3-24
Kirchhoff, E. A., and D. D. Bowman	Plainview	320 (11-26-46)	Hale	11,360	500	Remainder					File 41
Kirchhoff, Edwin H.	Plainview	320 (11-20-45)	Swisher	11,680	500	3,180	10	Sold through Dallas Exchange (12-26-45)		12-26-45	File 16-A

Name	Location	Acres (Date)	County					Notes	Reference
Kirchhoff, Edwin H.	Plainview	640 (1-4-46)	Hale	24,000	500	7,500	10	Hale County State Bank, Plainview (2-15-46)	2-15-46	File 17
Kirkpatrick, Willie R.	Spring Lake	160 (8-8-44)	Floyd	8,400	500	2,500	10		11-19-45	File 38 Dev. 31, Files 60, 47
Knoy, W. J.	Lockney	120 (6-6-44)	Floyd	7,100	500	1,600	10			Files 106, 131
Knuckles, L. J.‡	Chillicothe	119.40	Floyd							Dev. 3-34, File 40
Koeninger, J. H.	Hedley	320 (4-4-44)	Hale	13,400	500	4,300	10	Sold through Dallas Exchange (6-13-47)	6-13-47	File 42
Kornegay, A. W.	Plainview	320	Hale	11,680	500	5,180	10	Hale County State Bank, Plainview (10-14-49)	10-14-49	File 136
Langfeldt, A. P.	Aiken	City lots (3-18-46)	Floyd	1,200	450		5	Canceled due to Company error		
Langford, J.A.‡	Lockney	159§ (8-27-45)	Floyd	6,360	500	1,860	10			File 61
Langford, J.A.	Lockney	153.33§ (9-8-45)	Floyd	6,133.20	2,133.22		10		11-28-45	File 61
Larson, Theodore‡	Hudson, Wisc.	160	Swisher							Dev. 3-1
Latta, E.‡			Hale							Dev. 4-4, File 45
Lewellen, Clayton W.	Plainview	440 (1-23-43)	Hale	11,000	300	Remainder				File 34-A
Lewis, Charlie	Floydada	407.12 (2-5-43)	Floyd	11,195.80	750	Remainder			3-10-43	File 140-C
Lindsey, W. A.	Plainview	80 (11-13-43)	Hale	6,000	500	2,500	10	Hale County State Bank, Plainview (11-22-43)	11-22-43	File 105
Line, James L	Dallas	320 (1-9-46)	Hale	11,840	500	Remainder			2-3-46	File 23
Lowe, Ray F.	Plainview	160 (1-29-43)	Hale	5,800	300	Remainder			2-4-43	File 160
Lowe, Ray F.‡	Plainview	320	Hale							File 86
Lowe, W. F.	Plainview	150.85 (11-20-24)	Hale	22,000	18,000			Texas Land and Mortgage Co.	1924	Dev. 1

† The person or persons were not the original purchasers of part or all of this land.
* All places listed are located in Texas unless otherwise specified.
‡ This was to be a standard development by the company and/or by some special arrangement.
§ There were some developments on this property.

Purchaser	Residence*	Acres Purchased (Date)	County	Amount of Purchase (in Dollars)	Down Payment (in Dollars)	Amount Due with Delivery of Deed (in Dollars)	Annual Payments Remaining and/or Special Arrangements	Purchaser of Notes Still Financed by TL & D (Date)	Next Disposition (Date)	Date TL & D Fully Paid	Dev. and/or File No.
Lucas, O. A.	Plainview	80 (4-19-43)	Hale	6,000	300	1,200	10			8-13-45	Dev. 78, File 128
Lundgren, Mrs. Gust. E.†	Wausa, Neb.	85.39 (1917)	Hale						Reconveyed		Dev. 3-15
Lundgren, Gust. E.	Wausa, Neb.	85.39 (3-23-16)	Hale	10,673.75	668						Dev. 3-15
McBeth, James S.	O'Brien	320 (1-13-43)	Hale	11,840	1,000	2,000	10				File 126
Malone, J. M.	Plainview	157.21 (8-28-20)	Hale	9,432.60	500	1,932.60	10				File 150
Mason, C. H.	Plainview	109.3 (8-9-45)	Hale	3,600	200	800	10	Hale County State Bank, Plainview (10-14-49)		10-14-49	File 105
Mason, Clarence†	Plainview	85.39 (8-9-45)	Hale	7,000	200	1,300	10	Hale County State Bank, Plainview (10-24-49)		c. 10-24-49	Dev. 3-15
Mason, Otis F. and Gladys Ruth	San Diego, Calif.	190 (8-22-46)	Hale	8,500	500	2,050	10	National Farm Loan Assoc. (9-3-46)		9-3-46	File 132
Miller, C. D.	Pampa	320 (5-4-44)	Swisher	12,480	500	3,580	10			9-13-50	File 6
Miller, Judson, and Ben J. Tye	Plainview	640 (7-15-46)	Swisher	23,360	500	6,560	10	Hale County State Bank, Plainview (8-3-47)		8-3-47	File 49
Miller, Phil T. and Geneva†	Plainview	74.52 (1-26-46)	Hale	7,000				Fed. Land Bank Houston (1-16-50)		1-16-50	Dev. 3-24
Mills, J. M.	Plainview	135.7 (5-17-44)	Hale	5,225	500	1,125	10	Traveler's Insurance Co. (8-23-46)		8-23-46	File 101
Moore, Sam S.	Lockney	160 (3-30-44)	Floyd	8,800	500	2,500	10			12-1-49	Dev. 69, File 19
Moore, Sam S. and Carla†	Lockney	160 (11-13-45)	Floyd	5,600	500	1,600	10				File 19-A
Morgan, W. L.	Lockney	60 (11-20-46)	Floyd	?	3,200	700	Remainder by 11-20-47	Traveler's Insurance Co. (2-?-47)		2-?-47	File 25-D

Name	Location	Acres (Date)	County						Notes	Date	File
Morris, R. M.	Lockney	160 (11-17-43)	Hale	10,000	500		2,000	10			File 150
Morrow, E. C.	Lockney	31.38 (3-4-40)	Floyd	3,800	100	Remainder				3-8-40	File 114
Morrow, J. B.	Plainview	120 (11-15-43)	Hale	?	500		1,500	10			File 150
Mudget, Wiley	Lockney	159‡ (8-3-20)	Floyd	10,000	2,500			10	Sold to Paul V. Kern		File 61
Muncy, A. B.	Lockney	59.75 (8-28-26)	Floyd	3,734.38	200	734.38		10			File 140
Murphy, C. W.	Lockney	206 (8-14-20)	Floyd	12,875	500		2,730.15	10	Sold to S. T. Cooper	3-?-29	Files 21, 19
Neanover, Wm. H.		80	Floyd								File 11
Neill, J. M.	El Paso	320 (2-9-20)	Hale	9,600	2,400			10	Canceled		File 100
Neill, J. M.	El Paso	320 (2-18-20)	Hale	9,600	2,400			10	Reconveyed (1923)		File 100
Newton, A. S.	Kress	320- (7-27-43)	Swisher	11,000	300		2,700	10			File 16-A
Nichols, Claude	Williams, Ariz.	320 (2-18-46)	Hale	12,800	500		3,300	10		6-?-47	File 42
Nichols, W. C.	Bernardino, Calif.	160 (8-14-20)	Floyd	10,400	500	500	2,500	10	First Trust Joint Stock Land Bank, Dallas, Texas	12-12-27	File 87
Nowlin, C. S.	Booker	320 (2-28-46)	Hale	12,000	500		3,100	10	Hale County State Bank, Plainview (10-24-49)	10-24-49	Dev. 4-4, File 45
Pace, Homer A.	Wink	255.44§ (9-16-29)	Swisher	9,723.44	923.44			10	Reconveyed (1936)		Dev. 3-48, File 106
Pace, J. C.	Stanford	320 (1-6-43)	Hale	12,000	300	Remainder					File 40
Painter, Albert	Hale County	200 (12-31-42)	Hale	5,200			5,200	Remainder by 5-1-43		2-8-43	File 34-A
Painter, W. A.	Plainview	145.4 (3-13-43)	Hale	4,700	300		1,400				File 101
Painter, W. A.	Plainview	160 (2-6-43)	Hale	5,000	300		4,700			2-26-43	File 44-A

† The person or persons were not the original purchasers of part or all of this land.
* All places listed are located in Texas unless otherwise specified.
‡ This was to be a standard development by the company and/or by some special arrangement.
§ There were some developments on this property.

Purchaser	Residence*	Acres Purchased (Date)	County	Amount of Purchase (in Dollars)	Down Payment (in Dollars)	Amount Due with Delivery of Deed (in Dollars)	Annual Payments Remaining and/or Special Arrangements	Purchaser of Notes Still Financed by TL & D (Date)	Next Disposition (Date)	Date TL & D Fully Paid	Dev. and/or File No.
Parsons, Thrane		400 (7-9-46)	Hale	16,000	600	4,500	10		Gt. Southern Life Insurance Co. (10-7-46)	10-7-46	Files 108, 120
Patillo, W. L.	Lubbock	320 (6-26-46)	Hale	11,200	500	1,100	10		Sold to D. W. Ashburn	4-24-48	File 13-B
Patillo, W. L.	Lubbock	640 (7-1-46)	Hale	22,400	500	2,700	10		Sold to D. W. Ashburn		File 56
Perkins, D. H.	Floydada	160 (11-17-43)	Hale	9,200	500	2,000	10	Hale County State Bank, Plainview (11-28-45)		11-28-45	File 35
Perkins, G. J.	Plainview	160	Floyd	8,000	500	1,500	10	Hale County State Bank, Plainview (4-19-45)		4-19-45	File 74
Phillips, Everett P.	Hale Center	640 (7-15-46)	Hale	22,700	500	2,920	10	(2-22-47)			File 116
Pinkerton, Robert	Plainview	160 (2-28-46)	Swisher	5,840	500	1,340	10			5-5-48	File 12
Poage, Raymond C.†	Kress	186.9 (6-25-46)	Swisher	11,214	500	2,500	$812.50 by 7-20-17 10			9-18-46	Dev. 3-39, 3-50, File 106
Poissant, Octave	Minneapolis, Minn.	100‡ (7-20-16)	Hale	13,000	812.50				Reconveyed (12-3-19)	12-7-48	Dev. 102, File 62
Powell, D. L.	Snyder	201.4 (12-7-43)	Floyd	8,400	500	2,000	10				File 76
Pratt, E. T.	Lockney	160 (6-25-30)	Floyd	6,600	400	1,400	10				File 63
Pratt, E. T.	Lockney	160 (8-28-37)	Floyd	8,000	200	800	8			5-2-44	File 63
Price, Wasson S.	Plainview	160 (11-26-45)	Hale	5,100	500	Remainder		A. M. and J. F. Buchanan			File 1
Pyle, E. M.	Lockney	80 (4-3-44)	Floyd	4,600	500	1,100	10			12-11-45	Dev. 20, File 115
Race, Paul S.†	Floydada	320 (8-3-45)	Floyd	11,600	500	5,100				7-5-45	File 109
Rains, Clyde A.†	Plainview	160 (10-15-45)	Hale	8,800	200	2,200	10				Dev. 101, Files 9, 9-A

Name	Location	Acres (Date)	County					Hale County State Bank, Plainview (11-15-44)		Dev./File
Rambo, E. E.	Odessa	160 (11-6-43)	Hale	7,600	500	2,000	10		11-15-44	Dev. 3-26, File 102
Randolph, E. M.†	Lockney	400	Hale					Reconveyed (11-3-27)		Files 110, 47
Rankin, Ira B.	Plainview	160 (2-6-46)	Hale	5,280	200	800	10		8-13-47	File 9-B
Reed, Clifton	Kress	84.3 (9-4-43)	Swisher	2,334	100	634	10		11-13-43	File 20
Reed, Clifton	Kress	166.5 (11-13-45)	Swisher	5,661	500	3,161	10		8-5-46	File 20
Richardson, S. C., Jr.	San Diego, Calif.	115.15 (3-20-43)	Swisher	6,800	200	1,800	10		1-28-46	File 114
Roach, C. J.	Lockney	80 (3-31-43)	Floyd	6,000	300	700	10		1-7-44	Dev. 47, File 11
Roberson, J. C.	Plainview	160 (4-10-43)	Hale	7,640	300	1,740	10		7-24-44	Dev. 3-6, File 78
Roberson, J. C.	Plainview	80 (6-27-46)	Hale	2,940	200	800	10			File 97
Roberts, R. W.	Hale Center	200 (11-22-43)	Hale	9,700	500	2,500	10			File 2
Roberts, Tom	Plainview	160 (8-4-42)	Hale	5,100	100	Remainder				File 98
Robertson, G. W.	Hale Center	268.65 (5-2-44)	Hale	15,000	500	2,500	10			File 150
Roper, Elisha	Plainview	960 (2-19-43)	Hale and Swisher	32,160	500	11,500	10	Remainder within 12 months from date of deed	2-24-43	Files 37-B, 5
Rook, Homer A.†	Plainview	170.7 (11-5-43)	Hale	6,120	500	500	10			File 150
Rook, Homer A.	Plainview	317.21 (11-5-43)	Hale	13,800	500	Remainder				Dev. 3-22, File 150
Rook, Homer A.	Plainview	110.54 (8-9-45)	Hale	4,500	500	Remainder			9-10-45	File 150
Rydell, Ernest A.	Minneapolis, Minn.	80‡ (8-1-16)	Hale and Swisher	10,000	100			$750 by 8-1-16 $625 by 3-13-17 12	Canceled (9-29-17)	Dev. 3-46
Rydell, Ernest A.	Minneapolis, Minn.	113.22‡ (3-1-18)		10,996.60				Down payment was $1,250 he had paid under previous contract	Reconveyed (12-8-25)	Dev. 3-18

† The person or persons were not the original purchasers of part or all of this land.
* All places listed are located in Texas unless otherwise specified.
‡ This was to be a standard development by the company and/or by some special arrangement.

Purchaser	Residence*	Acres Purchased (Date)	County	Amount of Purchase (in Dollars)	Down Payment (in Dollars)	Amount Due with Delivery of Deed (in Dollars)	Annual Payments Remaining and/or Special Arrangements	Purchaser of Notes Still Financed by TL & D (Date)	Next Disposition (Date)	Date TL & D Fully Paid	Dev. and/or File No.
Sammons, Mrs. Eura Lee	Austin	160 (5-17-44)	Floyd	8,800		4,000	10				File 11
Sanders, C. H.	Meade, Kansas	86 (5-10-44)	Floyd	5,500	2,500		10	C. L. and Fannie Beebee			File 136
Saul, Doyle	Kress	640 (6-25-46)	Hale	27,200	500	8,700	10			1-10-48	File 13-A
Schreiber, Otto	Plainview	87 (4-12-44)	Hale	6,000	500	3,500	10			8-31-44	Dev. 98, File 62
Schreiber, Otto†	Plainview	100 (3-28-46)	Hale	4,200	500	1,700	8				Dev. 102, File 62
Schrivner, Lee	Plainview	160 (2-22-46)	Hale	12,080	500	2,580	10		Part sold to R. C. Cox; part to E.Latta; part retained	8-25-47	Dev. 4-4, File 45
Schrivner, Lee	Plainview	200 (7-6-46)	Hale	7,000	500	1,000	10			10-3-47	Dev. 3-30, Files 94, 121
Schrivner, Lee	Plainview	169 (7-6-46)	Hale	8,682.50	500	2,182.50	10			10-3-47	Dev. 3-23, Files 94, 121
Schrock, A. H.‡	Plainview	320 (8-31-45)	Hale	13,440	500	1,500	10	Fed. Land Bank (9-22-48)		9-22-48	File 39
Schrock, John†	Plainview	640 (8-23-20)	Hale	38,800	9,700		10		Reconveyed (8-9-25)		File 39
Seago, H. E.‡	Lockney	160 (10-11-45)	Floyd	10,400	500	1,500	10	Prudential Insurance Co. (2-10-47)		2-10-47	Dev. 23, File 38
Shannon, W. F. and Linnie	Plainview	84.17 (1-2-43)	Hale	6,150	300	1,700	5			7-24-43	File 105
Shannon, W. F.	Plainview	64.46 (4-18-44)	Hale	3,200	200	800	10				File 105
Shelton, T. J.	Plainview	120 (5-12-30)	Floyd	5,700	310	1,890	10		.60 acres sold for highway right of way (5-15-30) Remainder to L. J. Knuckles (1-22-41)	2-19-41	Files 106, 131
Shipp, T. A.	Hale Center	160§ (6-13-46)	Hale	7,200	200	2,000	10	Fed. Land Bank Houston (7-19-46)		7-19-46	File 153

Name	Location	Acres (Date)	County				Notes	File
Shurbet, H. C.	Lockney	320 (9-9-20)	Floyd	17,250	1,000	3,350	10		File 124
Sidebottom, M. E.	Plainview	320 (6-3-42)	Hale	10,000	200	2,300	10		File 113
Sikes, R. E. for the A. A. Huntingtons	Eastland	170.7 (10-18-19)	Hale	10,242	200	2,360.50	10	Reconveyed (11-5-43)	File 150
Simpson, C. O.‡		40	Floyd					5-28-27	Dev. 47, File 110
Simpson, Ira†	Lockney								Files 110, 47
Simpson, J. Scott	Plainview	320 (10-27-42)	Hale	8,480	500	2,580		Z. T. Huff (Fall 1943) Reconveyed Fall 1943	File 34-B
Smith, A. J.	Lockney	320 (5-20-20)	Floyd	17,400	500	3,900	10	Reconveyed (8-10-26)	File 109
Smith, E. J.	Morrisville, Mo.	160‡ (7-19-16)	Hale	18,400	2,300		12	Exchanged for a different 160 acre tract since could not irrigate satisfactorily	Dev. 2-3, File 22-A
Smith, J. J.	Lockney	158 (8-31-20)	Floyd	9,060	500	1,860	10	Reconveyed (2-4-24)	File 140
Sparkman, Paul H.	Plainview	100 (6-12-44)	Floyd	6,500	500	1,500	10		Dev. 91, File 136
Spears, Johnie	Devol, Okla.	80 (9-5-36)	Floyd	7,000	100	700	10	Transferred to J. R. Belt, Jr. (9-6-43)	File 128
Spilman, Wm. B.	Silverton	294.85 (8-11-44)	Hale	13,000	500	Remainder		(9-19-44)	Dev. 4-3, File 101-A
Springer, Daniel M.	Kress	160 (1-6-26)	Swisher	5,600	500	Remainder			File 6
Springer, L. M.	Plainview	132.9 (12-3-29)	Hale	4,651.50	400	Remainder		(12-9-29)	File 134
Standefer, W. D.	Plainview	60 (4-27-44)	Hale	5,400	400	1,000	10	(1-18-47)	File 136
Stansell, John W.	Memphis, Tenn.	80‡ (3-7-16)	Hale	10,000	625	625	12	Canceled for forfeiture of earnest money (9-12-18)	Dev. 64

† The person or persons were not the original purchasers of part or all of this land.
* All places listed are located in Texas unless otherwise specified.
‡ This was to be a standard development by the company and/or by some special arrangement.
§ There were some developments on this property.

Purchaser	Residence*	Acres Purchased (Date)	County	Amount of Purchase (in Dollars)	Down Payment (in Dollars)	Amount Due with Delivery of Deed (in Dollars)	Annual Payments Remaining and/or Special Arrangements	Purchaser of Notes Still Financed by TL & D (Date)	Next Disposition (Date)	Date TL & D Fully Paid	Dev. and/or File No.
Stephens, Elmo	O'Brien	160 (11-19-43)	Hale	5,600	500	1,500	10	Z. T. Huff (8-18-44)		8-18-44	File 10-A
Stephens, G. W.	Erick, Okla.	218.6 (8-14-44)	Hale	11,300	500	3,000	10		Sold by Stephens (12-14-44)	12-14-44	Dev. 3-3, File 81
Stephens, J. L. and Lee	Plainview	640 (7-6-20)	Hale	37,800	5,000	15,000	10		Contract never consummated		File 39
Stephens, Lee and Amanda	Plainview	640 (1-10-30)	Swisher	22,400	400	Remainder				1-11-30	File 4
Stewart, J. H.	Plainview	320 (7-7-20)	Hale and Floyd	20,488	1,000	5,240	10	Second lien by Dallas Joint Stock Land Bank	TL & D allowed land to go by default (1-1-34)		File 130
Stockton, Lonnie H	Kress	80 (8-27-46)	Swisher	3,200		Remainder					File 36-D
Stout, O. A.	Hale Center	160 (5-9-30)	Hale	6,500	500	1,000	11			3-3-34	File 22-B
Stout, O. A.	Hale Center	160 (11-23-37)	Hale	5,600	200	1,400	10			8-8-38	File 22-B
Stout, O. A.	Hale Center	160 (11-27-37)	Hale	Exchanged for 160 acres he owned							File 22-B
Stout, O. A.	Hale Center	480 (7-9-46)	Hale	18,400	500	9,500	10			7-26-46	Files 22-B, 22-A
Stovall, Wallace R.	Kress	320 (9-21-42)	Swisher	8,000	200	1,800	10	Fed. Land Bank (1942)		1942	File 16-C
Stovall, Wallace R.	Kress	320 (7-17-46)	Swisher	11,680	500	2,480	10			9-8-49	File 16-C
Taylor, J. B.	Lockney	80 (8-12-44)	Floyd	5,100	500	3,600	10			8-31-44	Dev. 5-3, File 53
Terrell, W. E.‡	Lockney	80 (10-20-45)	Floyd	8,000	500	Remainder					Dev. 28, File 18-A
Thomas, E. J.	Lockney	160 (7-12-37)	Floyd	8,000	200	4,600	10				File 88
Thomas, J. L.	Plainview	160 (3-25-44)	Hale and Swisher	8,800	500	2,300	10			2-11-48	File 97
Thomas, Roy L.	Hale Center	160 (1-21-43)	Hale	4,560	300	1,860	Remainder in 60 days				File 10-C

Name	Location	Acres (Date)	County					Notes	Reference
Thompson, A. W.	Marlow, Okla.	319.5 (5-20-43)	Hale	11,153.70	500	2,510	10		Files 92-151, 44-A
Thompson, I. J.	Plainview	80 (11-29-43)	Floyd	4,900	300	500	10		Dev. 48, 93, File 77
Thompson, I. J.	Lockney	80 (2-10-45)	Floyd	5,100	500	4,600		2-15-45	File 77
Thompson, I. J.	Plainview	160 (3-9-45)	Hale	9,000	300	1,700	10		Dev. 5, File 77
Tierce, J. E.	Lockney	33 (3-16-40)	Floyd	1,150	500	500	5		File 136
Tipps, Charles E.	Plainview	312.75 (5-31-44)	Hale	11,880	500	2,580	10	10-5-44	Files 117, 129
Tipton, D. T.	Kress	320 (10-28-44)	Hale	13,000	500	Remainder		11-7-44	File 118
Tivis, J. E.	Floydada	160 (7-27-44)	Floyd	8,800	500	2,300	10	Sold by Tivis to W. F. Culpepper before deed delivered.	File 107
Tye, Ben J. (see Judson Miller)									
Vance, John C.	Streator, Ill.	154 (3-24-16)	Floyd	17,710	1,800	$415 by 6-25-16	12	Reconveyed (3-29-20)	Dev. 72, File 19
Walker, Riley L. †	Elkhart, Kansas	80 (10-24-45)	Hale and Swisher	3,200	500	700	10	8-5-46	Dev. 3-33
Weathersby, R. L.	Plainview	60 (4-30-27)	Hale	16,150	500	2,500	10		File 26
Weathersby, R. L.	Plainview	9.34 (5-4-27)	Hale	607				Prorated into 10 annual payments in contract above	File 26
Weathersby, R. L.	Plainview	59.18 (7-7-27)	Hale	4,250			10		File 26
Welander, Eddie	Oakland, Neb.	80‡ (3-10-16)	Hale and Swisher	10,400	650	$650 due 3-10-17	12	Canceled 1917 due to trouble with irrigation	Dev. 3-33
Wells, Herbert	Hart	160 (7-15-44)	Hale	8,637	500	2,130	10		File 102
Wheeler, C. M.	Plainview	80 (4-10-43)	Hale	5,000	300	700	10		Dev. 3-32, File 105

† The person or persons were not the original purchasers of part or all of this land.
* All places listed are located in Texas unless otherwise specified.
‡ This was to be a standard development by the company and/or by some special arrangement.

Purchaser	Residence*	Acres Purchased (Date)	County	Amount of Purchase (in Dollars)	Down Payment (in Dollars)	Amount Due with Delivery of Deed (in Dollars)	Annual Payments Remaining and/or Special Arrangements	Purchaser of Notes Still Financed by TL & D (Date)	Next Disposition (Date)	Date TL & D Fully Paid	Dev. and/or File No.
Wheeler, L. C.	Hale Center	160 (1-21-43)	Hale	3,760	300	1,660	Remainder in 60 days				File 10-C
Whitfill, Ed	Aiken	11 City lots (11-20-43)	Floyd	500		500					File 136
Williams, Edward P.†	Hale Center	154 (11-14-45)	Floyd	9,100	500	1,320	10	Prudential Insurance Co. of America (3-22-47)		3-22-47	Dev. 72, File 19
Williams, H. C.		113.22 (c. 3-1-20)	Hale						Reconveyed (12-9-25)		Dev. 3-18
Williamson, A. G.	Plainview	320 (11-16-43)	Hale and Swisher	11,520	500	2,420	10				Dev. 3-51, File 97-A
Wilson, Geo. T.	Plainview	476.68 (4-3-43)	Hale	26,000	500	7,300	10			5-17-44	Dev. 2, 3, 3-B, File 26
Witkowski, Frank	David City, Neb.	80 (1-22-16)	Hale and Floyd	10,000	650		$650 due 1-22-17 12		Reconveyed (3-26-18)		Dev. 67, File 25
Womeldorf, R. J.	Plainview	320 (2-13-46)	Hale	24,640	500	5,540	10	Ct. Gen. Life Insurance Co. (11-?-47)		11-?-47	File 13-B
Wright, Clint M.		1,280	Hale								Dev. 41, 42, 43
Wright, D. L.	O'Brien	160 (4-19-44)	Hale	7,680	500	2,180	10			12-6-47	Dev. 29, File 18-B
Wright, Edward P.	O'Brien	320 (11-2-43)	Hale	11,200	600	3,000	10				File 10-B
Yarbrough, R. C. and Essie B.	Plainview	400 (4-17-44)	Hale	20,000	500	5,500	10				File 25
Yearout, E. J.	Lockney	40 (10-17-27)	Floyd	4,300	400	700	10				File 79
Young, Edgar C.	Swisher County	160 (10-18-46)	Swisher	6,480		Remainder					File 36-D
Young, Thomas and Pearl	Swisher County	160 (10-18-46)	Swisher	6,480							File 36-D
Zimmerman, Milton	Mendon, Mo.	160§ (7-24-14)	Floyd	16,800	100		$900 due 3-1-15 $1,000 by 12-1-15 $2,200 by 7-24-16 6		Reconveyed (c. 1-3-20)		Dev. 23, File 38

† The person or persons were not the original purchasers of part or all of this land.
* All places listed are located in Texas unless otherwise specified.
§ There were some developments on this property.

BIBLIOGRAPHY

Manuscript Collections

The Bain Files, Plainview, Texas

These items are in the possession of Mrs. Luther R. Bain, daughter of the late Winfield Holbrook. The collection consists of numerous letters written to and by her father; pictures; newspaper clippings; one tape interview between Mrs. Bain and Keith Catto, recorded May 31, 1958; and one very valuable item to anyone interested in Plainview in 1914—a complete copy of one issue of the *Daily Plainview Advertiser* (January 1, 1914), a sort of Domesday Book of Plainview as of that date.

The Brunson Letters, Southwest Collection, Texas Tech University, Lubbock, Texas

This collection contains approximately two hundred letters to and from former employees and officials of the Texas Land and Development Company; relatives, friends, and possible acquaintances of former employees and officers; bankers; attorneys; railway officials; chambers of commerce; commercial firms; college officials; real-estate agents; members of fraternal organizations; historical societies; ministers; government officials (including postal officials, county clerks, county surveyors, provincial officials); and friends. The letters were written to people in Canada, Mexico, and the United States. The bulk of the letters were written by the author or to him. However, there are a few letters that were given to the author by Mr. Clyde Emerson Craig of Raymondville, Texas, and by Mrs. A. B. Cox of Plainview, Texas. Mr. Craig donated two or three letters that had been written to him by the late Winfield Holbrook, and Mrs. Cox donated one from Mr. Robert S. Charles.

Also included in the Brunson Letter file are the papers of the Texas Securities Company, Limited.

The Clinkscales Collection, Plainview, Texas

This collection belongs to Mrs. F. W. Clinkscales of Plainview, Texas, whose late husband was a Plainview banker and businessman. The collection is made up of a large number of pictures, chamber of commerce brochures, newspaper clippings, and the most valuable item as far as the present study has been concerned, the often-cited brochure prepared by Milton Day Henderson entitled "Texas Land and Development Company." A microfilm copy of this brochure has been placed in the Southwest Collection.

The Randolph Files, Plainview, Texas

This collection contains hundreds of letters, legal documents, judicial reports, brochures, and newspaper clippings. Also included is a transcript of record, Staked Plains Trust, Limited, v. Commissioner of Internal Revenue, Fifth Circuit Court of Appeals, 1937. Most of the letters were written by Mr. Peyton B. Randolph (a few were written in the early period of the company by his father, H. C. Randolph) or to him by officials of the Texas Land and Development Company, the Staked Plains Trust, Limited, Texas Prairie Lands, Limited, Prairie Lands Trust, Limited, and to (or from) many others who were not connected with any of these companies, but who had come into contact with one or more of them for some reason. A wealth of information was obtained from this collection (primarily from the letters). Without the use of this collection it woud have been infinitely more difficult to have written the present work.

Smyth Collection, Panhandle-Plains Museum, Canyon, Texas

The Plainview Chamber of Commerce, "The Great Plainview District Where There Is Nothing Shallow but the Water."

The Texas Land and Development Company Papers, Southwest Collection, Texas Tech University, Lubbock, Texas

This collection is composed of well over ten thousand pages of materials that were donated to the Southwest Collection primarily by Mrs. Luther R. Bain, Mr. Peyton B. Randolph, and Mr. Hugh R. Partridge.

Mr. Randolph gave items to this collection in February and April 1958. Contained in this collection is correspondence dated from 1913 to 1947; legal instruments of various types; newspaper clippings; some annual reports of the Staked Plains Trust, Limited; all deeds of trust to Slaton and Randolph as trustees for Texas Prairie Lands, Limited; the sales contracts

Bibliography

and related correspondence; patents; releases; and the Texas Land and Development Company's minute book.

Mrs. Bain, in May 1958, gave these items: time books dating from November 15, 1918, to December 31, 1953; journals and ledgers of the Staked Plains Trust, Limited, dating from January 1, 1920, to May 1954; cash books dating from January 1, 1920, to March 31, 1954; ledgers of Baldwin, Slaton, and Randolph, and Staked Plains Trust, Limited; ledgers of the Staked Plains Trust, Limited, the Texas Securities Company, Limited, and Texas Prairie Lands, Limited; miscellaneous account books; well logs; pictures; and the "final correspondence."

The third part of this collection was given by Mr. Hugh R. Partridge of New York City in 1959 and contains the printed and bound volume of charters, indentures, and contracts cited in the body of the book as *Documents 1917*. This volume was invaluable to the present study and very appropriately, the trustees of the Staked Plains Trust referred to it as the "Green Bible" since the cover of the book is green. Also found in this part of the collection are the *Annual Reports* published by the Staked Plains Trust, Limited, from 1920 through 1955, with the exception of 1921. Presumably there was a report for 1921, but the number is missing from the collection.

The Texas Land and Development Company Papers also contain numerous miscellaneous items such as Field Book Number 360, which was given to the collection by the Hale County Surveyor, Mr. Jeff Williams; microfilm of various legal instruments taken from Mr. Randolph's files; and pamphlets and brochures given to the author by various other people.

INTERVIEWS

Tapes, Southwest Collection, Texas Tech University, Lubbock, Texas

Interviews were recorded on tape only when the person interviewed was closely connected with the company in an important capacity or when information was being collected for Chapter 1. All tapes in this collection were recorded by the author except that between Dr. Seymour V. Connor and Mr. Peyton B. Randoph.

Cited in the Notes

David Dell Bowman, June 27, 1958.
Fred Lowe, July 12, 1958.
Bob Martine, August 19, 1959.
Melvin Mise, August 20, 1959.

Clarence Rogers, August 21, 1959.
Homer Rook, August 28, 1959.
George Tolbert Perdue, July 14, 1958.
Hanley Wasson, August 19, 1959.
Fred Watson, July 12, 1958.
W. J. Williams, August 22, 1959.

Oral

Besides the tape interviews, approximately 150 oral interviews were conducted by the author with people living in Lubbock, Abernathy, Hale Center, Plainview, and Canyon, all in Texas. These interviews touched many phases of human endeavor. Included among the people interviewed were physicians, real-estate agents, attorneys, county and city officials, officers of fraternal organizations, farmers, housewives, secretaries, photographers, nurserymen, church officials, irrigation experts, dairymen, editors, historians, nurses, mechanics, abstractors, gin officials, construction men, painters, librarians, archivists, chamber of commerce officials, and automobile dealers. Notes taken during these interviews are in the possession of the author.

Cited in the Notes

William F. Carter, July 9, 1960.
Mrs. F. W. Clinkscales, January 3, 1960.
Dr. J. H. Crawford, February 22, 1960.
Mrs. Adella Drew, February 22, 1960.
Fay English, February 22, 1960.
Betty Evans, February 22, 1960.
George Green, October 25, 1958.
Reverend Corbie Grimes, February 22, 1960.
Leona Lloyd, February 22, 1960.
Mrs. Jess Lockhart, February 22, 1960.
Bob Martine, February 21, 1960.
Mrs. J. O. Osward, February 16, 1960.
Peyton Randolph, March 13, 1960.
Mr. Frank D. Travis, February 22, 1960.

NEWSPAPERS

The author searched through all available area and regional newspapers

Bibliography 235

in attempting to obtain information for this study. Only those papers from which some item has been cited are listed.

Amarillo Record, November 1913. Panhandle-Plains Museum, Canyon, Texas.

Daily Panhandle, 1912. Panhandle-Plains Museum, Canyon, Texas.

Daily Plainview Advertiser, January 1914. Bain Files. Through December 31, 1913, this paper was known as the *Daily Plainviewan*.

Hale County Herald (Plainview), November 1909. First Christian Church, Plainview, Texas.

Hale County Herald (Plainview), January 2, 1913, through June 19, 1914. Microfilm copy in main library, Texas Tech University, Lubbock, Texas. The original copies are in The University of Texas collection, Austin.

New York Times, June 1929.

New York Tribune, June 1929.

Plainview Evening Herald, June 23, 1914, through October 12, 1917. Microfilm copy in main library, Texas Tech University, Lubbock, Texas.

Plainview Evening Herald, sporadic articles 1928–1956. Panhandle-Plains Museum, Canyon, Texas. As far as could be determined there is no complete file of this newspaper (or any other Plainview newspaper) in existence. The *Herald* building burned around 1928 or 1929, and all papers to that date were, therefore, destroyed. Practically no papers for the years 1918 to 1928 could be located.

Plainview News, 1912, 1928. Estacado Junior High School Scrapbook, Plainview, Texas.

PUBLIC DOCUMENTS

Field Notes, Original Homestead Surveys, Book A-3, 4-5, field book no. 360. Office of the County Surveyor, Plainview, Texas.

Gammel, Hans Peter Neilsen, comp. *The Laws of Texas, 1822–1897* (10 vols.). Vols. VIII and IX. Austin: Gammel Book Company, 1898–1901.

Hale County Deed Record, I. H. E. (No person now remembers what the H. E. means. Vol. I is the only volume labeled with the H. E.) County Clerk's Office, Plainview, Texas.

Hale County Probate Minutes, Book 1. Office of the Justice of the Peace, Plainview, Texas.

Plainview Commissioner's Court Minutes, Term 189, Vol. 2. City Hall, Plainview, Texas.

United States. Department of Commerce. Bureau of the Census. *Eleventh*

Census of the United States, 1890: Statistics of Population, pt. 1. Washington, D. C.: Government Printing Office, 1895.
———. *Twelfth Census of the United States, 1900: Population*, pt. 1. Washington, D. C.: Government Printing Office, 1901.
———. *Thirteenth Census of the United States, 1910: Abstract of Census, Texas Supplement*. Washington, D. C.: Government Printing Office, 1913.
———. *Fourteenth Census of the United States, 1920: Population*. Washington, D. C.: Government Printing Office, 1922.
———. *Fifteenth Census of the United States, 1930: Population*, pt. 1. Washington, D. C.: Government Printing Office, 1931.
Vernon's Texas Statutes. Kansas City, Missouri: Vernon Law Book Company, 1948.

BOOKS, ARTICLES, AND THESES

Cox, Mary L. *History of Hale County Texas*. Plainview: Privately printed, 1937.
Crowther, Samuel. *The Romance and Rise of the American Tropics*. New York: The Country Life Press, 1929.
Dictionary of American Biography. Vols. XIII and XIV. New York: Charles Scribner's Sons, 1928.
Diocese of Northwest Texas (Episcopal). *The Adventure*, XXXVII, no. 4 (September 1959).
Ford, Herman. "The History and Economic Development of Hale County, Texas." Master's thesis, University of Colorado, 1932.
Kepner, Charles David, Jr., and Jay Henry Soothill. *The Banana Empire: A Case Study of Economic Imperialism*. New York: Russell, 1935.
Newman, Vernie. "A History of McMurry College 1920–1936." Master's thesis, Texas Technological College, Lubbock, 1937.
Paul, Jean. "The Farmers Frontier on the South Plains." Master's thesis, Texas Technological College, Lubbock, 1958.
Ratliff, E. C. "History of Irrigation in Hale County." Master's thesis, Texas Technological College, Lubbock, 1938.
Reed, S. G. *A History of Texas Railroads*. Houston: St. Clair Publishing Co., 1941.
Smyth, R. P. "The First Settlers and the Organization of Floyd, Hale, and Lubbock Counties." In *West Texas Historical Association Yearbook*. Vol. VI. N.p.: West Texas Historical Association, 1930.

———. [Undated and unnamed article.] Scrapbook. History Department Files, Estacado Junior High School, Plainview, Texas.

The Texas Almanac and State Industrial Guide. Dallas: A. H. Belo Corp., 1933, 1951.

Wallace, Ernest, and E. Adamson Hoebel. *The Comanches: Lords of the South Plains*. Norman: University of Oklahoma Press, 1952.

Who Was Who in America, 1897–1942. Vol. I. Chicago: The A. N. Marquis Company, 1942.

INDEX

Agricultural Adjustment Act (1933): 139
Alexander, D. L.: 73
alfalfa: experiments in growth of, 65–66, 67; methods of planting of, 97; on tenant farms, 115; effects of droughts on, 118; Depression crops of, 138, 139–140
Allen, Oscar Leroy: 74
Alley, Robert: 78
Alley Brothers (real-estate agents): 51
Amarillo, Texas: 11, 14, 51, 160
Amerada Petroleum Corporation: 161
American Locomotive Works: 74
American Sugar Beet Company: 100
Anderson, Jennings: 73
Archer, Virginia: 8
Ausable Forks, New York: 7
automobiles: introduction of, 12–13, 13 n., 45
Ayres, Walter S.: in charge of sales program, 52–53 n., 52–54, 55, 58, 59; mentioned, 89

Baldwin, Leroy W.: 32, 36–37
Bank of Scotland: 32
bankruptcy: avoidance of, 33, 40
banks, local: chartering of, 12. SEE ALSO First National Bank of Plainview
Baptist Church: 14
Barber, P. B.: 97, 101
Barcus, Dr. Sam: 14 n.
Beaver Park Irrigation Project (Colorado): 100
Bexar County, Texas: 6
Black, Zenas E. (publicity agent): 44, 53–54
Bledsoe Oil and Gas Company: 126, 127
Boise, Idaho: 54
bond issues: sold to Dunn, Fisher and Company, 31–32; and formation of Staked Plains Trust, 35–36; issued by Texas Prairie Lands, 31–32, 92, 105
Bonham, Texas: 8
bookkeeping: TLDC system of, 49, 53, 96, 164
Boston, Massachusetts: B. W. Palmer from, 36; investors from, 37, 39 and n., 58 n., 58–59, 89, 93, 99; mentioned, 19. SEE ALSO Old Colony Trust of Boston
Boulder, Colorado: 51
Bowman, David Dell: manages dry-land farms, 100–101, 113–115, 158; mentioned, 133, 134
Brask, Karl: 75
Brown, Bufor R.: 172 n., 172–173
Buffalo Gap, Texas: 8
Burdell Oil Company: 164
Bureau of Internal Revenue: investigates TLDC tax returns, 154, 164–166
business establishments: types of, in early Plainview, 11–12, 15. SEE ALSO real-estate business

California: 15
Canada: controlling corporations in, 22–24, 32
Catholic Church: 14
cattle raising: 10. SEE ALSO ranches; stock farms
Catto, Keith: 73
Central Plains College and Conservatory of Music: 13
Central Plains Holiness College: 13
Chamber of Commerce (of Plainview): and irrigation, 15; supports TLDC, 172; Winfield Holbrook in, 175
Charles, Robert S.: becomes officer of TLDC, 26; resignation of, 31 and n., 87; as vice-president, 43, 44; in charge of development, 44, 53, 61–

62, 67, 70, 71, 73, 94; becomes general manager, 53, 85–87, 94; wife of, 175
Charter engine: 80
Chicago, Illinois: TLDC office in, 52–54, 58–59
Church of Christ: 14
churches: establishment of, in area, 13–14; as asset of Plainview, 45, 46; employee activities in, 174. SEE ALSO entries for individual churches
Colgate, Oklahoma: 9
colleges: as asset of Plainview, 15, 45, 54
Colorado: sales contacts in, 51, 55; Winfield Holbrook in, 100
Colorado City, Texas: 7
Columbus, Ohio: 50
Comanche Indians: 6–7, 7 n.
construction: cost of, on TLDC land, 83 n., 83–84. SEE ALSO Texas Land and Development Company, development of
Cooke County, Texas: 8
Cooper, J. West Rulon: 133–134 n.
Country Gentleman (magazine): 55
Cox, Mary: 133, 134, 175
Craig, Clyde Emerson: as general manager, 88–90, 95, 96, 97–98; and Winfield Holbrook, 99; wife of, 174
Crosby County, Texas: 9
Cuba: 88, 94
cultivation: of TLDC lands, 80–81. SEE ALSO Texas Land and Development Company, development of

Dairy Farm: 97
dairy farming: failure of, 89–90; mentioned, 45, 97
Dallas State Fair (1912): 47
Daly, U. de B.: 31
DeLay and Burch (real-estate agents): 51
DeLoach, A. B.: on duties of directors, 29 and n.; as secretary-treasurer, 99; resignation of, 177
Demonstration Farm: first mortgage on, 36; as part of development program, 62–67; amount spent on, 67, 83; irrigation on, 79; as source of income, 85; grain crop of, 90; and 1919 reorganization, 97; sale of stock from, 114; as site for college, 127–130
demonstration farms: Prairie Lands Trust acquires, 39; mortgage on, 39, 103 n.; as part of development program, 62–67; cost of development of, 67; typical house on, 75–77; irrigation on,
77–81; appraisal of contributions of, 171–172; mentioned, 50. SEE ALSO Demonstration Farm; Pioneer Park Farm
Denver, Colorado: 50, 51
Depression, the. SEE Texas Land and Development Company, effects of Depression on
Disciples of Christ Church: 14
Dowden, E.: 15, 58
drought: effects of, on company operations, 117, 118, 137, 139–141, 142–143; mentioned, 144, 170
dry-land farming: use of, 85, 113, 116, 118; Watson manages, 90–91, 96–97; Bowman manages, 100–101, 113–115, 158; failure of, 140
Dublin, R. C. (Chess): 62, 77–78
dugouts: as homes, 10
Duncan, Laura: 8
Dunn, J. H.: 21
Dunn, Fisher and Company: 31–32, 33

Eastland, Texas: 7
El Paso, Texas: 19, 20
El Paso Milling Company: 19, 20
Empire Trust Company: U. de B. Daly and, 31; as trustee of bondholders, 32–38; waives default of payment, 33–34; and formation of Staked Plains Trust, 35, 37; forces reorganization, 91, 92, 107; controls reorganization, 93; and liquidation of Texas Prairie Lands, 102–103; representative of, as trustee of Staked Plains Trust, 111
Episcopal Church: 14, 174
Epworth, Texas: 7
Epworth Chronicle: 12
Estacado, Texas: 7
experiment farms. SEE demonstration farms

Fannin County, Texas: 8
farmers, independent: role of, 3; early products of, 10–11, 47; and early real-estate boom, 13, 14–15; F. S. Pearson and, 21; TLDC contributions to, 44–45, 66–67, 171–172
Farm Relief Program: 139
federal farm programs: and company operations, 138–139, 141–142, 144
Feeney, William F.: investigates Plainview office, 94–98; becomes secretary-treasurer, 98–99; as representative of Staked Plains Trust, 112 and n., 133 n., 159; as president of TLDC, 159; mentioned, 135

Index

fencing: 83
Fife, W. S.: 73
First National Bank of Plainview: company account in, 22, 25, 27; mentioned, 15, 99
Fleming, Henry S.: and 1919 reorganization, 93, 94, 105; as representative of Staked Plains Trust, 111–112, 112 n., 128–129, 150
Floyd County, Texas: TLDC lands in, 22, 42, 114, 125; mentioned, 8
Fort Collins, Colorado: 51, 54
Fort Scott, Kansas: 7
Fort Worth, Texas: 65, 85
Frisco railroad system: and proposed West Texas line, 20 and n., 61; H. I. Miller and, 30; mentioned, 26
frontier: on South Plains, 3, 5–6
fruit trees. SEE orchards

Garden City Sugar and Land Company (Kansas): 100
Garrison, J. E.: 15
Gladney, Dr. L. L.: 13, 13–14 n.
government, federal: Depression relief programs of, 138–139, 140, 144; interest of, in tenant farms, 141–142; TLDC tax difficulties with, 154, 164–166
Graham, R.: 78
Grant, Dr. James Walker: as real-estate agent, 12, 17; as company officer, 26; resignation of, 31 and n.; wife of, 175
Graves, Horatio: as first settler in Hale County, 7–8, 14
Great Britain. SEE London, England
Green, George: and first irrigation well, 15–16; and F. S. Pearson, 21; contributions of, to irrigation, 171
Green Machinery Company: 79 n., 79–80
Guantanamo and Western Railroad (Cuba): 88
Gulf Coast Irrigation Company: 52, 89

Hale, John C.: 6
Hale Center, Texas: growth of, 9; mentioned, 7, 78
Hale Center Live Wire: 12
Hale Center Messenger: 12
Hale City Globe: 12
Hale County: establishment of, 6, 9; settlement of, 6–7; early banks in, 12; economic and cultural development of, 12, 13–16; first irrigation well in, 15–16; TLDC lands in, 17, 22, 42, 114; cited in company advertisements, 47; hog raising in, 66–67; and land title problems, 125; mentioned, 147
Hale County abstract building: 10
Hale County court house: 7 n.
Hale County Fair Association: 174
Hale County Herald: on irrigation, 16; on farming methods, 44–45; advertising in, 50
Hale County Hesperian: 11
Hall, W. R.: 51, 52
Hamburg, Arkansas: 8
Happy, Texas: 16, 54
Hart, Francis R.: as trustee of Staked Plains Trust, 36, 93, 125, 150; as reorganization manager, 93, 102
Havana, Cuba: 88
Hefflefinger, Dennis: 129
Hely-Hutchinson, Maurice: 110–111, 161
Henderson, Milton Day: conceives plan for company, 17–18; interests F. S. Pearson, 18 and n., 20, 21; purchases land, 22, 25, 26 n., 42–43, 62; becomes company officer, 26; as sales manager, 26, 29, 43–44, 50, 94, 177; as company president, 28, 29 and n., 30, 42; as vice-president and general manager, 31 and n., 43, 45 n., 94; as trustee of Texas Securities Co., 42–43; contract of, 52, 52–53 n.; resignation of, 53; model farm proposed by, 63; supervises demonstration farms, 64; as civic leader, 174; mentioned, 55, 169, 172
Hess, Joe: as local sales manager, 44, 50–51, 54, 55, 58
Hess-Wilkes-Otto Company: 51
History of Hale County Texas: 175
hogs: successful raising of, 66–67; used to puddle lake, 70; and dairy farming, 89; failure of raising of, 90
Holbrook, Winfield (Captain): as general manager, 98, 109, 112–113, 114, 116 n., 119, 120, 127–128, 145, 146, 158, 159; education and experience of, 100; in charge of sales, 120; and proposed college site, 127–128; and Depression salary reductions, 133–137; and collection of overdue notes, 146, 148; as company treasurer, 159; and liquidation of company, 160 and n.; and sale of mineral rights, 160, 164; contributions of, to irrigation, 171; as civic leader, 175–176; contributions of, to success of company, 177
Holland, Mr. (farmer): 78
Hooper community: 73
horticulture: discussed in brochure, 47

hospital: 13
Hotel Missouri (in Plainview): 52
houses: sod, as first on plains, 8, 10; early, types of, 10; of stock farmers, 45; company, standard plan of, 75–76, 77
Houston, Texas: 79
Hubbard, Charles E.: 99
Hubbard, Charles J.: as company president, 59, 88–89, 98; display of wealth by, 176

Imperial Valley, California: 54
irrigation: attracts company, 5, 16, 17, 78; drilling of first well for, 15–16, 78; interest of F. S. Pearson in, 21; as selling point in advertisements, 46–47, 50, 54; R. S. Charles's faith in, 61–62; and lakes, 62; on demonstration farms, 64–67; and growing of alfalfa, 66; importance of, to development program, 72, 78–80; drilling of wells for, 77–80; equipment needed for, 79–80; expense of equipment upkeep for, 80, 83 n., 116; slowdown in company program of, 86; depreciation of system of, 90; Winfield Holbrook and, 100; on tenant farms, 115, 141, 143; drought proves value of, 118, 140, 141, 142–143; need for education in use of, 119; failure of, and repossessions, 122, 123; Texas Tech to "demonstrate," 128; appraisal of company program of, 171–172; mentioned, 56, 57, 101, 157, 170, 177

Johnson, Rev. N. B.: 14 n.
Jones, Clifford B.: 5
Jones, J. C.: 75
Jones, Thornton: 11 and n.

Kansas: 45 and n., 50, 100
Kansas City, Kansas: 45 and n., 50
Keith, Henry M.: 98 and n., 159
Keith, Minor Cooper: as trustee of Staked Plains Trust, 36, 40 n., 93, 109–111, 125, 129, 150; as trustee of Prairie Lands Trust, 39–40, 93, 110; as reorganization manager, 93, 102; as director of Empire Trust, 93; as investor, 178
Klinger, William J.: as secretary-treasurer, 99, 159; as civic leader, 175
Krueger, A. M.: 64–65
Kunesh, Joe: 73

Lake Plainview: development of, 67–72; as source of income, 68–69, 85; mentioned, 73
lakes: and land purchases, 62
Lancaster, Judge Joe E.: 172
land companies: establishment of, in South Plains, 3, 5. SEE ALSO Texas Land and Development Company
Las Cruces, New Mexico: 89
Lash, J. J.: 51
Layne, M. E.: 80
Layne-Bowler Pump Company: 79–80
legislature, Arkansas: 8
legislature, Texas: establishment of counties by, 6, 7; and college site, 127
Littlefield Lands: 5
Llano Estacado: 6
London, England: investors from, 21–22, 24–25, 37, 38, 39 n., 93, 110–111; Dunn, Fisher and Company in, 31–32
London County and Westminster Bank, Limited: 34
Longstreth, John Walter: as development assistant, 62; and demonstration farms, 64, 65–67, 86; as supervisor of cultivation, 80, 94; as general manager, 87, 94; wife of, 174
Lowden County, Tennessee: 8
Lowe, Edwin Lowden: as founder of Plainview, 8–9; and establishment of stores, 11
Lowe, Fred: farming operations under, 101, 113–115; resignation of, 158–159
Lowe, W. P.: 133, 134
Lower Rio Grande Valley: 52
Lubbock Leader: 11
Lyford, Texas: 89

McDonald, Rev. W. G.: 14 n.
Mackenzie, Colonel Ranald Slidell: 6–7, 7 n.
McNaughten, J. N.: 16
Madeira Company, Limited: 30
Malone, Charles: 15
Marshall, E. E.: 150–151
Mason, W. H.: as purchasing agent, 26, 27, 62, 74; resignation of, 31 and n.; civic activities of, 174; wife of, 175
Massachusetts Institute of Technology: 18
Maxwell, Z. T.: as founder of Plainview, 8–9; and establishment of stores, 11
Medina Dam project: 52
Medina Valley Irrigation Company: 52, 58
Merrill Farm: 85, 90

Index

Methodist Church: and settlement of Hale County, 7–8; establishment of church by, 7–8, 14; college operated by, 13, 13–14 n.
Mexico: 18, 19
Mexico Northwestern Railway: 20, 30
Miller, Harry Irving: as director of Texas Prairie Lands, 26; as president of TLDC, 30, 36, 37, 43; wife of, 30–31 n., 175; as trustee of Staked Plains Trust, 36, 125, 150, 151; and Lake Plainview, 67; display of wealth by, 176
Milton, Massachusetts: 36
Mise, Melvin: 74
Montague County, Texas: 8
Monteith, Mr. (auditor): 96
Morrison, J. W.: 7
Morrison, T. W.: 7
mortgage-finance business: 5
Motley, J. Lothrop: 98
Myers, Charles F.: as general manager, 59, 87, 88, 94; resignations of, 87, 88; as vice-president in charge of sales, 88

Nance, J. B.: 51
Nazarene Church: 13, 14
New Mexico: 89, 100
New Rhodes, Louisiana: 69
newspapers: founding of, 11–12; company advertising in, 49–51, 54–58; excursion trips reported in, 51, 52; trespassing notice in, 81–82; educational articles on farming in, 171–172; support for company in, 172
New York (city): Texas Prairie Lands office in, 29–30; investors in, 37, 39 and n., 58, 89, 93, 99; Texas Securities Company office in, 43; chief officers to be located in, 98–99; mentioned, 19
Norman, Bradford, Jr.: 133 n.
Northwest Texas Methodist Conference: 13

O'Brien, Edward: 85
oil fields: in Plainview area, 160–161
Oklahoma: 55
Old Colony Trust of Boston: as agent for sale of prior lien notes, 34–35; prior lien notes held by, 38, 39; and formation of Staked Plains Trust, 35–36; and formation of Prairie Lands Trust, 39, 41; president of, supervises TLDC officer, 59; and liquidation of Texas Prairie Lands Trust, 103 and n.; and liquidation of Staked Plains Trust, 167
Olin, Clark, and Phelps (law firm): 151
orchards: possibilities of, advertised, 45; on demonstration farms, 63, 64; halt in experiments with, 87; mentioned, 75

Pacific Securities Company, Limited: 21
Palmer, Bradley W.: 125, 150
Panhandle: division of counties of, 6; real-estate boom in, 13; mentioned, 14. SEE ALSO South Plains
Panic of 1907: 13
Paris and Great Northern Railway: 20 n.
Parker, W. A.: 15
Partridge, Hugh R.: as trustee of Staked Plains Trust, 109–111, 129, 132, 133, 133–134 n.; and London investors, 111
Pearce, Rev. William M.: 14 n.
Pearson, Dr. Frederick Stark: and M. D. Henderson, 18 and n., 20–21; background of, 18–19; arranges for purchase of lands, 21–22; makes final arrangements for company, 26; responsibility of company to, 27; and H. I. Miller, 30; invests in Texas Prairie Lands bonds, 32 and n.; and cancellation of Texas Securities Co. debt, 34; son of, and Staked Plains Trust, 36, 38; loses direct control of company, 37–38; death of, 38; and W. S. Ayres, 52; and development program, 61–62; efforts of, to acquire capital, 169; interest of, in Plainview area, 174; display of wealth by, 176; losses of, as investor, 178. SEE ALSO Pearson Syndicate
Pearson, Ward Edgerly: as trustee of Staked Plains Trust, 36, 38, 40 n., 125, 150; as trustee of Prairie Lands Trust, 39–40
Pearson Engineering Corporation, Ltd. SEE Pearson Syndicate
Pearson Syndicate: F. S. Pearson's operations through, 18 and n., 19; funds from, for purchase of lands, 21, 33, 42, 170; and establishment of Canadian holding company, 23; R. S. Charles and, 26; effects of World War I on, 38; H. I. Miller and, 43; and opening of TLDC Chicago office, 52; and source of development supplies, 74; Texas Securities Co. as part of, 104
Perdue, George Tolbert: 94, 98
Perry, E. H.: 78
Pioneer Park Farm: as demonstration

farm, 62–67; irrigation installed on, 79; as source of income, 85; dairy operation on, 89–90; and 1919 reorganization, 97; sale of stock from, 114
Pipkin, James Walkup: as general manager, 87 and n., 94; wife of, 175
Pittman, J. H.: 146–148
Plainview, Texas: TLDC begins in, 5–6, 16, 26–27, 28; established as town, 6–9; Indian scare in, 7 n.; growth of population of, 9–10, 14; types of early homes in, 10; early economic development of, 10–16; churches established in, 13–14; described in company advertisements, 14–15, 17, 45–49; proposed railroad through, 20; F. S. Pearson comes to, 21; H. I. Miller in, 30, 30–31 n., 43; Lake Plainview offered to, 71–72; importance of irrigation to, 78; M. E. Layne in, 80; company support in, 82, 170, 172–173; head officers removed from, 98; company investments in, 126; competes for location of Texas Tech, 127–130; effects of 1934 drought in, 141; effects of Depression on land sales in, 144; oil developments in area of, 160–161; contributions of company to, 168, 170–176; Winfield Holbrook as mayor of, 175
Plainview Cotton Gin Company: 126–127
Plainview Evening Herald: establishment of, 11–12 n.; R. R. White advertises in, 57–58; sales policy explained in, 59; on Lake Plainview, 71–72
Plainview National Bank: 134
Plainview News: 11, 11–12 n.
plowing: 65–66, 80–81
poultry raising: 45
Prairie Lands Trust, Limited: organization of, 39 and n.; assumes joint responsibility for TLDC, 39 n., 39–41, 40 n.; controls TLDC, 59, 89, 94; and Empire Trust foreclosure, 91; and 1919 reorganization, 93; liquidation of, 101, 103–104; consolidated with Staked Plains Trust, 106; profits of investors in, 107; mentioned, 178
Presbyterian Church: 14
Price, Henry B.: 111, 132, 133 and n.
Price and Boswell (real-estate agents): 51
prospectors: prospective buyers called, 51 n.; brought in by train, 51; character of, 57; and controversy with Dr. White, 56; and demonstration farms, 62, 67; mentioned, 50
public utilities: as asset of Plainview, 45

Quaker colony: 7
Quanah, Texas: 20

railroads: coming of, to South Plains, 5, 10, 12, 13, 15; sales excursion trips on, 5, 51–52, 53–56, 55 n.; proposed, through West Texas, 20, 30, 61; Charles F. Myers and, 87, 88, 94
ranches: 3, 5, 7
Randolph, Halbert Cyrus: as company attorney, 22, 27–28; as trustee for Canadian company, 22, 23, 24; as trustee of TLDC, 25–26, 26 n., 32; as trustee of Texas Prairie Lands, 36–37
Randolph, Peyton Beaumont: as company attorney, 22, 55 n., 110, 135–151, 159; on resignation of M. D. Henderson, 53; and land-title problems, 125-126, 149; and Santa Fe Grant, 130–131; collection of overdue notes by, 145–148; on trustee-payment question, 150–151; as assistant secretary-treasurer, 159; wife of, 175
real-estate business: early boom in, 12–13; promotes Hale County land, 17; use of excursion trips by, 51; R. R. White in, 56–58
Reorganization Agreement of 1919. SEE Texas Land and Development Company, 1919 reorganization of
Restriction Street, Plainview: 10
Rock Island Railroad: and proposed West Texas line, 20; H. I. Miller and, 26, 30; W. S. Ayres and, 52
Runningwater Cattle and Land Company: 7
Runningwater Draw: 8
Runyon, George: 75

St. Louis, San Francisco, and Texas Railway: 20 n.
Salem, Oregon: 54
San Angelo, Texas: 146, 160
San Antonio, Texas: 52
Santa Fe Railway: bonus raised for, 12; coming of, 12, 15; sponsors excursion train, 51; irrigation well at station of, 67–68, 71, 72; right-of-way grant to, 130

Index

schools, public: establishment of, 13; as asset of Plainview, 15, 45, 46, 54
Seth Ward College: as Methodist institution, 13, 13–14 n.; mentioned, 54
Shady Glenn Farm: 90
Sherman, Texas: 8
signboards: used by R. R. White, 56–57
Sinclair Prairie Oil Company: 161–162
Slaton, John Henry: irrigation well on farm of, 15–16, 17, 78, 79; as trustee of Canadian company, 22, 23, 24; as trustee of TLDC, 25–26, 26 n., 32; as trustee of Texas Prairie Lands, 36–37
Smyth, R. P.: 78
Snyder, P. E.: 78
Soash, W. B.: 5
South America: 19
South Plains: late settlement of, 3, 5; division of counties of, 6; early real-estate boom in, 13; Plainview as center of, 14–15; F. S. Pearson reports on, 18–19, 20; as stock-raising region, 45, 47; market for crops of, 65
Spade Ranch: 5
Spur Ranch: 5
Springfield, Missouri: 8
Staked Plains: 6
Staked Plains Trust, Limited: formation of, 35–36; limits of Texas law on, 36; character of backers of, 37; and formation of Prairie Lands Trust, 39–41, 40 n.; and Prairie Lands Trust, 39 n., 39–41, 40 n.; and consolidation of operation, 41; and 1919 reorganization, 89, 91, 92, 93; and Empire Trust foreclosure, 91, 92; becomes controlling company, 101, 102–108; liquidation of indebtedness by, 105 and n., 109, 131, 153, 156; summary of post-reorganization role of, 108; post-reorganization trustees of, 109–111; improvements under control of, 119; land-title problems in trusteeships of, 124–126; and location of Texas Tech, 127–130; rights-of-way granted by, 130–131, 143; effects of Depression on salaries authorized by, 132–137; comments on tenant-farm conditions, 141–142; in dispute over land titles, 149 and n.; payment of pre-1919 trustees of, 150–151; liquidation of, 153, 154, 159, 160, 166–168; retention of mineral rights by, 154; interest of, in oil developments, 160–161; income-tax difficulties of, 164–166. SEE ALSO Texas Land and Development Company
Stamford College: 14 n.
stock farms: as major early industry, 10; South Plains described as region of, 45, 47; discussed in advertising brochure, 47; mentioned, 5
Sunset (magazine): 55
surveying: and development program, 72–73
Swisher County, Texas: company land in, 22, 42, 113–114, 125

taxes: real-estate, owed to state, 135; income, problems of, 154, 164–166, 167
tenant farms: as source of company income, 85, 86, 89, 90–91, 117–121; company terms regarding, 85; crop-production prizes for, 86; charges of inefficiency in operation of, 96–97; overseeing of, 113–115; choosing of tenants for, 114–115; crops grown on, 115; use of irrigation on, 115, 141, 143; buying of, encouraged, 123, 156; effects of Depression on, 132, 137; government relief programs for, 139; interest of federal government in conditions on, 141–142; termination of program of, 153; appraisal of company policy toward, 173–174; mentioned, 170
Temple, Texas: 56
Texan Press: 11
"Texas Land and Development Company" (brochure): 45 n., 45–49, 49 n., 177
Texas Land and Development Company: compared to other land companies, 5; unique fiscal structure of, 5, 39–40, 41, 178; original idea for, 17–18; charter of, 27, 28–29, 61; role of early directors of, 28–30; effects of Texas law on operations of, 36, 110, 125; investors in, in Staked Plains Trust, 36–37; role of British backers of, 37; trusts assume joint control of, 39–40, 40 n.; move to consolidate operation of, 41; appointment of officers of, 28–29, 30, 31 and n., 42, 43, 53–54, 58, 59, 87–88, 94, 98–99, 159; bookkeeping system of, 49, 53, 96, 164; Chicago office of, 52–54; repossessions of land by, 121–123, 143, 144–148; effects of bank failure on, 134; land-title difficulties of, 149 and

n.; mineral rights of, 150, 154, 160–161, 162–164, 166, 167; official dissolution of, 159, 160, 168; contributions of, to Plainview area, 170–176; appraisal of negative aspects of, 176–178; as example of free enterprise capitalism, 178–179

—, development of: irrigation program of, 5, 16, 78–80, 86, 90, 171–172; funds for, 33, 38–39, 41, 85; effects of World War I on, 38–39, 85–87, 88, 94; and formation of Prairie Lands Trust, 39–41, 39 n.; R. S. Charles in charge of, 43, 44, 61–62; newspaper articles on, 44–45; effects of tight-money policy on, 58–59; and control of Boston backers, 58–59; officers in charge of, 61–62; importance of lakes to, 62; original five-year plan for, 60; and cost of demonstration farms, 67; types of cultivation and, 65–66, 67, 80–81; Lake Plainview as part of, 67–72; surveying program of, 72–73; drilling program of, 72, 77–80; construction operations of, 72, 73–77, 82–83, 83 n., 83–84; employees involved in, 73–75; source of supplies for, 74–75; standard set of improvements for farms in, 75–76, 77, 78; fencing as part of, 76–77, 83; problems in, with trespassers, 81–82; local hinderances to, 82–83; amount of money spent on, 83 n., 83–84; change in crop policies of, 87; changed to contract basis only, 88; failure of dairy-farming program of, 89–90; reasons for failures of, 91, 92–93, 176; demonstration-farm program of, 89–90; stock-raising experiments in, 90; and company-operated farms, 90; and rapid turnover of general managers, 94; charges of inefficiency in, 96–98; tenant-farm operations of, 96–97, 173–174; during period of reorganization, 101 and n.; reorganization provisions for, 112; Winfield Holbrook takes charge of, 112–113; cost of, after reorganization, 113; effects of Depression on, 132

—, effects of Depression on: development by, 132; salaries of, 132–137, 139; payment of real-estate taxes by, 135; land repossessions by, 122, 143, 144–148; crop income of, 137–143; land sales of, 143–148; collection of notes by, 145–148, appraisal of, 170

—, farming operations of: types of plowing in, 65–66, 80–81; inadequate supervision of, 97; by tenants, 114–115, 119; effects of drought on, 115–116, 117, 139–141; dry-land and irrigated, compared, 116; improvements in, cut losses, 118; amount of land used in, 119–120; effects of Depression on, 137–143; hail-storm damage to, 138; dry-land, failure of, 140; sugar-beet experiment of, 140–141; during 1940's, 155, 156–158; effect of heavy rains on, 157; failures of experimentation in, 176; mentioned, 128

—, financial backing for: sought by M. D. Henderson, 18; role of F. S. Pearson in, 18–28 passim, 38; and distribution of shares in, 27; through sale of Texas Prairie Lands bonds, 32–35, 37, 92, 102; role of Prairie Lands Trust in, 39–41, 85, 104; and formation of Staked Plains Trust, 35–37, 85; and sale of prior lien notes, 37, 103; effects of World War I on, 38–39; temporary loan arranged for, 38–39, 41; role of Texas Securities Co. in, 43; complicated maneuverings for, 88, 92; and mortgage of demonstration farms, 103 n.; appraisal of, 169–170, 178–179; mentioned, 5

—, income of: from Lake Plainview, 68–69; from unsold lands, 84–85; sources of, during development period, 84–85; tenant farms as source of, 85, 86, 89–91, 117–121, 156–157, 158; from company farming operations, 113, 117–121, 133, 137–143, 151, 156–157, 158; from land sales, 121, 122–124, 143–145, 155–156, 157–158; effects of Depression on, 133, 137–143, 152; from mineral rights, 160–161, 163–164, 166, 167; and tax problems, 164–166

—, indebtedness of: from sale of bonds, 33–36; and formation of Staked Plains Trust, 35; from farming operations, 85–86; forces reorganization, 91, 102–108; for payment of early trustees, 150–151; retirement of, 156, 166–167; and interest in oil developments, 161

—, investments by: in Plainview companies, 126–127, 145; in government bonds, 126, 127, 145; rights-of-way grants regarded as, 130, 143; effects of Depression on, 145; program of, during 1940's and 1950's, 154

—, 1919 reorganization of: reasons for forcing of, 91, 92–93, 96–98; role of

Empire Trust in, 92, 102–103; managers of, 93; preliminary proceedings of, 93–94; and investigation of Plainview office, 93–98; program of, for more efficient operation, 98; local operation of, 99–101; and liquidation of Texas Prairie Lands, 101–106; Staked Plains Trust assumes control under, 102–108; and interest in oil developments, 161; mentioned, 150, 153, 177

—, organization of: Plainview as site for, 5–6; original idea for, 17–18; F. S. Pearson interested in, 20–21; complicated financial arrangements for, 22–25, 24 n., 27, 31–41; legality of arrangements for, 36; purchase of lands for, 22, 33, 42–43, 61, 62; role of Texas Securities Company in, 23–25, 23–24 n.; effects of Texas law on, 25–26; appointment of trustees for, 25–26; completion of arrangements for, 26–28; and distribution of shares, 27; official date of, 28; role of Prairie Lands Trust in, 39–41

—, promotion and advertising of: assets of Plainview cited in, 14–15; staff acquired for, 44 and n.; in newspapers, 44–45, 123, 164; brochure used for, 45 n., 45–49, 49 n., 177; variety of crops emphasized in, 47, 48; amount spent on, 49, 50, 58, 59; in publications, 49–51, 54–58; sales trips made for, 50–51, 55; irrigation emphasized in, 50, 54; use of excursion trips for, 51–52, 53–56, 55 n.; Chicago office takes charge of, 52–54; controversy with Dr. White over, 56–58; for sale of mineral rights, 164

—, sales of land by: as security for mortgage, 36; to furnish operating capital, 38–39; M. D. Henderson takes charge of, 43–44; terms of, 44, 46, 47–48, 53, 54, 55–56 and n., 59–60, 78; amount of, 1913 to 1916, 55–56 and n.; halts in program of, 59, 88, 121; removed from Chicago office, 59; amount of, 1916 to 1919, 59–60; importance of development program to, 72; failure of, and reorganization, 92–93; 1920 high point in, 120–121; land-title problems and, 124–126; effects of Depression on, 133, 143–145; completion of, 153, 160; during 1940's, 155–156, 157–159; tax problems of, 166; appraisal of difficulties of, 169, 170; negative aspects of, 177

Texas Northern Land and Irrigation Company: 22–23
Texas Prairie Lands, Limited: role of, in establishment of TLDC, 23–25, 27 and n., 28, 29–30, 29 n.; 1912 bond issue of, 31–32, 92, 105; avoids near bankruptcy, 33–34; sells prior lien notes, 34–35, 103; transfers holdings to Staked Plains Trust, 35–36; becomes inactive, 37; borrows money for development, 42; relation of Texas Securities Co. to, 43; liquidation of, 99, 101–106; mentioned, 178
Texas Press Leader: 11
Texas Securities Company, Limited: role of in organization of TLDC, 23–25, 23–24 n., 27 n., 29 n., 33, 104; debt canceled by, 34, 104; and formation of Staked Plains Trust, 36, 37; M. D. Henderson and, 42–43; relation of, to Texas Prairie Lands, 43, 104 and n.; end of, 104 and n., 106
Texas Technological College: proposed site for, 127–130; mentioned, 5
Toronto, Ontario, Canada: 23
transportation: early difficulties of, 11, 12, SEE ALSO automobiles; railroads
trees: planted on Staked Plains, 8; planted on demonstration farms, 64. SEE ALSO orchards
Treub, A. M.: 31
truck farming: discussed in brochure, 47; on demonstration farms, 64–65; as source of company income, 85; on tenant farms, 117; mentioned, 75, 172
Tulia, Texas: 146, 147

United Fruit Company: 36, 178
University of Colorado: 100
University of Wisconsin: 73
Utah: 100

Valley View Farm: 90
Vaughn, J. L.: 51, 52
Ven-Severin engine: 80

Waco, Texas: 65
Walsenburg, Colorado: 51
Wasson, Hanley: 73–75
Watson, Fred: as superintendent of dryland farms, 90–91, 96–97; mentioned, 101
Watson, John F.: 87
Wayland Hotel: 10
wells, water: early, in Plainview, 8, 10–11; as part of development program, 72, 75, 77–80

wells, irrigation. SEE irrigation
wells, oil: in Plainview area, 160–161
West Texas: development of, 5. SEE ALSO Panhandle; South Plains
White, Dr. R. R.: advertising controversy with, 56–58
White River: 8, 63
Whitney, Henry F.: as trustee of Staked Plains Trust, 111, 132, 133, 133–134 n.; as president of TLDC and Staked Plains Trust, 159
Williams, W. J.: 73
Wilson farms: 97
World War I: effects of, on money market, 38, 58, 169–170; effects of, on development program, 85–87, 88, 94; mentioned, 73, 98, 99, 171
Wychoff, J. O.: 15–16

Yellow House Land Company: 5

Zehnder, Charles H.: as trustee of Prairie Lands Trust, 39–40, 93, 110; as reorganization manager, 93, 102; as trustee of Staked Plains Trust, 109–111, 150; and proposed college site, 129